PRAISE FOR **MATTHEW BERRY AND *FANTASY LIFE***

"As a longtime fan of Matthew Berry, I'm happy he's finally collected the most inane and hilarious things people will do in pursuit of fantasy glory. If I was in a fantasy league where you drafted people who write about fantasy leagues, I would draft Matthew first. Also, I would need to make some major changes in my life."

• Seth Meyers, *Saturday Night Live* head writer and three-time
fantasy champion in a league you don't care about

"You don't have to play fantasy sports to enjoy Matthew Berry's Fantasy Life. *You don't even need to be a sports fan. If you like great writing, if you appreciate irreverent humor, if stories about friendship, family, backstabbing, and regrettable Justin Bieber tattoos warm your heart, you'll love this book."*

• Harlan Coben, #1 *New York Times*–bestselling author

"I am a bad fantasy football player and worse fantasy baseballer. I am heartened after reading Fantasy Life *that this apparently does not matter. Matthew Berry's book proves that there are lots of people out there like us: people who don't use fantasy sports to escape from life, but rather to live it with more fun."*

• Peter King, senior writer, *Sports Illustrated*, and owner,
Montclair Pedroias, New Jersey Suburban League

"If I had to choose between playing real football and fantasy football, I honestly don't know what I'd choose. (Just kidding.) For players like me, fantasy sports are an obsession, an escape, and a great opportunity to trash talk each other. Matthew Berry is THE guy (other than me) everyone listens to and texts for advice during drafts. Fantasy Life *is a must-read for fantasy sports fans, athletes, and anyone who loves ridiculous stories."*

• Maurice Jones-Drew, All-Pro NFL running back,
host of *Running with MJD* on SiriusXM Fantasy Sports Radio

"I don't care about fantasy sports, and unless it involves a player shooting another player on the field like in The Last Boy Scout, *I don't want to hear any stupid fantasy stories. But Matthew Berry did the impossible: He wrote a book about fantasy football that was hilarious and interesting to people who don't even like fantasy football. I loved this book."*

• Tucker Max, #1 *New York Times*–bestselling author of *I Hope They Serve Beer in Hell*

"Football can be broken down into X's and O's, but at the end of the day, we're all after drama, human interest, and a great story. Matthew Berry's Fantasy Life is a great story. I know sports can make a difference in people's lives; Matthew Berry has shown that fantasy sports can, too."

• **Ron "Jaws" Jaworski, ESPN NFL analyst, and proud owner of multiple fantasy championships under the name "Jawbreaker"**

"For those of us who compete in fantasy sports, it's a fraternity. And this book IS fantasy sports. It covers the highs and lows, the good and bad, in victory and in defeat. And it's told by the only man who could tell it: Matthew Berry, the Talented Mr. Roto himself."

• **Dale Earnhardt Jr., NASCAR driver and 12-team Dirty Mo Posse league champion**

"I was excited to see that Matthew was writing a book about fantasy sports. As a pro athlete I've seen fantasy sports blow up in the last ten years, and he's been in the middle of all of it. Thank you, Matthew Berry, for writing such a funny book—and for being my personal consultant for the Cardinals' fantasy football league."

• **Matt Holliday, All-Star outfielder, St. Louis Cardinals**

"Matthew Berry has gleefully documented everything that is so great about fantasy sports—the celebrations and the punishments, the conniving and backstabbing, the agony and the ecstasy. He's got an amazing story for any situation you find yourself in. It's the Kama Sutra of fantasy. If you've ever watched The League, you will love this book. Matthew shows in hilarious fashion that fantasy is like life—just better."

• **Jackie and Jeff Schaffer, creators of The League**

"One of the people who makes it so much easier for you to enjoy success in fantasy sports now explains why we all enjoy playing fantasy sports. Draft this book early in your first round."

• **Keith Olbermann, four-time New York Times–bestselling author, nine-time fantasy baseball pennant winner**

"Matthew Berry's personal journey in fantasy football is a lesson in a reality of life. Now, you can separate fantasy from reality in a fascinating read."

• **Chris Mortensen, ESPN Senior NFL Insider and "always in the money!"**

"Matthew Berry's Fantasy Life is touching, gripping, addicting. There's nothing like it."

• **Adam Schefter, ESPN NFL Insider**

FANTASY LIFE

FANTASY LIFE

The Outrageous, Uplifting, and
Heartbreaking World of Fantasy Sports
from the Guy Who's Lived It

MATTHEW BERRY

RIVERHEAD BOOKS   *a member of Penguin Group (USA) Inc.   New York   2013*

RIVERHEAD BOOKS
Published by the Penguin Group
Penguin Group (USA) Inc., 375 Hudson Street,
New York, New York 10014, USA

USA · Canada · UK · Ireland · Australia
New Zealand · India · South Africa · China

Penguin Books Ltd, Registered Offices: 80 Strand, London WC2R 0RL, England
For more information about the Penguin Group visit penguin.com

Library of Congress Cataloging-in-Publication Data

Berry, Matthew, date.
Fantasy life : the outrageous, uplifting, and heartbreaking world of
fantasy sports from the guy who's lived it / Matthew Berry.
p.   cm.
ISBN 978-1-59448-625-8
1. Fantasy sports.   I. Title.
GV1202 F35B47   2013   2013009331
796.1.—dc23

Photograph on page 12 courtesy of *Northfield News*
Photograph on page 40 courtesy of Club Risqué
Photographs on page 45 courtesy of DavidHillPhoto.com

Printed in the United States of America
1   3   5   7   9   10   8   6   4   2

BOOK DESIGN BY NICOLE LAROCHE

*Penguin is committed to publishing works of quality and integrity.
In that spirit, we are proud to offer this book to our readers;
however, the story, the experiences, and the words
are the author's alone.*

6.6%

**of all Americans watched
the 2012 *American Idol* finale**
(Nielsen)

8.2%

of all Americans play golf
(National Golf Foundation, 2012)

13%

of all Americans play fantasy sports
(Ipsos Public Affairs, 2012)

A QUICK NOTE ABOUT THE BOOK

Hiya. Thanks for taking a leap of faith and buying the book. Or having someone in your life who gave it to you. Or just thumbing through it while killing time waiting for a plane because the line at Starbucks is too long. I get it and I thank you.

Just a few quick notes. Some of the things in this book I have written about before, in different forms, on ESPN.com. They've all been rewritten, updated, and expanded upon, but yes, I spent more than 12 years writing about myself and my life in a weekly column before writing this book, so yeah, there's some overlap.

Every story you are about to read is, to the best of my knowledge, 100 percent true. Now, I've had to change some names and details to protect the not so innocent, but as best I could, I've verified everything in here. That said, what am I, a detective? In some of these I am relying on the accounts of people who were actually there. But look, it's a book about fantasy sports. Don't sweat it. Put your feet up and enjoy the ride.

To my parents, Nancy and Len Berry,

for always encouraging me to go for the dream,

and to my wife, Beth, and kids, David, Matt,

Connor, Samantha, and Brooke,

for helping me achieve it

CONTENTS

PART ONE

THE LEAGUE

1.

It Starts with a League

Everyone Remembers Their First Time

They were in a hot tub, and they were drunk.

Good friends from college, they played in a 10-team fantasy football league together. And as the drinks kept flowing, so did the trash talk.

"Everyone in the league was a college athlete, so egos are pretty big," Quin Kilgore remembers. "No one could even consider the thought of losing."

Trash talk leads to bets, and bets lead to rules, and by the end of the evening the group had come to a very simple, but very real, agreement.

Last place in the league . . . has to get a tattoo.

Not some lame-ass henna tattoo that fades in a few weeks. No, we're talking a legit, full-on, chosen by the winner, for-the-rest-of-your-life tattoo. Nights that start drunk in a hot tub often end in regret, but "sobering up the next morning, we stuck with it," Quin tells me. "One of the guys in the league, Spud Mann, was in law school at the time and drew up a contract dictating size, placement, and tone of the tattoo."

The basic parameters: embarrassing tattoos are allowed, racist ones are not, and no going all Mike Tyson and putting it on the face. "Just before the draft that year, we all signed it. And of course, the first year the loser was the guy who drew up the contract . . . Spud Mann."

Basically, the way the Tattoo League works is, in weeks 15 and 16, the top four play for the right to choose the tattoo and the bottom four are playing to avoid the tattoo. In year two, the loser was a guy named "Ron."

And in year three Adam Palmer got the, uh, honors.

Now, sometime between two-time league winner Dusty Carter explaining to a tattoo artist exactly what a "Tebowing Care Bear" should look like and then a year later trying to find the best picture of Justin Bieber to copy, JJ Dunn was in Spokane, Washington, working on one of his 10 fantasy football teams.

"I had stayed up an hour longer than I was planning to adjust my roster, and because of that I was able to hear a very quiet sound coming from my son's room in the basement."

JJ decided to check out the sound before he went to bed. "I found my 13-year-old boy without a pulse. I started CPR and yelled for my wife to wake up and call 911. Paramedics got there quickly, and after a lot of effort, Jake's heart started pumping on its own. Jake has since been declared all but a miracle kid, suffering no brain damage. If it wasn't for fantasy football, I never would have been up at that hour and heard that. It may seem like hyperbole, but fantasy football helped save my son's life."

Getting the word LOSER permanently inked on your body and being the reason your child is still alive are polar opposite stories, but in the world of fantasy sports I got news for you: neither one surprises me. When you're done with this book, you'll realize the same thing I did:

From birth to funerals and everything in between, there is no aspect of life that fantasy doesn't touch.

Most important, it touches people. I've said this a million times in interviews over the years. Long before Twitter, Facebook, or even MySpace and Friendster, fantasy football was the *original* online community. And now there are millions of people with the same shared experiences.

From friends from high school, college, or work, to couples, families, and even people you've only "met" online . . . I know of leagues from every walk of life. Heikki Larsen and the "Margarillas" play while on tour with Jimmy Buffett. Many major league baseball players have a clubhouse fantasy football league with their teammates, including CC Sabathia, who would like you to know he's the 2012 New York Yankees clubhouse champion. There are leagues with prison inmates and leagues done on Army bases overseas. Dr. Melanie Friedlander plays in a league of all orthopedic surgeons. All 10 owners in Don Carlson's league are from Fire Station 1 in the Los Angeles Fire Department. And Miss January 2010, Jaime Edmondson, plays in a league with fellow *Playboy* playmates.

I've heard of leagues in the White House and US Senate; leagues with all female lawyers, with Hollywood agents, and high stakes ones comprised of Vegas casino owners. David Bailey runs a 12-person league with six real-life couples. The trash talk gets pretty intense in that one. The cast of the Broadway play *Rock of Ages* has a league, as does Petty Officer 2nd Class Dick Shayne Fossett and the squadron aboard the *USS George H. W. Bush*. Jay-Z plays in a high-stakes league with music producers, record execs, and the people who run the 40/40 club. In fact, many celebrities play. *Saturday Night Live*'s Seth Meyers is a longtime player, as are actors Paul Rudd, Jason Bateman, Ashton Kutcher, and Elizabeth Banks. Daniel Radcliffe, "Harry Potter" himself, once told my podcast audience that Anquan Boldin was his "Fantasy Voldemort." Dale Earnhardt Jr. and the pit-crew guys at Hendrick Motorsports have a league, and there are tons of high-stakes Wall Street leagues. Priests, Rabbis, and Ministers sounds like the start of a joke, but it's actually three different fantasy leagues I know of.

The best part of fantasy is that it gives people who normally would not have a reason to interact an excuse to talk. From the CEO and mailroom guys to long-lost cousins to everyone in between, they all have one thing in common:

Fantasy brings them together. And it keeps them together too. That feeling of belonging is certainly what drew me to the game.

From the time I was born in Denver to when we moved to Richmond, then Atlanta, then Charlottesville, Virginia, and finally to College Station, Texas, I had moved around a lot as a child by the age of 12. My big frizzy hair didn't help, nor did always being the new kid. Add thick glasses (I'm nearly blind without contacts), plus a general sense of being socially awkward, and the prom king I wasn't.

Now, College Station is known for lots of things: Texas A&M University, where my father is a professor, is the big one. The George Bush Presidential Library, its sister city of Bryan, Texas, and the fact that singer Lyle Lovett got his start there all make the Wikipedia page.

But among the things College Station is *not* known for?

Jewish kids.

Only a few handfuls of them live there, so that was yet another thing that made me feel different when I arrived. For as long as I live, I'll never forget one of my first days in Texas. I was sitting at lunch with some classmates, including a girl I had just met. It was during Passover week, and I mentioned that the odd bread I was eating was called "matzoh" and that I was Jewish:

ME: What?

HER: What what?

ME: You're staring at me.

HER (genuine curiosity): I'm trying to see your horns.

ME: Horns?

HER: My dad said all Jewish people have them.

Half the table nodded. True story. Welcome to Texas, Berry.

So as a bit of an outcast, perhaps it was only natural that I would be drawn to a brand-new, niche game like fantasy baseball and that I was so willing to try something, anything . . . as long as it included me.

It was early spring in 1985, and I was actually a high school tennis player. Yes, that's right. In football-loving Texas, I played tennis, a sport you play without teammates. Looking back, it's amazing I had any friends at all.

I took tennis seriously. Won some tournaments, ranked as a USTA junior in the state of Texas, went to the state finals in high school, etc. This is only important to our tale for this lone fact:

As a result of being good at tennis, I took private tennis lessons. And that's only important because of the guy I took them from, the local tennis club pro, a man named Tommy V. Connell. Or as I prefer to call him, owner and general manager of the always plucky TV Sets.

I was walking up to see him for my lesson one day, and he was talking to his best friend, a guy I would later come to know as Beloved Commissioner for Life Don Smith, owner of the Smith Ereens. They were talking in a strange language that felt newly familiar, and going through names of guys they could ask "to join." What they were discussing would set my life on a course I'd never imagined.

"Are you guys talking about Rotisserie League Baseball?"

They were just as shocked that I knew what they were talking about as I was that anyone besides me read *Rotisserie League Baseball,* a weird little green book that had just been released detailing the rules, spirit, and advice about how to play "The Greatest Game for Baseball Fans Since Baseball."

Don, Tommy, and their friends were forming a league, and they needed a 10th guy who had both heard of this weird thing and was willing to try it. It was to be a National League–only fantasy baseball league. They would have to do stats by hand because in 1985 there was no Internet, no one had cell phones, and people still bought magazines for their porn.

I was 14 years old.

The other guys in the league were in their twenties and thirties, and I was a freshman in high school. But we've all been in leagues where you just need one more guy—any guy—to play, and that first year the Fat Dog Rotisserie League was no exception.

I joined because it seemed like a helluva lot of fun.

Almost 30 years later, I can confirm it is, in fact, ONE HELL. OF A LOT. OF FUN.

Fifteen years after my initial fantasy auction (blurrily pictured here), I would get my first job writing about fantasy sports. Four and a half years after that, I would start TalentedMrRoto.com, and in 2006, just a scant 22 years after this picture was taken, I sold the site and came to ESPN as its senior director of fantasy sports.

Along the way, a bunch of things happened. There were wars and presidents, and apparently some big wall overseas fell at some point, but probably most important, fantasy sports became not just mainstream but a way of life.

Fantasy sports are popular for lots of reasons. The competition with your friends, family, and even strangers. The rooting interest it gives us in sporting events we would normally never care about or the athletes we never dreamed of cheering for. The ease of it, thanks to the Internet and other technology.

But more than anything, it's *fun*.

For many people—and I'm in this group—it's all about your league. The guys and gals who are your league-mates. The good times, the bad times, the highs and the lows, it all comes back to someone's league. A bad league ruins the experience for so many, which is why I was so lucky that the Fat Dogs, my original league, is such a great one.

It's where I learned not only how to play but how to play the right way, to enjoy the game with a good group of guys who want to win, sure, but who mainly just want to laugh and have fun.

We draft on the same days every year. (Traditions are crucial for any good league.) The Friday after opening day we do the Lone Star American League auction (started the year after the Fat Dogs). Then on Saturday we do the National League. We sit in order of last year's standings, with the champion at the head of the table, second place sitting to his right, third next to second, and so forth.

Twelfth place gets to throw the first guy out for auction, and the pizza is delivered promptly at 12:30. Even though I live in Connecticut now, I fly back to College Station every year. That's right—the league still exists.

In fact, get this: 6 of the original 10 guys from 1985 are, many, many years later, still in the Fat Dog League. And two others have been in it for 20-plus years. For all the amazing advances the Internet has made to help the growth, popularity, and ease of fantasy sports, I see one major downside. That folks no longer have to be in the same room to draft. It's just not the same.

Especially when you get to draft with people you've known for more than a quarter-century. Because when you do something embarrassing at the draft—and we all have over the years—it gets remembered. Forever. And the amount of trash talk is both hilarious and awe-inspiring.

To this day, fellow Fat Dogger Woody Thompson, owner of the Thompson Twins, is reminded of the year he tried to draft promising youngster Ryan Howard to his minor league team, only to be told Howard was already owned. By him.

When we started, we didn't draft with personal computers because they didn't exist. Standings came once a week . . . by mail.

As for transactions, well, let Beloved Former Commissioner for Life Don Smith tell you.

"Originally, if someone wanted a player, they just called the commissioner. First to get to me, first served. Anyway, one Monday during that first year I was sitting in my office, and I heard a commotion. My brother Terry, owner of Smitty's Grills, was running down the hall with his five-year-old daughter in tow. 'C'mon, Heather, hurry, we've got to see Uncle Don! Hurry!' There were no cell phones, of course; it was about 8:30 AM, and he was taking her to school, but he'd heard on the radio that San Diego had a new starting outfielder. He was huffing and puffing, dragging his kid into my office. 'I claim Carmelo Martinez!' he wheezed as his confused daughter looked at her out-of-breath father. The Grills got their outfielder but Heather didn't make it to school on time. And we enjoyed the craziness of that moment for the next 26 years."

Yeah, we did, Don, and it was with great sadness to all the Fat Dogs when Terry passed away in March of 2011. I'll never forget Terry dragging his young daughter down the hall.

You know, since that first year, I've lost my glasses and a good chunk of the hair, I've gained experience, perspective, and weight, but most important, I have played in hundreds of fantasy leagues covering all kinds of sports and entertainment. I'm pretty sure I even played fantasy hockey once. What can I say? I was young and experimental.

But the best league I've ever played in is still the first one. As a league, we've been through marriages and births, heart attacks and deaths, and a three-week email war over who owned Manny Ramirez. They are great guys, they are pains in the ass, and I wouldn't trade my sense of community with them for the world. Recently, in a public study, ESPN found that the average *sports fan* spends more than six hours a week with ESPN on one of our many platforms—TV, radio, dotcom, the magazine, our mobile apps, etc.

But the average *fantasy player*?

He or she spends *over 18 hours a week* with ESPN. *Almost a full day a week!*

Oh yeah, people are into it. But while stats like that are impressive and speak to the broad appeal of fantasy, the truth is it's all about the people. It's not the draft, it's not the trash talk or the punishments, it's not even the winning (okay, maybe it's a little bit the winning). It's the people. It's the people who make the draft and the trash talk and the punishments and the winning what it is.

Consider the story of Kevin Hanzlik from Northfield, Minnesota. His team, Hanzie's Heroes, lost in the finals of his 2011 10-team fantasy football league. It happens. The fact that he lost to his 87-year-old mother, Pat Hanzlik? Not as common. Grandma Pat, as she is known, rode Cam Newton's rookie year and 16 touchdowns from Calvin Johnson to a title for G-Ma's Marauders.

Look at that picture. Come on. She's 87 years old. Get better than that.

Because of fantasy sports, I've had amazing experiences that I would have never thought possible. And I'm not alone. What follows are stories about me, stories about players, and stories about, to paraphrase Daniel Okrent and the founding fathers, "the greatest game for sports fans since sports."

So whether you are a lifelong fanatic, have never played before and want to understand what the fuss is about, or just have an afternoon to kill and need something with a bunch of small, easy-to-understand words, you'll soon realize what everyone else does.

Fantasy sports is outrageous, poignant, obsessive, heartwarming, heartbreaking, frustrating, crazy, uplifting, life-changing, monstrously fun, very addicting, and, quite simply, the best thing ever invented.

You'll see.

TIME-OUT:

Lessons of the Fat Dogs

The key to a great fantasy experience is a great league. And the lessons of the Fat Dogs are as good a blueprint as I've found in 30 years of playing:

We play fair: We all want to win, but we also play for fun. A victory you had to cheat to get isn't a real one. And as you'll see in upcoming chapters, people will do insane things to try and win a league. However, a league where no one cheats is a happy league. With the Fat Dogs, only one person has to report a trade. Every other league I've played in has to have both teams confirm. When I asked Beloved Commissioner for Life Don Smith about this early on, he said, very simply, "Well, if you're lying about the trade, we'll all find out pretty quickly." We've never had a problem.

Now THAT's a trade deadline: Our trading deadline is the final out of the All-Star Game. Every year a bunch of the owners gather to watch the game, and those of us who can't make it call in knowing that everyone who needs to trade will be checking in. Trade talk really heats up around the eighth inning, and nobody wants a one-two-three ninth. Of course, technically, the trade deadline in 2002 still hasn't passed. What are you gonna do? It's a double-edged sword. Bottom line, make sure you have a trade deadline party, whether it's the last minute of the Monday Night Football Game or the All-Star Game or even just midnight on a specific

Saturday night. The league that trades together is a league I wanna play in.

Have characters: Not character. *Characters.* That's a rule from Rick Hill, owner of the Zydeco Jukers. He brings a voodoo hand on a stick, Mardi Gras beads, and an iPod and large speaker to every draft. And every year, when the Jukers roster a player, loud Zydeco music blares as Rick waves the hand and shakes the beads. I've seen it for 30 years. It never gets old. Seriously. All leagues need silly and fun. Bring out your inner Juker.

No one tanks: Nothing—and I mean nothing—drives me more nuts than someone who stops playing or paying attention once their team is out of it. It's not only the wrong thing to do, it's bad karma. Even if you're out of it, your play has a bearing on the outcome of the league for others. And next year, when you're in the title hunt, you'll appreciate everyone else playing the season out and keeping your opponents honest. You're not always gonna win, but you'll always have your fantasy pride.

Of course, the Fat Dogs don't just rely on karma. We're a keeper league, so after the auction we do a minor league draft, where every year at least one Ryan Howard joke about Woody will be told. And first pick belongs *not* to the last-place team but rather the team finishing sixth, or just out of the money. So even if it's not your year, you still compete to try and finish sixth. It's no unicorn tattoo, but it works for us.

A league that eats together stays together: Just like the founding fathers did at La Rotisserie Française, our league eats lunch together every Thursday, rain or shine, at Jose's Mexican Restaurant in Bryan, Texas. During the second half of the season, this is also where we have a once-a-week, blind, free agent acquisition budget (FAAB) bidding on available free agents. If I am visiting my folks for a weekend, I will try to come in on Wednesday night, just so I can make Thursday lunch. Lotta laughs, trade talk, and studying of the standings.

Your league's traditions can be simple or, as you'll soon see, wildly elaborate. What they are isn't important. The important part is that they exist at all . . .

2.

Great Rules and Traditions

or

Every Team Has to Be Named After a Weird Kid from High School

For the Dartmouth Rotisserie Baseball League, the draft that year was perfectly normal. And the drinking was very typical. In fact, everything that happened that weekend was exactly as expected. Everything, that is, except one small thing . . .

Founded by 10 Dartmouth graduates in the late nineties, the league travels to different cities every year for their draft and parties all weekend. Mike Fleger explains that the "winner of the DRBL gets to choose the city. We've drafted in Las Vegas, South Beach, New York, Boston, Washington, DC, Chicago, Key West, and even Columbus, Ohio."

Draft weekend actually starts when they get to town on Wednesday night, and they go strong until they leave on Sunday. "The group of guys all live up to the tradition of 'Dartmouth boys'—hard-drinking, party-ing guys' guys," Mike says.

And so, with the draft done, Mike and the gang went to a bar and, following the natural progression of life, did what guys do at bars. "A guy in the league was hitting on a girl, and someone took a photo of the two of them. In the picture, they are grinning ear to ear as if they each won the one-night-stand lottery."

After the picture, the rest of the league went back to drinking and left their buddy to hang out with his new friend. And everyone forgot about the night.

Until the next year's draft.

"We'll find any reason to give a guy shit," Mike says, "and in this case it was easy. The girl from the bar had certain features . . . *masculine features.*" That's right. Their drunk buddy hooked up with a dude. So what does the league do? Let him forget it? Of course not. They all get T-shirts made up with a picture of this guy and his "date" and *wear them to the draft.*

I'm guessing these shirts don't get a lot of repeat wear. But it was a success that night. Not only did they manage to give their buddy tons of grief, but it ended up becoming a great opening line to girls afterward. "How many men do you see in this picture?" Mike and his buddies would ask as they approached. "Fifty to 60 percent responded, 'Two.'"

I've seen a close-up of the photo, and I assure you, gentle reader,

40 percent of the women that night were wrong. It is *definitely* two guys in the picture. And just to be clear, I have no issue with someone hooking up with a dude if a dude is who you *want* to hook up with. Love who you want. But if you think you're hooking up with a woman . . .

I told you last chapter . . . you do something embarrassing in a fantasy league and it gets remembered. Forever. At least it does in good fantasy leagues. And the DRBL is a great league. I love that they all travel to a different city to draft together every year. I love that they took the picture, all got T-shirts with it, and then *waited a year* to wear them. All for the sole purpose of giving one guy in the league crap.

But mostly, I love that they are all great friends from college who use this league as a way to keep in touch.

Because I can relate. Not only do I fly back to College Station for my original fantasy baseball league every year, I am still, more than 20 years later, in my original fantasy football league, which I joined when *I* was in college.

Half of my high school graduating class stayed local and enrolled at Texas A&M University. The other half headed to Austin, where they attended the University of Texas. Neither was an option for me. My parents wouldn't allow it.

Dad, or as he's known to the rest of you, Dr. Leonard L. Berry, grew up in Fresno, California. My mom Nancy was from Long Island. Dad went to the University of Denver, Mom went to CU in Boulder, and that's where they met. "You need to learn to be on your own," my folks told me when it was time to start applying. "There will be times when things get tough in college and you shouldn't be able to just drive home, do your laundry, and escape it. You need to be on your own and learn to figure it out for yourself."

And so it was settled. They were forcing me to go out of state. And thank goodness they did. So because they had a good communications program, I chose Syracuse University. Go Orange!

When I went to Syracuse, I was like a fish taken out of its bowl and dropped into the sea. It's like . . . Whoa! There are others like me? Who knew? Unlike small-town Texas, Syracuse had tons of Jewish kids, and I finally realized there was a genetic reason I was neurotic and talked with my hands.

I dove into everything I could there. Being a morning DJ at the student radio station? Done. Writing a humor column for the student newspaper? You bet. And most important—producing a show at the student TV station. Not just any show, but a sitcom.

Producing a sitcom is hard enough, but it's almost impossible on university TV. There weren't a lot of resources or equipment in 1988 when I was a freshman. Most of the TV shows they did at that time were what I called "one camera, one host, one plant." Literally, they were all music video shows or sports highlight shows. One person would sit next to one potted plant and talk into one camera about the new R.E.M. album for about fifteen seconds. And then play a Midnight Oil video. When I told the kids running the student station that I wanted to shoot a living, breathing, fully scripted, three-camera sitcom, shot in their studio, which was no bigger than a walk-in closet, they told me I was nuts. Plus, it's college: kids don't want to work that hard; they want to drink and party. They said I'd never get enough help with all the things a show needs—scripts, costumes, props, a crew, you name it. "How about doing a video countdown show?" they suggested.

Themes that would show up throughout my life suddenly surfaced: If you tell me I can't do something, I immediately set out to do exactly that. And no journey is taken alone.

I printed up flyers and posted them all over. I went to a bunch of classes and made my case. "They say this has never been done, they don't think it can be done, I'd like to prove them wrong, who is with me?"

Turns out, a lot of kids just wanted someone to say, "Hey, we're meeting Saturday at three." We got more volunteers than we needed.

Now, this wasn't just low-budget; it was no-budget. We had to bring in a remote news camera for our three-camera sitcom, which meant that every third shot was a little grainier than the others. We had college kids playing all the parts, no matter how old the character was supposed to be. And we only had enough money for one wig. There was lots and lots wrong with it, but we had a really funny cast, and if nothing else, it made us laugh. We ended up doing 20 half hours of the show, it won some student awards and got syndicated nationally on a college TV network, and many of the kids who worked on it went on to Hollywood careers. But the biggest thing for me was that I belonged.

There were lots of late nights setting up the studio, longer days shooting, and even more laughs, but through it I developed a good group of friends who worked together, hung out together, and played fantasy football together. And that's why this story is in here. One of the guys who worked on the sitcom was my friend AJ Mass, now a fantasy analyst at ESPN. He's the commissioner of the Doug Logan League (named for the longtime former radio broadcasting voice of Syracuse sports). I decided to co-own a team with the star of our sitcom, my college roommate and one of my best friends, a guy named Chris Lindsay.

You already know I stayed in the league, but I am proud to say, 21 years later, 11 of the original 12 members are still in it. It's been a great way to keep in touch with everyone, especially Chris, since we live on opposite coasts. Every week we're talking, texting, or emailing to set our lineup, prep for the draft, make pickups, or discuss the latest terrible trade offer. Neither of us needs to co-own a team, but I wouldn't want to do the league without him, and vice versa.

The bonds of fantasy leagues formed in college run deeper than most. And they exemplify the spirit of fantasy as well as anything.

In an odd way, a league is like a college. You have your own rules, language, and inside jokes. So whether it's ultra-specific scoring, unique rules, or strange traditions, a fantasy league, like college, is a universe unto itself.

Take, for example, Ryan Lents's CFL Fantasy League. Going into year 12 with 10 best friends from the Newman Center at Ball State University, they have a pretty good tradition.

"A month before the draft," Ryan tells me, "we all start growing out mustaches." And then Ryan went one step further. "I take pictures of all the guys' 'staches, and throughout the season I make vintage 1970s-era football cards for each of them with their league nickname and their actual NFL team of choice. It's been an epic hit."

Of course it was. As someone who actually collected cards in the seventies, these look damn authentic. I'm not even *in* Ryan Lents's league, but after Ryan sent me this . . .

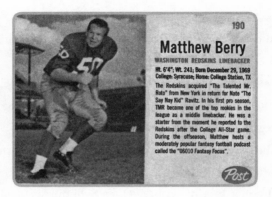

190

Matthew Berry

WASHINGTON REDSKINS LINEBACKER

Ht. 6'4"; Wt. 241; Born December 29, 1969
College: Syracuse; Home: College Station, TX

The Redskins acquired "The Talented Mr.
Roto" from New York in return for Nate "The
Say Nay Kid" Ravitz. In his first pro season,
TMR became one of the top rookies in the
league as a middle linebacker. He was a
starter from the moment he reported to the
Redskins after the College All-Star game.
During the offseason, Matthew hosts a
moderately popular fantasy football podcast
called the "06010 Fantasy Focus".

Post

. . . how could I *not* feel a kinship with them? I drew the line at grow-ing a '70s mustache.

A '70s mustache rule, meanwhile, might be the only thing the Ducal Crown Fantasy Football League *doesn't* have. Formed by fraternity brothers who went to the University of Virginia, the league is so popu-lar, commish AJ McGraw tells me, that they have a waiting list. "It's a group of guys who play in a separate league that we pull from when needed. Kind of like a fantasy farm system."

The Ducal Crown guys have a six-page, fully vetted and ratified constitution, an off-season rules meeting, and AJ writes a weekly blog during the season. But what really sets them apart is the trash talk. The *constant* trash talk. They do so much tweeting about the league, in fact, that the whole league created separate, private Twitter accounts for the *sole purpose* of trash-talking each other. Brilliant. Deranged and obsessive, but brilliant.

Now, on Twitter, these "@Ducal" accounts just follow each other, so the only people who see the trash talk are the guys in the league. At least, that was the idea. Until one day, out of nowhere, there was a new Twitter account following all the guys in the league: "@DucalSchefter."

Oh yeah. It's a parody account of ESPN NFL reporter Adam Schefter. But unlike the real Schefter, who reports on the entire NFL, this one has a very simple beat he covers: the Ducal Crown League.

"Yep," says AJ. "Our league has its own 'Insider.'"

And if you think that's obsessive, wait until you hear this. According to AJ, "We don't know who is running the account."

That's 50 shades of genius right there. One of the guys in the league started this account in secret, and now he's alternately helping and screwing the guys in the league.

"Yeah," AJ explains. "He'll direct-message you for information about your trade talks. Then he'll report on it."

But, as AJ notes, talking with "@DucalSchefter" is playing with fire. You can potentially get good insider info on what other owners are doing and this "Insider" allows you to sneak false information to another owner. But since no one knows who it is, you could be sneaking info to the same guy you're trying to deal with!

Personally, I love that they have an anonymous "Insider" reporting on and talking to everyone in the league. Very simply, whoever started that account is among the most clever fantasy minds ever. Diabolical, even.

Whether it's Twitter handles or football cards or even producing a league-only podcast (several leagues I've heard of do this), I'm a fan of any tradition that makes the league and the experience more memorable, more special, more . . . fun.

Jeremy Gurvits's Gizmo League from Newton, Massachusetts, arrives at their draft in a stretch limo, all dressed in mandatory formal attire, and they're videotaped as they walk down a red carpet. After each pick is announced by Jeremy, the owner comes to the podium for handshakes and a photo holding a copy of the player's jersey. Think that's over the top? Andrew Foster's TGKL League has an anthem (yes, an anthem) that they *all sing* before the draft. And Anthony Bouressa is in a longtime 14-team league from Kaukauna, Wisconsin, that requires all owners to eat a live moth to gain admittance and maintain membership in the league. You read that right. A live moth. Tattoo is sounding better by the page, isn't it?

Sometimes the traditions are what make a league unique; other times it's the rules. Michael "Duca" Manduca finished second so many times in his Sacramento, California–based league that they enacted "the Duca Rule," where first and third get paid out but second gets nothing. I know of leagues where you get two points every time your kicker makes a tackle, leagues where you can't draft a Yankee, leagues where the team that finishes last gets kicked out forever, and one league where every team had to be named after a weird kid from high school. In the St. Clair Rescue League out of St. Paul, Minnesota, John Palmersheim explains that the top two teams from the previous year do a "draft" in the off-season to decide who is in their division with them. Love the idea of choosing your own division and debating the merits of your league-mates right in front of them. "I'll take Keith, the human black hole. Where running backs go to die." "That's fine. Gimme Charlie. He just sucks."

And while that tradition is good for stirring up heated rivalries, there may not be a league rule that creates more of them than what they do in the Blut 3000 Fantasy Football League. Sal Iacono, better known as "Cousin Sal" from *The Jimmy Kimmel Show*, is a member of the league, an 11-team (yes, 11) league with a few celebrities and one very specific rule. "Whoever wins the league gets to vote a team *out* the following season, *Survivor*-style. Then the owner who was voted out gets to return the following season replacing the newly ousted owner."

The best (or worst) part of this rule? The champ doesn't announce his decision until the draft the following season. So all 11 team owners have to prepare and show up to the draft in September. Sal remembers that in 2010 "Jon Hamm of *Mad Men* fame texted me that he was going to be 30 minutes late because the shoot that day was running long."

Thirty minutes pass. More texts, more frantic calls. The shoot's still going. Finally, after two hours, Jon arrives. "He was out of breath and very apologetic (clearly having made an effort to be there), and then . . .

promptly voted out by the winning owner. In very cavalier Don Draper fashion, Hamm took a swig of beer, flipped the room the bird, and took off."

Great rule. Hilarious to 10 people and really annoying to one. And while Sal's league keeps one person from playing in the league that year, there's another league that has a different type of exclusion based on, well, I'll let "Jane" (not her real name) explain it.

"I've played in and commissioned an all-girls league for the past three years. We get together to watch the games, gossip, and drink martinis." And like lots of leagues, it was at those get-togethers that a specific tradition was born. One that I'm guessing isn't in most leagues. "You can't own a player you've dated. If you have dated a defensive player, you can't draft his team's defense," Jane explains. "We are a bunch of hot women who have dated a lot of NFLers in our days. So with this twist it makes us really think, *Do I want to draft him or 'date' him?*"

I am guessing there's lots of laughs and pointing at Jane's draft, especially when someone passes over an obvious pick. Either that, or some jealous turf claiming. "Oh really, Miss I already have two running backs? You better not be passing on Dez Bryant." "What? He's injury prone." "Mmmmhmmm. Sure he is. Excuse me. I got to make a call."

Adam Squires's 10-team Guinness Bowl League in Cleveland, Ohio, has been together for over a decade, and draft day is an all-day event where, Adam's wife Jennifer tells me, "I have one job: get the hell out of the house."

How big is draft day for the Guinness Bowl? Two years ago, it was on Adam's seven-year-old daughter's birthday. Take one guess which celebration got rescheduled. Hey, she was only seven. It's not like it was her 16th or anything.

Anyways, the Guinness League guys enjoy draft day so much, they don't simply analyze the draft right after, like many leagues do. No, they analyze *every draft in the 10-year history of the league.*

"Prior years' draft boards are dragged out of the basement and hung next to the current year's board," Jennifer tells me. Fueled by Bud Light and Jäger bombs, the guys crush each other's picks over the years and passionately defend their own all night long.

And that's what it's about. Spending time together. Whether it's eating a live moth, wearing a T-shirt of your buddy hooking up with a dude, or just sitting back, having a beer, and asking someone what the hell they were thinking in the third round seven years ago . . . these moments create memories and bond a group.

There may be no better example of that than the South Side Fantasy Football League (SSFFL) out of Kansas City. As Kyle Maciejczyk tells me, their commissioner, Bruce J. ("B.J.") Collins, "is the most genuinely nice guy in the world, a die-hard Chiefs fan who injects fun into everything we do." He would buy draft day T-shirts for everyone, personalized with their team names. B.J. had everyone over to his house to watch games and handed out customized scoring and matchup sheets along with a coaster featuring each person's favorite NFL team. Whenever there was an opportunity to make the SSFFL a little bit more fun, B.J. did it.

But a month before the season, Kyle tells me, the league got some terrible news. "B.J. was diagnosed with a cancerous tumor in his jaw."

"Due to the circumstances, we didn't even know if B.J. would be up to playing in the league, let alone running it." After talking to B.J., though, they realized that he desperately wanted to play that year—it was one of the few things he was looking forward to.

"So we brought the party to him and had the draft in the lobby of Good Sheperd Hospital in Bethlehem, Pennsylvania."

Most hospitals *only* allow family members to visit a patient. Which is exactly why the SSFFL was allowed to see B.J. . . . .

PART TWO

DRAFT DAY

3.

Drafting in Strange Places

or

"Turns Out, a Cheat Sheet Taped Inside My Beak Was Not Ideal"

Jeff Ralabate had a problem. As the commissioner of The League, a 10-team fantasy baseball league in the Buffalo area, he was used to problems. But this was a new one. And to make matters worse, he didn't have a lot of time to solve it.

The problem was Joe Bozek. Specifically, Joe Bozek's job. More specifically, the fact that Joe had been called in at the last minute to work said job. Two hours before the draft.

Jeff tried a bunch of different solutions, but they kept coming back to two main issues: One, this was the only time everyone in the league could get together for the foreseeable future. Two, the baseball season started the next day.

They say desperate times call for desperate measures, and this certainly qualified. So, Joe suggested, why not keep the draft time the same and switch the location?

To Joe's workplace.

Which was the chain restaurant Red Robin.

Where Joe would be *dressed as the Red Robin.*

Yep. They were running a promotion, and Joe had to wear the Red Robin suit, hand out flyers, and shake hands.

They let the Robin draft 10th so he would have plenty of time between picks. "Every few minutes," Jeff remembers, "he would waddle over to our table to see what pick we were on and who had been selected."

Joe explains that it wasn't easy. "Turns out, a cheat sheet taped inside my beak was not ideal. Nor was making picks quietly enough so children at nearby tables couldn't hear. It was, however, a fun and memorable experience." Jeff agrees. "It ended up being the most fun we've ever had at a draft."

I have no doubt. Is there any draft, anywhere, that wouldn't be improved by the addition of someone wearing a giant bird head? I was in a fantasy NBA league for a few years where a guy would come to every draft dressed in a head-to-toe Wookiee outfit. (Team name? The Wookiees, of course.) It was always funny. Always.

If you think about it—and by "think about it" I mean if you think about it with the goal of trying to make a flimsy connection between "real life" and "fantasy life"—draft day is the official start of your fantasy season, just like your first job out of college is really the official start of your professional life. Now, I never had to dress as a large bird, but dealing with kids? That I totally get.

After graduating Syracuse with a degree in writing for electronic media and having done the prestigious (as far as you know) student sitcom *Uncle Bobo's World of Fun!* I wanted to be a sitcom writer. So with my college writing partner (another big fantasy player named Eric Abrams), I moved to Los Angeles to try to break into television.

Which I accomplished, of course, by getting my first job at FAO Schwarz, the famed toy store. Sigh. A successful sitcom writer had told me to get a retail job. "Assistants in show business work long hours, rarely leaving time for writing. So with some nine-to-five retail job you can just concentrate on writing."

Which is very true. The problem is that once you're done writing, all you can really do is show your sample scripts to other toy store guys. You never meet anyone. Well, that's not true. I did get to wait on stars, including Arnold Schwarzenegger (at the height of *Terminator* fame), Denzel Washington, and many other celebrities. But none of them were looking for scripts from the guy wearing a hat made of Legos.

The job was no big red bird, but it was close. Since we had demos of every toy out, parents would just leave kids in the store to play. I couldn't believe it. Who just leaves kids unattended? And unattended kids do, well, what attended kids do, just more of it and with reckless abandon. Throwing things, breaking things, peeing everywhere. Seriously. I cleaned a lot of pee that first year. Hmmm. Maybe I *would* have been better off in a robin outfit.

I worked with lots of nice people, but I hated the job. My writing partner and I kept cranking out sample scripts and eventually I left FAO to get a job as a production assistant (read: gofer) on *The George Carlin Show.* I loved working for George, and a year later he wrote a recommendation letter for my writing partner and me to get into the highly regarded Warner Brothers' Writing Workshop. Through that I got my first sitcom-writing job on a show called *Kirk,* starring former teen heartthrob Kirk Cameron. I'm sure you're a big fan.

We were super-excited to officially be TV writers, but overall it wasn't fun. The only writers on the show were, frankly, writers who couldn't get jobs anywhere else. We were two newbie kids with a "Gosh, it's so awesome just to be here" attitude, which did not play well with grizzled, bitter comedy writers. Very tough year for a first gig. Anytime we'd try to be positive (or even pitch a joke), we were told to shut up.

But there were some positives. One writer on the show, Nancy Steen, was great, and I learned a lot from her. We managed to get an agent and kept writing scripts. And after that first year, the Parents Television Council declared *Kirk* to be the safest, most family-friendly show on TV. That's why I was so proud our next job was on the show they called the worst: *Married . . . With Children.*

Now, *that* show was a blast. I worked on 28 episodes, cowriting four, including the 250th episode and the last original episode to air (but not what's considered the "final episode").

It was 1996, and while I was writing on *Married . . . With Children,* I met and started dating a woman seriously. And when I wasn't spending time with her or working, I was becoming obsessed with fantasy sports. In addition to the Fat Dogs, the Lone Star League, and the Doug Logan League, I had joined a fantasy hoops league plus four more football and baseball leagues with some other LA-based Syracuse grads.

I remember being in the writers' room at work and putting possible lineups on the back of my scripts. During breaks, while everyone else was making calls, I was online, looking at stats and scrolling through player updates. I was winning a lot more leagues than not, and more important, I was not alone in my growing obsession.

Fantasy football was just starting to become semipopular. Fantasy would occasionally be mentioned in the mainstream media. Usually by an ex-athlete analyst who clearly didn't play. (Typical advice: "Hey, pick up rookie Karim Abdul-Jabbar!" Dude, it's week 15. He's been owned all season!) But at least it was a start.

There was actually a nationally syndicated fantasy football TV show back then that was on at odd hours (shout out to Brady Tinker!), plus a few segments on radio. The big websites like ESPN and Yahoo had just started offering fantasy sports columns, and Bill Simmons, the most popular sports columnist in the country, would occasionally write about fantasy. In fact, I believe Bill was the first (and only) mainstream national sports columnist to admit to playing fantasy in those days. But information was generally hard to find. And when you met someone else who played, it was thrilling, as if you two shared a secret life that most people hadn't heard about, let alone understood. It was like when you're a fan of an obscure band and you meet a fellow fan and you talk excitedly at them. "I know! I love their second album too!" "Did you see them at the Wiltern?" "I have the acoustic bootleg where they do a Jane's Addiction cover!"

Fantasy sports wasn't just invading my work life, it was also at home. While my girlfriend was watching TV, I was reading everything I could get my hands on. As my girlfriend waited for me so we could go out, I'd be on the phone with a league-mate, trying to pull a deal. While my girlfriend slept, I stayed up late studying free agents in my leagues like they were the Zapruder film. I was in double-digit fantasy leagues by that time, and my obsession was growing to the point that every single time I had a draft day I actually started to hide it from my girlfriend.

Just like Jacob Karp, whose "In It to Win It" fantasy football league draft got scheduled when he'd be on a romantic trip in Europe. "My girlfriend is a cool chick, but she wasn't going to be pumped on me spending time in Santorini drafting a fantasy football team," remembers Jacob.

But what initially seemed bad turned into a plus: the draft was scheduled for the middle of the night there. So what does Jacob do? Takes the girlfriend out to a nice dinner, orders bottles and bottles of wine, and gets her totally hammered. That's right. Jacob became the first man in history to get a girl drunk to *not* sleep with her.

Back at the villa, she passed out cold. Jacob quietly escaped to draft a fantasy team. He says, "The next morning my girlfriend awoke with a headache and, more importantly, zero suspicions. *Boom.*"

Boom indeed. As any fantasy owner worth his salt will tell you, you can't miss draft day. Because it's not just the best day of the year, if you want to compete that year, it's the only day of the year. That simple. Come hell or high water, you draft.

No matter *where you are.*

Even if you are in temple for the Jewish High Holidays? Even if you are in temple for the Jewish High Holidays.

It was Yom Kippur, the holiest of the Jewish High Holidays, and Michael Gottlieb's Syracuse, New York–based fantasy hockey draft was happening with or without him. He couldn't miss services, and since cell phones are not permitted in the sanctuary, he had to get creative.

"I positioned myself at the end of the aisle near the back of the synagogue. During each round, my buddy would stand outside and talk to the league. I told him to write each pick on a small piece of paper no bigger than his palm."

When it was Michael's turn, his buddy would walk into the synagogue, Michael would read over the names picked, and then whisper his pick to him. His family, Michael tells me, never knew. "I did, however, overhear someone say they thought someone was having explosive diarrhea because he was constantly leaving the service."

You see that, folks? People would rather be seen as having explosive diarrhea than reveal that they're drafting a fantasy sports team. We've come so far.

Michael continues: "I am proud to say that my team, Forsberg's Spleen, won that league convincingly."

There is one thing I definitely learned doing this book. No matter what you believe in religiously, there's someone who is happy to violate it for fantasy sports. In 2009 Matthew Mahn's church youth group went to a church in Tulsa, Oklahoma, to do a special youth service on his draft day.

So Matthew skipped out of church, *snuck into the pastor's office,* got on the pastor's computer, and quietly drafted a team. Remember, *he's visiting this church and doesn't know anyone.* But draft day went off without a hitch and no one was the wiser. Even better? Matthew won the league that year, his first title ever. He adds, "I've been in plenty of leagues since, and to this day the team I drafted in a church is the only one to ever win a title."

Huh. Both Michael and Matthew drafted their teams in houses of worship, and both won their leagues. Maybe the rest of us are doing it wrong by drafting at people's houses, at bars, at . . . the White House Situation Room?

Check out this passage from Michael K. Bohn's book *Nerve Center:* "Clinton's national security advisers, Tony Lake, Sandy Berger [both avid baseball fans], and others used [the Situation Room] to conduct their Rotisserie League draft during Clinton's first term." Tony Lake recalled their hobby: "We held our player drafts in the Situation Room, each of us chipping in twenty-three dollars to build a pot that went to the winning team at the end of the season."

Hard to top the room where national security decisions are made for a unique and crazy place to draft, but thanks to wi-fi and mobile technology, it doesn't mean people haven't tried.

Brandon Bruce drafted from Disneyland while his wife and kids were on rides. Jeremy Harshey drafted while at an outdoor Ted Nugent concert, and Alex Timmons drafted during a USC football game, sitting in the stands at the LA Coliseum. Matt Hediger drafted from his phone while sitting in court, as he was a witness in a robbery and got summoned to appear on his draft day. "Your honor, I saw the defendant . . . Dammit, he took Harvin!"

When Arthur Lenk was named Israel's ambassador to Azerbaijan, it meant he had to draft from Baku, Azerbaijan, with the rest of his league in Israel. After some technology issues, the only way he could do the draft was by phone, and a lengthy call from Azerbaijan to Israel cost much more than any prize money he could have won in the league. He still made the call.

In August of 2000, Dr. Satch of the Long Island, New York–based Wiley Football League was doing his residency as an orthopedic surgeon. League-mate Jonathan Stulberg tells it like this: "Kid comes into the emergency room with a displaced fracture in his arm. Doc gives the kid a Novocain shot to numb the area. Doc's just about to reset the kid's arm when his cell phone buzzes. Doc says, 'Excuse me,' walks to the corner, and answers.

"'Give me Derrick Alexander.'

"He calmly shuts the phone and walks over to the couple. 'Sorry, very important call. Novocain should be working now.' Mom is still somewhat astonished, while Dad looks at him. 'Nice pick, doc.'"

Dante Gorrindo had to draft during a good friend's bachelor party.

Problem was, no one else at the party was in the league. So Dante did what he had to. He brought his laptop *into the strip club*. "I made my picks while watching my friend have the time of his life." Dante shrugs. "Was I distracted by the situation, you ask? Well, I finished middle of the pack. . . ."

Ah, drafts at strip clubs. Was wondering when those stories would show up. "Duncan's" Northern California–based league always holds its draft at the local strip club. "After the eighth round, the girls dance and lose all their clothes. Guys get the sticker of the player they want to draft," Duncan explains, "and put the sticker on their nose and approach the stage. Then the stripper removes it with her boobs."

"Best story is a few years ago one guy who is usually kind of reserved got a little crazy. Stickers on his crotch, girls bouncing on him to take them off, etc. So then he decides to place a sticker on his nose, lies on his back, and the girl sits down on his face to pick up the draft sticker. Pretty awesome . . . until he had to explain to his wife how he got pink eye."

You know, for a league filled with guys, it seems like a perfect setup. Drafting fantasy football while surrounded by beautiful women. What could possibly go wrong?

"Jerry A" is in the Murphy Fantasy League, a 20-year league from the Philadelphia area. They usually hire strippers to perform a "show" in the middle of the draft. But last year his commish decided the league was going to up the ante and hold their draft at an *actual* strip club. "So he called a local club and made arrangements for the league to do the draft in the upstairs room."

Which sounds great. Until they got there. "As I walked up the stairs I felt as if time had slowed down, like the moment before a car crash. On the walls were life-sized photos of muscled guys in cliché outfits like 'the fireman,' and 'the policeman' . . . That's right. Our commish didn't know the upstairs he booked was, in fact, a *male* strip club.

At that point, Jerry's commissioner went into damage control, but after much pleading, the best that could be done was the guys got free admission into the female club after their draft.

"Rescheduling would have been impossible, so we drafted surrounded by various dudes pumping up, oiling up, the smell of man sweat . . . the whole thing was very distracting."

But did it stop folks from drafting? Of course not. If you've learned anything from this chapter it's that it doesn't matter where you are. If it's draft day, you draft. Period. Whether you are in a Red Robin outfit, whether you are at a male strip club, or even if you are overseas *fighting in a war* . . .

You heard me.

I cohost a daily fantasy football podcast for ESPN called *Fantasy Focus,* and we have a very popular 16-team "Man's League" where listeners play in a league against our producer, Jay Soderberg, aka "Podvader." In 2011 Chase Magann was among the 15 people selected to play in it.

Unlike the 14 others, however, his day job was fighting a war. "My buddy Jake Rettig and I were stationed in northern Iraq at FOB Warrior, just outside the city of Kirkuk. We work as a scout weapons team. Our main mission was to protect the base from rocket attacks, paired with a ground patrol inside the city of Kirkuk." The guys were excited to be selected for the league, but to put it mildly, it would not be easy.

"Iraq was eight hours ahead of the eastern United States in time. And we were concerned that we would have to fly mission during the actual draft. So we devised a plan: we'd wake up around 4:00 AM, fly the mission, and be back in time to draft. The entire schedule was worked out for our day to revolve around this auction."

So they took off just as the sun rose, but it didn't matter. It was still crazy hot. "September in Iraq is not fall. Sitting in the Kiowa Warrior with no doors on and all our body armor and gear made it even hotter. We flew like that for seven hours. As we did our mission, Jake and I discussed who we liked for the upcoming draft. Jake liked Matthew Stafford; I wanted to avoid Peyton Hillis. We war-gamed how much we were willing to spend on each position and sleepers we thought we could get cheap." They landed back on the base just before the draft. (Think about that. They had to do their entire prep for this draft *while flying over hostile territory during wartime in Iraq.*)

So now Chase and Jake go to the computer room that was designed for soldiers to use to keep in touch with their families. The auction was going along fine for a while, Chase recalls, until disaster struck. "I was about to hit pass on Peyton Hillis [in his last year with the Browns] when the Internet froze. We couldn't do anything. Instantly we decided to go back to my room for the draft, where the Internet wasn't as reliable but was run by a different server."

Annoying but reasonable, right? Except the computer room they were in was in a hangar, Chase tells me, that "was surrounded by giant concrete barriers and baskets filled with dirt and sand. They are all designed to protect from rocket attacks that happened on the base."

That's right. Rocket attacks. You have the same concerns where you draft, right? Unfortunately for Chase, "the fastest way to our living quarters was through this maze of barriers. But we had no choice. So I took off running. I hadn't had time to change out of my uniform from earlier, so I had on my ACU patterned flight suit, combat boots, and my 9mm pistol strapped to the side of my hip as I jumped on the side of barriers trying to get to our living areas."

Personally, I get tired from repeated trips to the fridge in shorts and a T-shirt, but for Chase and Jake? "It took about two minutes to run at a full sprint back to our rooms about a quarter-mile away. Once I got there, I flipped up my computer and saw that at that time I was missing money and had filled a roster spot. That roster spot was now filled . . . with running back Peyton Hillis. He was auto-auctioned onto our team at a much higher price than we could afford."

These guys woke up at 4:00 AM, flew all day over Iraq, ran through concrete barriers that were open to potential rocket attacks, completely *risked their lives serving our country,* and what was their reward?

Just 10 games played, three touchdowns, 717 total yards. Peyton Freakin' Hillis. Remember when Hillis couldn't play one week that year because he got a cold? Jake and Chase were flying over Iraq in 100-degree heat. I'm glad it's Chase and Jake protecting our country, not Peyton Hillis. Just saying.

Jake, Chase, Dick Shayne Fossett, and everyone in the military (special shout-out to those who play fantasy), I thank you for your service, and I'm thrilled that fantasy sports allow you guys a bit of much-deserved distraction and fun. Even if your draft story is crazy.

Of course, crazy doesn't mean surprising. Because this is not a surprising story. As you're about to see, it's not just a weird or inconvenient location, there is nothing—and I mean *nothing*—that will stop people from drafting.

TIME-OUT:

Picking the Draft Order

Obviously, draft day is the biggest day in any league. And an important part of draft day, of course, is what order you draft in. Picking the draft order is one of the most fun traditions of draft day itself, or even as an event prior to the day. It's also among the most creative.

Dave Armstrong let a kid's soccer team kick 10 numbered balls to determine his Eagle Mountain, Utah–based league's draft order: furthest ball gets first pick. The funniest part is that one of the kids totally whiffed on his ball. Can you imagine? "Wait, I got pick 10 because my kid was Count Dorkula?"

Austin Strelinger is the GM of The Fozzie Bears. And his Denver, Colorado–based Live Free or Die Nasty keeper league has found a way to keep the action going all year round. In January, right after fantasy football season, they all start watching *The Bachelor*. Every week. After the first week, in reverse order of standings from the regular season, each team chooses one hopeful woman. The longer the woman lasts, the higher the fantasy football draft pick the next year. "It's funny," Austin says. "Picture a bunch of guys in mid-February, yelling, 'I can't believe Ben sent Rachel home this week!'"

There's no end to the creativity when it comes to picking draft order. I've heard of leagues that race horses, pigs, even each other. Travis Knoll's BIG League from Bigfork, Montana, has a fun tradition. "We buy 10 rubber duckies, paint them different colors, and race them," Travis tells me. "First place in the duck race gets first pick, second gets second, and so on." That makes sense. But that's not my favorite part of the story. It's what they have to do to race the ducks.

"The entire league jumps a chain-link fence, passing numerous TRESPASSERS WILL BE PROSECUTED signs, and we illegally drop the ducks into a waterway. Throwing rocks behind your team's duck to give it a boost is legal, and bombing rocks at opposing ducks to stop them is encouraged. Meanwhile, a video camera is placed at the finish line so we can decide photo finishes by replaying it in slow motion."

That's right. They not only do this whole thing, they tape it and *watch it back*.

"Even though we all go to college in different states, we still all gather in Bigfork for the annual Rubber Duck BIG League draft race."

It's awesome that all of them travel back home specifically to jump a chain-link fence to race plastic ducks. But they're not the only league that travels to pick the draft order.

Brian Bentley's Lone Star fantasy league started with a group of friends from Baylor University in 1997. Every summer they put 10 Ping-Pong balls, each with a team's name on it, into a hat to determine draft order. "We've held the draft lottery at Texas Ranger games, family cookouts, and the side of the road, but on June 16, 2007, the Ping-Pong balls traveled to Santa Fe, New Mexico, for the wedding of one of our owners where half of the league was present."

So what made this lottery so special?

The bride made the picks.

Between the ceremony and the reception.

In her wedding dress.

Amy Chalfant, the bride, is in the league and her West Frisco Honey Badgers are former champions. But even still, why on earth would a woman interrupt the biggest day of her life to pick a draft order? Because draft day is that important. Because draft day is that special. Because, as Beloved (now Former) Commissioner for Life Don Smith has said to me every single time the Fat Dogs all get together for our draft, "It's only the best day of the year."

4.

Drafting by Any Means Necessary

—————— *or* ——————

"They Have Free Wi-Fi at the Krispy Kreme!"

The first thing you should know is that we are witholding his last name.

Because the second thing you should know is that everything here is very, very real.

"Dan N." you see, is a repo man. A repo man who works nights. A repo man who works nights who wants to keep his repo man job. Hence the first name only.

The story starts one random night in August of 2011. "My fantasy league was drafting at 9:00 PM during my shift, which meant I was going to be drafting live from the repo truck. Not an ideal situation, but I figured I could make it work," Dan tells me.

"My partner knew I'd be drafting, so we agreed to go after a car we'd been trying to find for weeks but had never seen. We called it 'The Loch Ness Monster.' Obviously, we wouldn't see it tonight either, and I could draft in peace and quiet."

Of course, if that's what had happened, this story wouldn't be in the book, now would it?

"My draft is ready to begin, and the freakin' car shows up. My partner decides to hook it, but we get seen, and the owners jump in the car, refusing to get out. Now I'm in a pickle, as my draft is starting, we've got a car hooked up, and we've got an irate woman and her husband trying to get us to put the car down."

Yeah, that's a situation it's hard to mock for.

"I go back to the truck and start my draft. What else was I supposed to do? The husband comes to the truck to try and convince me to put the car down. But then he sees that I've got your rankings up on my computer and that I'm about to draft. 'Draft Vick,' he says. 'I agree with Berry: he's going to have a huge year.' I take that as a sign and pull the trigger on Vick at eight."

Yeah. Sorry 'bout that.

"So the wife sees the husband involved with our draft, and she is still sitting in her car, so now she's *really* pissed. She decides to try a different tactic to get us to put the car down. She calls the cops."

Things are going smoothly, then?

"The draft continues, the cops show up and demand to know what's going on. My partner explains the situation. 'I'm trying to repo the car,' he says, 'while that woman is trying to drive it off the flatbed and my partner is trying to draft his football team.' The cop, doing his civic duty, demands that I tell him the round and scoring system, then proceeds to tell me my pick of Vick was a mistake and I need to grab Bradford as a backup. Sweet, now I have gotten advice from another repo man, a deadbeat, and a cop."

I love how fantasy can bring the most unlikely people with such diverse interests together. And that the cop was even more wrong on Bradford than I was on Vick. Anyways, back to Dan.

"All of us finish the draft together, and now that it's over, we get back to the repo and come to an agreement. We get the car, the cop writes it up as an amicably resolved civil disturbance, and I agree that if I win any money, I will send the husband half. Deal."

"Meanwhile, the woman realized that the four guys at the scene (two repo men, a cop, and her husband) cared more about my third-round pick than they did about her sitting in a car on my flatbed. So as we were leaving, she went inside and locked him out of the house."

Relationships are like car bills, you have to take care of them.

"I'm not 100 percent sure, but showing more concern for the fantasy draft of a dude you've never met who is repo-ing your stuff ahead of the satisfaction of your wife is probably not going to win you Husband of the Year. And if it does, I've been doing this whole marriage thing wrong.

"Epilogue—I went out of the playoffs in the first round, so the husband lost his car, my league, and quite possibly his wife, due to one bad fantasy draft."

So you're saying Vick in the first round wasn't his worst judgment of the night? Fair. Drafting while getting yelled at by an angry wife, dealing with a cop, and trying to tow a car is, shall we say, not optimal. But whatever. Dan found a way. For those of us obsessed with fantasy, there is no such thing as no. There are only challenges to be overcome.

That's always been my attitude. And when something important in my life and fantasy would intersect, well, I would always choose fantasy. Which meant making sure that my wedding day wouldn't conflict with any fantasy sports. That's right, wedding day. The girlfriend had recently turned into a fiancée who, in the summer of 1999, would become my wife.

It was still a few weeks before my wedding and as usual I was reading every fantasy article I could find. I had read in a column somewhere that *The Sporting News* was starting up its own independent fantasy service. I emailed Matt Pitzer (*SN*'s lead fantasy guy at the time), asking for help, and he gave me the email address of a man named Mike Nahrstedt, who was starting the whole thing up.

One of the reasons for fantasy's appeal, of course, is proving how smart you are. And I think everyone who is human has some insecurity. Look, I'd been in Hollywood, and it's a tough town. Between pounding the pavement for a few years to find a job and experiences like *Kirk*, I was getting mentally beat up a lot. So with those issues and a need to constantly prove myself, what could be better than getting my own column and having a legitimate sports website call me a "fantasy expert"?

I was a reasonably successful Hollywood writer at that point, having sold movies and working steadily in TV, and yet, there I was, on my honeymoon, running from the beach to dial up to my email in my hotel room to see if Mike had responded. (There wasn't even fast Internet, let alone email, on your phone in 1999.)

When Mike said, sure, give him a call, he was amazed I would do it from my honeymoon. Frankly, I was amazed he was amazed. I was so into it and excited, I assumed tons of guys must have been banging down his door. My interview went well, and I convinced him of my passion. I wanted to be a columnist for him, a "fantasy expert." How could I get in on the ground floor of this, I asked?

Would I write news blurbs, like the ones on Rotonews? You bet. Would I work dirt cheap? You bet. (I wasn't giving up my movie-writing jobs, I thought, so who cares what they pay? I just want to do this for fun on the side.) Could I move to St. Louis, because they needed me in the office?

And that's where I had to say no. My wife, who had a great job as an executive in show business, wasn't moving to St. Louis, and I couldn't ask her to.

But just the idea, the mere possibility of writing about fantasy sports, of somehow having a national fantasy website declare me an analyst, got me more pumped than I had been in quite some time. So I started looking all over the Internet for another opportunity.

There were two websites I used all the time back then. Rotonews .com (which later became Rotowire.com) and a similar site, a news gathering and commenting site called Rotoworld. One day in the fall I noticed Rotoworld was advertising for fantasy writers. My heart started racing. "Know fantasy sports? We're looking for a few good writers! Email us!" the ad screamed, along with a link to do just that. So I wrote this long, impassioned email. How I was a professional writer in Hollywood. How I not only loved fantasy sports but lived and breathed them. That I'd do it for free. Please, I begged, is there any way I can try out?

And after pouring my heart out in this email, I quickly heard . . . absolutely nothing. Follow-up emails got no response. Emails asking to be turned down just so I knew someone had read me were also ignored.

But whatever. That's not a no, right? It's just a challenge that needs to be overcome.

I had read the site enough to know that its head writer was a guy named Matthew Pouliot. So I emailed him directly, saying I had a fantasy advice question, but not one he usually got. The advice I wanted was how could I get a job at Rotoworld?

I mentioned the unanswered emails and that I was a sitcom and movie writer but obsessed with fantasy sports. Could he give me advice on how to get my foot in the door there? If I wrote a sample column, could he get someone to look at it? Or help me get an interview with someone? Anything?

Matthew wrote me back the very next day, saying he was actually in charge of hiring. The jobs email had been so overflowed with applicants that he just hadn't had the time to sift through everything.

Anyways, because I sent my message directly to Matthew's personal email, he had taken a look, and the professional writer thing intrigued him. He said he looked me up on IMDB.com to see if I was telling the truth. As it turns out, *Married . . . With Children* was his favorite show of all time. And just like that, I was hired.

(Little known Rotoworld fact: in the early years, every update, on every player, was done . . . by Matthew Pouliot. All him. For multiple years. Others made a lot more money off that site than he did, but he's the reason that site had early success. Truly an unsung hero of the fantasy sports industry.)

Obviously, 1999 was a much different time. You still had to dial up to get online. People weren't online all day like they are now . . . you checked your email maybe once a day. Nothing was mobile. It was much more prestigious in those days to write for a newspaper or magazine. And like I said, Rotoworld (it turned out) was really just a one-man shop in terms of the content. So the fact that I was a professional writer carried a decent amount of weight, given that few, if any, of the columnists on the site had any formal training. But still . . . no sample, no anything?

I asked Matthew: Don't you want to see what I can do? Prove I know something about fantasy? He wrote back something very smart that I later used when hiring my own writers. "The readers will tell us if you do," he said. "If you don't, they won't read you. And that will be that. In the meantime, you're hired."

Getting that "you're hired" email was among the happiest days of my life. I literally pumped my fist in the air when I read the email. I called my wife. I called my parents. It was unreal. I was a 29-year-old man, I had a successful script-writing career, and yet I was doing backflips because I was getting to write for free for a website most people had never heard of.

But, man, was I fired up. I would have done anything for that job. Which isn't shocking behavior. Many of us who play fantasy are like that with our enthusiasm and focus: We do whatever we have to compete, to win, and especially . . . to draft.

But it's not just about funny or weird places. It's about overcoming any obstacle. About not taking no for an answer. About finding a way to draft . . . *by any means necessary.*

Just ask Zach. In March 2009, eight members of Zach's 14-team fantasy baseball league, The Gentlemen's Club, planned on doing their draft in Vegas. Scheduled for Saturday, they drove in from LA on Friday night. "We basically drank and gambled until about 5:00 AM," Zach says, shocking absolutely no one.

Like many college students in Vegas, they were hungover and very poor the next morning. Unlike many college students, however, they also had a draft. So, told by the concierge that there was free wi-fi at a coffee shop in Planet Hollywood, they headed out. Once there, they found no wi-fi, with only an hour until draft time.

Zach continues: "Keep in mind, none of us had smart phones. We are now too far away to walk back to our hotel by draft time, and we have no money for cabs. It would be impossible to convey the enormity of our challenge. We had to find a place with Internet without using the Internet, assemble our crew of eight, and walk there while hungover within the next 60 minutes."

Actually, Zach, I think you conveyed it pretty well. Looks like you're screwed. "Clutching our laptops, we cast about, calling everyone in our phone books to see if they knew where to find Internet within 45 minutes' walking distance of Planet Hollywood." They started assaulting passersby on the street like creepy zombies with bed head and bloodshot eyes. "Internet! Where can we get Internet?"

Then Zach hears a rumor. "They have free wi-fi at the Krispy Kreme!" Now, time is getting short, and the store is located in the Excalibur, which is far down the road, but doable. "So," Zach tells me, "we went for it, dodging traffic and throngs of people on the streets. What should have taken 30 minutes to walk took us 10. While hungover. But we made it, and true to the word, they had free wi-fi. We cracked open celebratory tall boys and began another glorious fantasy baseball season."

Hungover, sleep deprived, no money, no Internet, hauling laptops through Vegas an hour before the draft? Pretty sure this is what Rudy Tomjanovich meant when he said, "Don't ever underestimate the heart of a champion."

And you know what else Zach told me? "It has now become tradition. Every year since, we make the pilgrimage to the Krispy Kreme. We bring tall boys, make stupid parlay bets on March Madness, and once again vie for the position of Gentlemen's Club champion."

I applaud an entire league working together like that to make draft day happen. Like Tony Seidman's Quebec-based Solly's Fantasy Baseball League out of Quebec. In the year 2000, they had a problem with their auction. Normally done in person, a few guys in the league had moved away that year. Back then, long distance wasn't cheap like it is today, and you couldn't do a 10-way conversation via IM, video chat, or web messenger like you can now. So what were they to do? Eventually, they came up with a solution.

"We all decided to log on to a porn site and hold our draft in one of their sex chat rooms. Needless to say, we had several visitors to our chat room who did not understand what 'Barry Bonds for $8' meant. Our auction, which normally takes about five hours, took us about ten as we would constantly be interrupted with 'Are there any horny girls in here?' or guys 'yelling' at us, saying we weren't talking about sex enough." Odd. Never an issue at any of my drafts. Tony continues: "Somehow we got the whole auction done."

There are endless stories of people going above and beyond to draft a fantasy team. Brendan Dennis drafted while driving a tugboat, veering off his charted course to steal wi-fi from an oil rig. His boat showed up three hours late to the dock, but he got his draft in. While he was at work, Brian Kleckner's neighborhood was forced to evacuate because of a nearby wildfire. But it was draft day, so Brian snuck past police to break into his house, grab his computer, and sneak back out, past police again, to do his draft. And Drew's auction draft was the day after Hurricane Irene and there was no power. So he used his parents' small battery-powered generator to power his laptop and drain his folks' generator. "With the generator useless, my parents had to just sit in the dark while I did my draft."

What proud parents they must be.

Many great draft day stories, from what people have risked to what they've overcome. But the one I like the most might also be the simplest.

Scott Warren had just moved to Atlanta and, wanting to socialize with league-mates in person, found a league with an opening on Craigslist.

"It was an eight-team mixed keeper league that had been running for about 10 years. Fifty bucks to get in. Yeah, kind of small, but I just wanted to play. So I started looking over strategies for eight-team leagues and doing my homework to crush the competition."

Scott did more than that. Custom, in-depth spreadsheets, rankings, projections, depth charts . . . all loaded on his computer. As Scott says, "I love being the most prepared person at the table."

But when Scott gets there, there are only six other guys that will draft. Now it's a seven-man league apparently. *Great*, he thinks. *What a waste of my time.* Scott continues: "The commissioner then says $150 would be going to the website they host the league on. Ouch! That left just $200 to win on a $50 investment. My hopes of enjoying this league at all were dwindling."

But then Scott learned that of the remaining $200, $100 would be taken out and put into a girl's fund for college. He's just about to leave when he learns why.

"The league name was the George Braitsch Memorial League. This league first started with some work buddies, and Mr. Braitsch had dominated this league for years. Tragically, some years ago Mr. Braitsch unexpectedly passed away midseason, leaving behind a wife and young daughter. The members of the league decided to name the league in honor of their friend."

In fact, Scott learned, George was the eighth owner. "His team is filled with minor leaguers and benchwarmers, but he will always be a part of this league. The members decided that they would take $100 from the pool every year and put it in a trust for his daughter to have after she graduates high school to help buy books for college or whatever she needs. And before we drafted, the commissioner gave everyone an update on the young girl, how she was doing, and what extracurricular activities she was involved in.

"I was amazed at how truly touching the whole story was. It reminded me that playing fantasy baseball wasn't about winning money or proving who was the best, it was just about having a good time with good people. I could tell the rest of the guys were here for that reason. No one had a laptop, only a couple had a magazine, and most just had a few handwritten notes. So for the first time ever in a draft, I packed up my laptop, yanked a cheat sheet out of a magazine, and just started to scratch off names as they were called.

"It wasn't about proving anything. It was just about having a good time."

PART THREE

THE SEASON STARTS

5.

The Questionable Ways People Try to Win

or

"So I Invited Ricky's Ex-Wife to Join the League . . ."

"You *play* to *win* the *game!*" screamed Herm Edwards at a postgame press conference. Coach Edwards was speaking about the NFL, of course, but in this oft-repeated quote, he could just as easily have been speaking about fantasy sports.

Friendship is great. So is competition. Camaraderie, smack talk, league traditions, all fun and wonderful. But at the end of it, you play. To win. The game.

It's a noble pursuit, of course, except when it comes to how far people will go to win. And that's when the area, you see, turns gray.

"Travis" had done it the right way. As the commissioner of a work league in 2010, he had finished first in the regular season. And then, in the first round of the playoffs, he squeaked out a victory, winning by two points.

Or did he?

Late on Monday, the NFL ruled that in his week 15 game against the Jets, Steelers running back Rashard Mendenhall rushed for 99 yards instead of the 100 he was originally credited with. The NFL changed his official stats. That meant, in Travis's league, his team had four points taken away (one for the yards and a three-point bonus for 100 yards total). As a result of the stat change a day later, Travis actually *lost* his playoff game by two points.

He felt the way you or I would. "I was incredibly upset and felt cheated."

Of course, the way Travis reacted is probably different from the way most of us would.

"I went in that night before I thought anyone noticed and changed the totals. I tried to make it look like I had won by the same amount. However, because commissioner changes are listed, some guys noticed. They confronted me, and I admitted what I had done and changed it back. They then told everyone at the office about my cheating."

I know what you're thinking. You're thinking that's pretty bad. But guess what? That's not the worst part. Tell them the worst part, Travis.

"I am a pastor."

You heard him. A pastor.

"At the time, a staff pastor for a big church in Oklahoma, as is the rest of the league."

That's right. Travis cheated in a league *full* of pastors. And you know what? He wasn't alone!

"In that same 2010 season, two of the other pastors did a lopsided trade that was ridiculous. There was another case of one team benching its lineup to help another team make the playoffs. . . . It all really came to a head after I cheated to try to win. We were in our weekly pastoral staff meeting, and we all started yelling at each other. Not really angry, just being aggressive and challenging each other's code of ethics. Our boss, the senior pastor, did not play in the league. He just sat there staring at us with this look like, *I can't believe I hired these idiots to help me pastor this church.*

Honestly, I sorta can't either.

Travis continued: "I have since become the lead pastor at a church in another state, but I still run that league. And I often wonder if the people in my church would lose respect for me if they knew I had cheated to try and win a fantasy football league."

I'm gonna say yes, which is why I altered your name.

"PS—I finished first in the regular season again this year and once again lost in the first round of the playoffs, this time by only three points. God may love Tebow, but He frowns upon pastors cheating in fantasy football."

That antsy feeling Travis got when the Mendenhall stat got changed—the frustration, the restlessness that kept him up at night, the feeling this all seemed somehow unfair—is a feeling I can truly relate to. You see, after *Married . . . With Children*, Eric and I began our run of writing for a bunch of very talented people on some truly terrible sitcoms. We worked for people like Diane English and James Burrows—titans in the industry known for shows like *Murphy Brown, Cheers, Friends,* and *Will and Grace.* Except, of course, those weren't the shows of theirs we worked on. We were low-level writers for much of it, so we couldn't take credit or blame for most decisions. All we could do was pitch jokes and story ideas and hope for the best. Every year the show we were on would get canceled, and every year we were, once again, looking for work. It started to wear on me.

The shows were bad or the work experience was not fun or, well, it was always something. I kept telling myself that if we could just get on a hit TV show like *Frasier*, everything would be okay. We were good writers, and we were rehired by every show runner that ever hired us, but for whatever reason, we never caught that one big break. Eventually, my writing partner and I turned to movies.

Around that time, I was getting more and more into fantasy sports professionally. When I started writing my column on Rotoworld, I decided I needed a title. The names of columns on Rotoworld at that time were all fairly generic sports terms—things like "Red Zone" and "Balls and Strikes." I knew my column name shouldn't be sport-specific, as I wanted to be an analyst in multiple sports.

Since the site was called Rotoworld ("Roto" was short for Rotisserie League Baseball), I figured my name should have "Roto" in the title. So I wanted to be known as "The Roto Whore," because I thought it was funny. And then the first of many lucky breaks went my way. The guys running the site hated "The Roto Whore." Wasn't family-friendly enough, they claimed (I assume "roto" was the offending word). I was upset at first, but I'm a big believer that everything happens for a reason. So I went back to the drawing board. I told my wife that I wanted something that would make me seem like an expert but not one who took himself too seriously. A name with a wink, equal parts silly and "experty." I was coming up with all sorts of terrible, obvious names . . . "Mr. Roto" . . . "The Lord of Roto" . . . "The Roto King" . . . "The Czar of Roto." Just brutal, all of them.

Later that week, we were coming home from seeing the Matt Damon movie *The Talented Mr. Ripley*, and my wife just said, "How about 'The Talented Mr. Roto'?" That's hilarious, I said. Sold. It was just over the top enough that people would know not to take it seriously. It stood out and had name recognition because of the movie.

The silly, over-the-top name caught on, and the column grew in popularity and notoriety. Radio producers who were fans started asking me to come on their shows. At first, I hid my involvement. We wanted movie producers to take us seriously as writers. How could they if I was busy screwing around on some fantasy sports website? But eventually the truth came out, and instead of detracting from our movie career, we found that, oddly, my fantasy column started helping. Lots of executives and movie producers play fantasy, and when we'd have meetings, the first 15 minutes were spent helping them with their teams. It created a bond and better relationships for us with some big-name people in Hollywood.

One of the reasons we were getting all these movie meetings was because of a sample movie script that Eric and I wrote called *Undercover Elvis*. It's based on one of the most popular photos in the National Archives: a picture of President Richard Nixon, in the Oval Office, shaking hands with Elvis Presley, who is wearing a full-body purple jumpsuit. Of course he is.

In doing research on that photo, we discovered that Nixon had *actually* made Elvis an agent in the Bureau of Narcotics and Dangerous Drugs (the precursor to the DEA). In other words, it *wasn't* an honorary thing. You can look it up. Elvis Aaron Presley was really a full-fledged member of the BNDD. Nixon originally wanted it to be an honorary thing, but Elvis wouldn't do it without it being legit. Nixon, desperate for good publicity (and insanely thinking this would provide it), eventually agreed and sent him a badge. And so the King of Rock 'n' Roll became a government agent. The whole story is completely nuts, and it led us to write a script for a smart action comedy with this premise: "What if all the crazy stuff you knew about Elvis actually made complete sense when you realized he was really the world's greatest secret agent?"

We got great feedback on it, and it remains one of my favorite things we ever wrote. It didn't ultimately sell, but it did get us a lot of meetings and jobs, including a live-action adaptation of the cartoon *Johnny*

Bravo for Warner Brothers to star Dwayne "The Rock" Johnson (which sounded better than it probably does now). We started working on good projects and occasionally getting written up in *The Hollywood Reporter* and *Variety*. From a romantic comedy with the producers of *Elf* for Paramount to a rewrite for a Tim Allen Disney comedy, we eventually became movie writers.

Among the highest points of my writing career was when we were hired to do a new version of *The Muppet Show* for Fox. (I'm a Muppets freak.) And then one of the lowest was when the script went through the entire network with no notes, everyone loved it, until it got to the head of the network, who read it and said, "It's really funny. But does it have to be The Muppets?" True story.

One time a studio called us and asked us to work up a pitch for a project they wanted us to do. We spent a month on it. Only to find out, just before we pitched it, that they had hired someone else to write it. "Hey! You requested *us*." Another time, a writer we used to work with called us. He couldn't get a job; he couldn't even get his agent to call him back. He had written a sample pilot for free (called "on spec") and would we please help him punch it up? We felt bad for him, so we ended up helping him rewrite it significantly. Then with this new script, we gave it to some people we knew and got him a much better agent who ended up selling the script for more than half a million dollars. We then worked on the pilot and, at his request, came up with a bunch of future episode ideas. We were promised a high-level job on the show and had been told to turn down other job offers because we were working on this show. And then when the show was picked up to go on air he got full of himself. He didn't hire us but still used the episode ideas without telling us. He didn't want to share the spotlight, so he turned on us. By then, all the other jobs were filled. So not only was it horribly disheartening and depressing and we had nothing to show for our three months of free work to turn this guy's career completely around, but being nice to this guy and helping cost us other jobs. When the dust settled and people found out about what happened, two different studio executives called to formally apologize to us for his behavior and he was forced to give us story credit on one of the ideas he used. But it wasn't nearly enough for what he did to us. To this day, everyone I've told the full story to has said they think it's one of the worst Hollywood betrayals they've ever heard.

It was my worst, but I wish it were the only one.

My writing partner and I got taken advantage of many, many times. By sitcom producers, by movie producers, and by Hilary Swank, who once wasted a year of my life. Seriously.

There's a reason Hollywood is known for screwing people over. It's because it happens. Very similar to fantasy sports in that respect. Anytime you have money, ego, and reputation at stake, you will also have chicanery, duplicity, skulduggery, subterfuge, treachery, double-crossing, misconduct, deception, hypocrisy, deviousness, malfeasance, fraud, intrigue, bribery, lies, grifting, ruses, false pretenses, wrongdoing, corruption, lawlessness, underhandedness, bamboozlement, deceit, hoaxes, extortion, trickery, swindles, breaches of trust, violations, misrepresentations, impropriety, rackets, hanky-panky, fast ones, flimflams, shady dealings, misbehavior, scandals, unscrupulousness, bending of the rules, gray areas, loopholes, cunning, and good old-fashioned cheating.

And perhaps the only thing that has been around longer than ethically challenged behavior is ethically challenged behavior involving pursuit of the fairer sex. Be it to eat an apple, inspire soldiers to hide in a big wooden horse, or just upgrade their pitching, it should come as no shock that men will do almost anything to win the affection of a young lass—and that women have used that to their advantage.

Jill knew that the youngest guy in the Los Vaqueros fantasy baseball league, "David," had a crush on her. Her team, Joe Girardi's Braces was in the hunt and looking to make a deal. "It was 2011, and I wanted to upgrade at shortstop. I was shopping Alexi Ogando, but no one would bite." But one night she sees David on G-Chat and nonchalantly asks what it would take to get Asdrubal Cabrera, with Ogando as the bait.

DAVID: Want Chipper Jones? Haha

JILL: No, I do not lol

DAVID: haha didn't think so . . .

JILL: I will be totally honest here. The only guy I want is Cabrera.

DAVID: Ogando, Barney, and a GREAT blow job, and I'll do it. I need the pitching.

JILL: Are you serious? Done and done

DAVID: I think it is worth it. And I need a blow job. =)

Jill continues: "I scored a top-10 shortstop by getting rid of two players I had planned to drop and, oh yes, a blow job that I never ever planned to give."

I would just like to pause for a moment to apologize for the stupidity of the male gender. Forget trying to negotiate for oral sex from someone you have no romantic relationship with. It was a terrible baseball trade. Okay, back to the story.

"I was nervous someone would protest the trade, considering the centerpiece was unwanted Alexi Ogando. While Ogando's raw stats were deceivingly good, a simple Google search would have turned off anyone because Alexi had sucked his last three starts and was rumored to be heading to Triple A."

Yes, Jill is a smart fantasy player. And she was very happy. But . . .

"I felt like a dirty whore. I knew I would not hold up my end of the bargain and justified it with the fact that he was *so* dumb that he deserved it. I'm sorry, but you should not play fantasy baseball with the little baseball bat in your pants." Underline that one, kids.

"I felt like that slut who sleeps with her boss to move up in the world. But instead, I took advantage of a college student. Which is terrible! In the end, I wanted everyone to know that I was successful without any favors. Including imaginary ones. But it didn't matter. I got what I deserved."

Fantasy karma's a bitch . . .

"After going undefeated through the first 23 weeks of the season, I lost the championship by one hit. To David, of course. Who had eked into the playoffs in the last spot. You have no idea how much I wish this story wasn't true. I am irrationally superstitious when it comes to sports, and part of me is afraid that the fantasy baseball gods will turn me into the Chicago Cubs. I think this means I either have to hook up with David or buy a goat. I am hoping for the latter."

Poor David. Or lucky goat. But while Jill only promised putting out to try and win, "Jessica" actually did. In a fantasy football league with her boyfriend "Nick," who had already clinched a playoff spot. Jessica needed a win against her boyfriend just to make the playoffs.

"Okay, so . . . it started off as just a joke," Jessica tells me. "He'd text me like 'Hey, wanna go out to lunch?' and I'd ask if he still had Greg Jennings in his lineup. He'd tell me yes, and then I'd respond, 'In that case, I am not free for lunch.'"

But by midweek it became clear that a couple of star players for Jessica had injuries and weren't playing that week. Without them in her lineup, she says, "I got desperate." So she went over to Nick's house. "I was wearing my too-small-for-me Bills jersey, and I started making out with him. And then at the worst time I'd pull back and be like, 'You really ought to sit Matt Forte this week . . . and I think Earl Bennett is going to be *huge* this week.' He, in his excited state, caught on and hastily agreed."

Of course he did. Men have crumbled for much less. "He got his laptop, and we worked it out. He continually needed 'encouragement' during the lineup setting because fantasy football is important to both of us and he wasn't happy about being corrupted. It wasn't easy." But eventually Nick started too many Browns (he's a fan, so it just looked like he was being a homer) and once his poor lineup was set, he and Jessica got down to business.

The way it worked out was that Jessica made the playoffs as the third seed and her boyfriend Nick was the fourth seed. And did Nick lose? Of course he did. Had he played his correct lineup, would he have beaten his girlfriend and been the third seed? Of course he would have. And had he been the third seed, based on what ended up happening over the next two weeks, would he have won the whole thing? Of course he would have.

The fantasy gods, man. Don't mess with them. "We learned our lesson," Jessica says. "And oh, by the way, please change our names. I'm pretty sure my dad will read your book."

Your secret is safe, "Jessica." And if it makes you feel better, you're certainly not the only one to try and take advantage of an existing relationship.

A college buddy invited Scott into a league where everyone else was close friends from high school. Scott completed a deal for a wide receiver that he felt put him over the top. Upon learning about Scott's trade, Scott's "buddy" got all his friends in the league to veto Scott's original trade, and then completed his *own* trade for the same WR the next day. Sketchy, right? Wrong. It's super-sketchy.

No one responded to Scott's complaints on the message board, but he needn't have worried. Fantasy karma had his back. The wide receiver who got "vetoed" off Scott's team? Plaxico Burress, just before he shot himself in the leg that year. Scott ended up winning the league and beating the shady owner in the finals. Once again, fantasy karma prevailed. Still don't believe in fantasy karma? Well, Gomez knows exactly what I'm talking about. Ricky and Gomez are best friends in real life, but "when it comes to fantasy sports," says Gomez, "we are mortal enemies."

One year the Balco Bombers League out of McKinney, Texas, drafted at Gomez's house. Ricky brought over a picture of Gomez and his ex-girlfriend lying on a beach. Everyone had a good laugh, but at some point in the middle of the draft Gomez couldn't find it. He asked Ricky where it was. Ricky just smiled and said good luck finding it. "My wife is an insanely jealous person," Gomez tells me. "Thank goodness I found the picture before she did."

Years after that, Gomez had the highest-scoring team. He had won the year before, and a repeat title seemed like a foregone conclusion. But then he got cocky and taunted the fantasy football gods. "Instead of staying humble, I took a picture of Ricky's ex-wife holding the trophy while sitting on my lap."

I try to tell people about fantasy karma. They never listen. So after posting that picture, there was a firestorm on his league's message boards, and what happened, Gomez? "The fantasy gods wiped my team off the face of the earth in the semifinal, due to my arrogance."

Exactly. But did Gomez learn? No, Gomez did not learn.

"Since the picture did not have the desired effect, I felt like I still owed Ricky some payback. That is when I devised the cynical plot to ruin Ricky's fantasy baseball draft this year. I invited Ricky's ex-wife to join our baseball league."

It was half evil, half genius to invite Ricky's ex-wife into the league. Especially because they hadn't seen or spoken to each other since the divorce a year and a half earlier. "The company line is we needed to fill an open slot; however, my personal intentions were much more sinister."

No kidding.

"She accepted, but then I felt guilty. So I wrote in to your podcast, asking, 'Did I cross a line by inviting her to play in the league, only to throw him off his game on draft day?'"

I remember. Your follow-up question was: "Should I tell him she is in the league or wait until draft day, where this will do the most psychological damage?"

"Right. When I emailed you, I knew I was taking the risk of Ricky hearing it on the podcast. Then my brother brought up a good point. Ricky has never finished higher than fourth place in fantasy baseball. Someone who is so terrible at fantasy baseball couldn't possibly listen to the ESPN Fantasy Focus 06010 podcast."

You don't have to suck up, Gomez. You're already in the book. So what happened?

"Well, Ricky heard the podcast and gave me an ultimatum: 'It is either me or her, you choose who you want in the league.' I told him to grow up and deal with it, because she had already accepted the invite and paid her money (in advance). She was champing at the bit to destroy her ex at something that she knew he loved."

Clearly, Gomez didn't learn his lesson from the fantasy gods. In the end, Ricky chose to quit the league, and his ex-wife destroyed everyone, winning the league by 11.5 games.

Game, set, match . . . fantasy karma.

But don't feel bad, Gomez. The game has been around for more than 30 years. Millions and millions of players and leagues covering every sport in the universe have been played. And fantasy karma is still undefeated . . .

TIME-OUT:

Texts from Last Night

(913): In a meeting downtown with the department of transportation. Hungover. Pretending to take notes on my laptop, but I'm really in the middle of my fantasy baseball draft. Yes, this is a mass text.

It's a mass text from the 913 area code, to be specific. It's kind of sketchy to be doing a fantasy draft in the middle of a work meeting, but if there's one thing that people do more often than having questionable behavior related to fantasy, it's texting their friends about it. How do I know this? Because Lauren Leto has made a small fortune off it. Leto and partner Ben Bator founded a website called TextsFromLastNight.com. People send in the embarrassing, awkward, funny, sad, brilliant, and what-the-hell-was-that texts they've received. Each text is anonymous, with only the area code it was sent from, and the site receives more than 15,000 submissions every day.

Given the obsession folks have with fantasy sports, along with the staggering number of submissions the site receives, it's no surprise that quite a few texts out there are related to fantasy sports. I asked Lauren to pull the funniest and most interesting. She came through like a champ.

(813): She just told me she was pregnant, will you look after my fantasy football team? There's $40 on the line.

(214): He woke up just long enough to set his fantasy football lineup and puke. Then he passed out again.

(914): We did a fantasy football draft together and then had sex . . . I found the perfect woman.

(801): Playing in my drug dealer's fantasy football league. When I win I'm making him pay me in weed.

(954): Last night my boyfriend wasn't able to have sex with me because he couldn't stop thinking about his fantasy football team.
(954): Is his team good?
(954): You're an asshole.

(727): I'm cooking Thanksgiving in lingerie and a matching apron, while screaming at the Texans D/ST for fucking up my fantasy team. I think I now qualify as a southern lady.

(716): So my girlfriend wanted to get freaky during my draft last night . . . I ended up with three kickers and no quarterbacks. Totally worth it.

(336): We thought you were passed out, but every time the announcer said the name of a guy on your fantasy team you gave a thumbs-up.

(218): I broke up with my fantasy football team today. Never share a team with your significant other.

(325): No more vodka for you until you can go a night without sobbing over your fantasy baseball team.

(276): He's winning his fantasy football league . . . I had to sleep with him.

(301): I think I told her that she'd never mean as much to me as Matthew Berry does.

6.

Fallout from Cheating

— or —

"Uh, Mom . . . Can You Bail Me Out of Jail? I, Uh, Sorta Beat Up Dad . . ."

It was Alex Moretto's junior year in high school when his dad had a parent-teacher conference with his history teacher. Alex hoped it went well, hoped his teacher had nothing bad to say, and hoped his dad didn't share any embarrassing stories from home.

As it turned out, both dad and teacher were huge Dolphins fans, and they really hit it off. Hit it off so well that dad invited the teacher to play in the family fantasy football league the next year. A league that Alex is also in.

The teacher had never played before but had always wanted to try. And so, after being invited, Alex remembers, "my teacher is thrilled, and my grade suddenly goes from a 75 to a 90." The only downside was the teacher coming to Alex's house during the summer for the draft. "Nothing better than seeing your teacher in the middle of the summer."

But the next season everything's going great until about the halfway point. Alex's dad then swindles Alex's teacher in a trade, preying on his inexperience and lying to him about the rules. "My teacher found out a few days later that he had been ripped off and 'initiated into the league' after being dealt a draft pick that he wouldn't be able to use." The teacher's team went from first to worst, and as the teacher's team dropped, so did Alex's grades. "My grade inexplicably dropped a staggering 15 percent in three weeks!"

I can truly appreciate Alex's feeling of helplessness. Of sitting there thinking, *Why am I being punished? I did nothing wrong.* But because someone else let his ego get in the way, Alex had to suffer. The only positive for Alex was at least no one else knew about it. In my situation, it was broadcast around the world . . .

It was a few days after Thanksgiving, and my writing partner and I were, once again, unemployed. We had just finished working as semi-low-level writers on a sitcom called *Union Square*. Executive-produced by James Burrows, among others, it had been an NBC Thursday night show slotted between *Friends* and *Seinfeld*. It couldn't miss. Except, of course, it did. The show was canceled, and we had five months or so to kill before "staffing season," the time when shows go about the once-a-year process of hiring new writers.

This was before we had written *Undercover Elvis*, before we'd ever done anything in movies, and as we were trying to decide what we wanted to do, our agent called with a simple question.

AGENT: You guys know who Paul Hogan is?

ME: Of course.

AGENT: You ever see *Crocodile Dundee*?

ME: Of course.

AGENT: Well, Paul Hogan is a client here. And he wants to do a third installment of the franchise. I'm one of the agents in charge of putting together writers to pitch him ideas for the film. If you want, I'll throw you guys on the list.

ME: But we've never written a movie before. We don't even have a spec.

AGENT: I know. You probably won't get the job. But it'll be good practice. And you never know.

So Eric and I thought about it and were like, "What the hell. Let's meet Paul Hogan. It'll be a funny story."

So we rewatched the first two movies. They're charming. They are not laugh-out-loud funny, and they don't have large elaborate scenes, like a car chase or something, but they're easy to watch. They're a series of small moments. Okay, got it.

The other thing we noticed was that Paul Hogan's character is much funnier reacting than acting. This is an important distinction that some writers fail to understand. Most comedic actors are funnier when they have the punch line or when they are the one forcing the action or doing the big, outrageous thing.

But in this case the comedy comes from this guy from another land (Down Under!) reacting to things that are normal to us but obviously not normal to a guy who has lived in the Australian outback. So, easy, right? Film of simple moments, loose plot, need him to react to stuff. Got it.

At this time, *There's Something About Mary* was the big movie, and R-rated comedies were "in." So we're like . . . uh, this isn't built to compete with movies like that. The only shot this movie has is if it's a family comedy that people who liked the original can take their kids to. That was our logic. Plus, we weren't getting this job anyway, weren't even sure we wanted it, so we didn't spend a lot of time.

All we knew was that Linda, Hogan's real-life wife and costar of the first two movies, had to be in it. And he wanted it to take place present-day, which is to say, 16 years after the last movie.

So, like a week later, we met him, and we didn't give the hard sell. Instead, we gave a very simple pitch. "In the first two movies you were dating Linda but never married. But you guys have been together all this time, so let's say you have a kid together. He's a little Croc. You did New York in the first two movies, so let's do Los Angeles this time. Your wife gets a great job offer in LA, and the kid has never been outside of Australia, so you decide to move to LA, and now you're showing the kid around because you 'know America.' It's the blind leading the blind. Eventually, you get a job at a movie studio as an animal trainer because you can 'talk' to animals. Turns out, there's some bad guys there, you save the day. At the end, you decide to marry her, so we end with a wedding. Everyone loves a wedding. But most of the time, you're in Hollywood. There's lots of craziness here, you'll wander around and react to stuff. I mean, come on, it's *Crocodile Dundee*. We'll make it funny."

And there was a long pause as he looked at us. And then he said, in that unmistakable accent, "Ah, you guys are the only ones who get me. You're hired."

What??!

Turns out he had met with like 30 other writers, and everyone else had pitched him crazy stuff. "Crocodile Dundee saves the world from a nuclear explosion," *Crocodile Dundee in Space*, or really raunchy humor to jump on the *Mary* bandwagon. Apparently we were the only ones who were like, "Dude, it's not hard. The movies are what they are. Put him in funny situations and let him react. That's the whole movie."

As we wavered on accepting, our agent pitched us on it: Look, this movie *will* get made. (It's almost impossible to get a movie, any movie, made in Hollywood. Especially from first-time writers.) You've never written a movie before. They will pay you to write one, and if it's good, you can use it as a sample. And guess what they want to pay you?

When we heard the amount, we almost choked. If you're gonna sell out, kids, sell out big.

I didn't love how the movie turned out—it was never going to be great given we were starting with a sequel to a 16-year-old movie—but the original script was much more self-referential and snarky. For example, the movie studio where Croc worked made nothing but "useless sequels for movies no one remembers." Lots of jokes like that, making fun of ourselves, making fun of Paul, that sort of thing, and all of it got cut. But, to be honest, the movie could have been much worse. It's definitely a watchable family movie. A movie you can sit your kid in front of without worry and the whole thing goes by quickly. You won't laugh a ton, but it's not a train wreck. It's just very, very vanilla.

But that wasn't the issue. The issue was writing credit. When we signed on to do the film, it was with the understanding that we would share writing credit with Paul. That was fine with us. And that's how we submitted it to the Writers Guild. But then Paul Hogan—that would be star, executive producer, in-every-single-frame-of-the-movie Paul Hogan, announced that he also needed solo writing credit and wanted our names taken off the script entirely.

Which would have been fine with us—it's not like we were proud of the thing. Except here's the problem: for significant financial reasons (residuals, certain contractual things, etc.) we *needed* to have writing credit. The whole reason we wrote the damn thing was money.

We were happy to share credit with Paul, but once he demanded solo credit, the line was drawn in the sand: us or him for credit. So we had to go through an arbitration process, where we submitted everything we wrote, Paul submitted the rewrite he did on our original script, and they compared both to the final script. And the three-person panel independently voted for us. Then Paul appealed. And we won again with a new set of people. And then Paul appealed the appeal. And lost for a third time.

Paul had his day in court. Nine different objective people ruled for us on three separate occasions, he's still getting tons of credit on the film, and he's still insanely rich. So he dropped it, right?

Wrong. Paul then goes public with it. He does an interview with *The Hollywood Reporter* and in every single radio/TV/press interview he does for the movie he talks about how he is going to take the Writers Guild to court (unheard of), and how we are getting writing credit that we don't deserve. So now we're in this very public legal fight to demand credit for something we didn't want public credit for and weren't real proud of to begin with. So awkward and terrible. "No, really, *we* wrote *Croc 3*! Yes, us! Why are you looking at me like that? I know it's a bad movie. What of it?" Sigh.

Now, normally, when you get credit as screenwriters on a produced movie, you're part of the marketing materials, you do some press, you get a good seat and table at the premiere and after-party, etc. We got none of that. You can only find our names on the movie in the one place Paramount was legally forced to put it. There was no mention of us anywhere in anything promoting the movie, we were shoved in the back of the theater, we weren't allowed to sit with the rest of the cast and crew. The whole thing was humiliating and horrible, and I hated almost every moment of it. Suffice it to say, I am not a fan of Paul Hogan, the human being. That movie bought me a nice big house in Los Angeles. But it was a painful, hurtful experience, and it taught me a very powerful lesson: doing something you don't care about kills you inside. And a lot of money won't change that.

You know, after the *Croc* episode I felt so damn beat up. I was never actually beat up, of course, I just felt like I had been. Hogan never actually sued the Writers Guild, he just talked about it (and us) nonstop until the movie came out. It was the spring of 2001, and I was just emotionally drained and embarrassed, and it really wore on me. And just like the stars in Hollywood chasing fame (or screen credit), pursuing fantasy glory has led some people to questionable behavior. And sometimes questionable behavior *does* include getting physical.

"Before each draft," Caleb Rappaport tells me, "the Balco Boys Fantasy League from Nashville drink . . . heavily! Pitchers and shots flow freely as we 'pregame' for hours before each draft. In past years laptop computers were drenched in beer and ruined due to out-of-control pre-draft antics, but it had never actually affected the draft. Until 2008."

In the first round of 2008, Caleb remembers, "I proudly put my sticker on the board and declared, 'The Buffalo Bills Bombsquad selects Adrian Peterson.'"

He sat down confident and happy. Then the next team went:

"Muzic City Mayhem selects *the Vikings'* Adrian Peterson."

Yep.

"In my drunken stupor, I had selected *the Bears'* Adrian Peterson! As we stopped the draft to discuss, the feeling was that I would be allowed to have the AP that was obviously intended. However, Jacob Schneier, one of my best friends, would not stand for it."

Apparently, Jacob is also the most belligerent, antagonistic owner of their group. "Since my hand had come off the sticker, Jacob demanded that the selection be made final. This led to much shouting, pushing, and eventually me throwing a right cross and two uppercuts."

A full-on brawl ensued.

And here's why you know Caleb and Jacob are such good friends. Twenty minutes after that fight, the two of them were cool again. Caleb was allowed to draft the Peterson he wanted, and order was restored. "We all laughed, rehashed the timeline of events, and of course did all kinds of shots in honor of 'Balco Brawl I.'"

I'm not sure *more* drinking was the solution at that point, but it seems to work for Caleb's league. "Yeah, we drink too much, go out way too much, get in far too much trouble for 30-plus-year-olds with families to be getting into, but love every second of it. College is over, but this is our fraternity now."

Speaking of punches being thrown, Matt Henehan relays a story that took place a long time ago, before cell phones, while he was in high school. During class one day, "a guy in our league, Kevin, was talking about picking up Felipe Lopez during class." Apparently they then mentioned this to another league member named Tom. Tom, in a move that is both ingenious and kind of weasely, faked being sick to go home early. Tom got Lopez. I've heard of lots of reasons to fake being sick over the years—avoiding a test being number one—but to pick up Felipe Lopez? (Career batting average: .264.)

Matthew continues: "Lopez ended up having a monster game that night. Kevin was so upset, he got into it the next day with Tom, who argued back just as hard." The argument continued with neither guy backing down and no solution in sight. And so, eventually, it was decided: they would box for the rights to Felipe Lopez.

Kevin ended up winning the fight, but the hilarious part to me is it all sounds so civilized. I bet, if you do the research far back enough, you'll find the Burr-Hamilton duel started over who got to draft Cornelius Waxford-Chase in the Gentlemen's Sporting Club Proprietary League.

Look, violence has no place anywhere, let alone fantasy sports, but obviously it still crops up. Fantasy will do that to people. And when there's violence, there are cops. . . .

In late 2010, there was an altercation on the mean streets of West Terre Haute, Indiana. Written about by both MyWabashvalley.com and Tribstar.com, the reports state that 40-year-old Michael All was arrested for getting into a fight with his 66-year-old father—

I'm gonna pause for a second to let a few keywords sink in. Words like "arrested," "fight," and "father."

According to the reports, the dispute arose over a payout from their fantasy football league. The dad suffered broken eye sockets, a broken nose, and several cuts and bruises. Michael was charged with battery resulting in serious bodily injury. Somehow this guy's life led him to not only play in a fantasy football league with his father (normal) but then to get into a knockdown, drag-out brawl over the winnings with dad (not normal). And from the least surprising part of the story department, a blood test showed Michael All was twice the legal limit at the time of his arrest.

Can you just imagine him being brought into the booking station? Wow. What was his one call? "Hey, uh, Mom . . . can you bail me out of jail? I, uh, kind of beat up Dad. . . ."

Sometimes people use their fists to rectify a wrong, sometimes it's their mind. After Kyle Benevides discovered that the commish of his Tiverton, Rhode Island, fantasy football league had cheated by changing the league settings midseason to benefit his own team, he decided he wasn't going to take it. Kyle and his league-mate Kiefer wrote an email that had a keylogger virus secretly embedded in it. (A keylogger virus basically logs *every* keystroke, so you can see exactly what someone's typing.)

They sent the virus email to the cheating commish and used the program to extract the commish's password. They then locked him out of his own email, changed the league settings back, and didn't let him back into his own email until he admitted what he had done and apologized in person to everyone in the league.

Yes, the advances in technology have made all sorts of new ways to cheat possible. Before Twitter and text alerts were the norm, Will Mullin created an entirely fake sports website that looked legit, wrote an article about how Drew Brees was missing the game, and sent his opponent the link Sunday morning. "It was working until he tuned in to the Fox pregame show, and Pam Oliver was doing an on-field interview with . . . Drew Brees."

I remember one time seeing a tweet from a guy that read like this: "RT @MatthewBerryTMR Arian Foster is Inactive!" Except I never wrote that tweet! Some guy had just written the whole thing, inserted my Twitter handle, pretended I wrote it, and sent it to his league-mate. I quickly tweeted the guy that this was incorrect, but still. Fairly clever on a Sunday morning when lots of info flies quickly.

Of course, there's technology and then there's old school. "Zac" (not his real name) is most definitely old school. Zac, you see, was working for the Florida Marlins in 2007, and toward the end of the year the Marlins were well out of the race. Zac's fantasy team, however, was very much alive. Playing for the title in a head-to-head fantasy baseball league during the last week of the season, Zac accompanied the Marlins on an end-of-the-year road trip to play the Mets in New York City.

The night in question was Friday, September 28, 2007, and all Zac needed for his title was one last great starting pitching performance along with a win. From John Maine of the Mets. Who was pitching the next afternoon at 1:00 PM versus the Marlins. It was against this backdrop that Zac and his buddy arrived that Friday night at a bar with some of the team and shared a drink with a few Marlins players. And after they all hoisted a few, an interesting, if not exactly kosher, idea occurred to Zac.

"All we need to do is get a few more of them drunk and my boy Maine should cruise through the lineup."

Fast-forward to midnight that night. "Some front-office staff, a lot of players, a couple of female sales interns, and myself meet up at a trendy bar called Whiskey Park. Drinks were flowing. The bullpen was buying . . ."

(Note to self: make friends with more relievers.)

". . . but I was buying more to make sure they got extra rowdy." After many shots of Patrón, lots of vodka Red Bulls, and, just to show how loaded they were getting, one drunken picture of a player licking salt off Zac's nipple, everyone headed back to one of the players' rooms at the hotel. Apparently, the party was just starting. . . .

"We proceeded to play 'Mexican Shotgun,' which was a game I made up on the spot. It consisted of shotgunning a beer and chasing it with tequila (courtesy of the minibar)."

Brilliant in its simplicity, Zac.

"The next morning I felt like shit, but I also felt confident in unleashing Maine as my last starter to grab a title. I also called all my compulsive gambler friends and let them know the Mets' money line was the play of the century."

Google the box score for the Mets-Marlins game on September 29, 2007. That day John Maine went seven and two-thirds, giving up just one hit and two walks, and the Mets cruised to a 13–0 win.

The box score credits the win to John Maine, but deep inside I know that W was earned by "Zac Smith." "I went on to win that final week of fantasy and the season, with the John Maine win and his sterling WHIP being the clincher."

And *that*, kids, is how you win a fantasy league!

PART FOUR

TRADES

7.

Crazy Things People Have Traded

or

"I Said I'd Take Stafford and Hernandez for Finley and Dibs on Amy"

It was definitely a problem.

And Tyler knew there was a solution.

He just didn't know what it was.

It was the 2011 season, and Tyler's team, "Can I get a B.J. . . . Raji?" needed a tight end. That was the problem. His good buddy had Rob Gronkowski *and* Jimmy Graham. That was the solution. In their Tuscaloosa, Alabama–based league you could play only one tight end, and with both Gronk and Graham having monster years, there was a valuable asset that Tyler could use and his league-mate could not.

But try as he might, Tyler could not pry away one of the tight ends. Quarterbacks, running backs, two-for-ones, three-for-ones, Tyler offered it all and was either rejected or ignored. And worse yet, he couldn't even get a counteroffer. What the hell did this guy want? "No offer was sticking," Tyler remembers, until one day when the guy called Tyler and said, "You know what? I'll trade you Graham for Scott Chandler and some of your clean piss."

Tyler rode Jimmy Graham to the championship, and Tyler's friend passed his work drug test. And *that*, kids, is why you don't do drugs. Someday you might need your urine to upgrade at tight end. Just think. If only Lance Armstrong played fantasy football, he'd still be a seven-time champion.

It goes to show, you never know how, when, or in what form opportunity will knock. Sometimes it's your clean living that brings an elite tight end, and sometimes it's just having a random meal with a friend.

In late 2003, I was having dinner with a friend who was a big Internet entrepreneur. He had successfully started and sold a famous website. And he had an opportunity. A different website was for sale and had been offered to him. A website that had, in the past year, made $60 million. Sixty million dollars *in one year*. And the asking price was just one year's profit—$60 million. Remember, this was when websites were selling for up to 10 times revenue, so it was an amazing price. The owners had apparently made so much crazy cash that they just wanted out—and quickly. My friend could easily get a bank to give him the money—it was a great price for a cash cow. There was just one issue.

It was an adult website. Specifically, the site was one of those "age verification" sites that, at the time, solved the two biggest problems that porn sites had: proving someone was of legal age to view the content and credit card chargebacks. Too often some guy would call the credit card company and say, "What is this charge? My wife and I are outraged! You need to reverse this immediately! There's no way I would ever watch teenage busty Asian cheerleaders!"

Right.

Anyway, this company had come up with a simple and ingenious solution. They went to all the adult websites and said, hey, we'll handle that hassle for you, charge a decent fee to customers (like $30 a month), take a slice off the top, and send you the rest. And they did this for a lot of websites. So, for $30, a customer actually got access to tons of different adult websites. For the websites, it solved a major headache and got more customers to their site than they might have drawn otherwise. Plus, under the group business plan, they were making money even if a customer didn't come to their specific website.

And for the guys running the verification site, it was genius. They didn't have to produce content. They didn't have to hire models or directors or anything. All they had to do was make sure people were of legal age and occasionally handle some annoyances from the credit card companies. Everyone else was making the content, and all these guys were doing was skimming some money off a very large pile to take care of fairly simple issues. It basically ran itself. It was (and remains) a brilliant business model. And it occurred to me . . . what other business has a hard-core, passionate fan base willing to spend money on premium content?

I called it RotoPass.com.

I had been getting more and more into fantasy sports at that point, writing two columns a week for Rotoworld and doing three different sports for them (NFL, NBA, and MLB fantasy). I had even been the senior editor of Rotoworld's first fantasy football magazine in 2003.

I didn't want to give up show business, especially when it seemed like things were finally moving in the right direction, but I saw an opportunity in the fantasy sports business space. Sure, I'd have to do a little work at the beginning to get it up and running, but once that happened, it would run itself. I could continue my movie-writing career, and I'd make some nice side money in fantasy.

That was the idea anyway. I was starting to think outside the box, starting down a path that would eventually lead me to trade one life for another. Just like we do in fantasy when our player goes down with an injury or underperforms, or when we're just bored and want to do *something* . . . there is no activity during the season that takes up more thought, discussion, time, and email than trade talk.

Ever since fantasy was invented, trades have been a huge staple of fantasy sports, happening in every league, every day, all around the world. It's a crucial way to improve your team, of course, but it's also a lot of fun. Thinking about trades, staring at other teams' rosters, negotiating back and forth . . . it's an important skill in fantasy, and it's a total blast.

But sometimes your skill isn't enough to pull off the deal you need. Or, more than likely, you don't have players who are good enough for the other person to want. Other than the occasional future draft pick, very few leagues allow you to trade anything other than a fellow player for players in return. But just because there's a rule against something doesn't mean people follow it. Not everyone needs clean piss, but they all need *something*.

In 2008, Dan was trying to trade with Dave for LaDainian Tomlinson at the deadline but couldn't beat a competing offer from Jason. "In addition to draft picks, Jason agreed to redo Dave's kitchen!" And in a work league, Jesse offered LeSean McCoy to his boss for a scrub and 20 hours of overtime. It was a part-time job for Jesse, and "the overtime was more money than the league prize."

Ryan Rummel told me a story from the early days of the Cincinnati Cactus League. "We had a late-season trade go down between one of the top teams and one of the bottom teams. The top team, just a QB shy of being unstoppable, got Brett Favre [circa 1998], and the other team got junk." Ryan questioned both guys. The guy who gave up Favre, it turns out, was someone who filled in as the 12th guy at the last minute and didn't really know football, so "I was convinced it was a case of a smart player taking advantage of a not-so-smart player. Not totally cool, but not against the rules."

Favre led his new team to a fantasy championship that year, and it was only later that Ryan learned the winner "may or may not have given the other guy a bag of weed" for Favre.

Sounds like the 12th guy was smarter than you thought. It's not like he had a shot at the title. . . .

Ryan adds, "Needless to say, we have a rule that came out of the 'pot-for-players' scandal of '98, a rule that stands today. I also give each year's winner a shirt that has our former champions' names printed on the back. 1998's champion has an asterisk next to his name."

An asterisk? Or a pot leaf? Because that's what I would have gone with. It's not always illegal things that get thrown into trades. Sometimes it's just . . . well, let Joe Kurczewski tell you.

Joe is a member of the 10-team Peter J. Harris Memorial Stifler Football Association out of Buffalo, New York. In 2011, Joe needed a QB badly. Not related to his need of a QB was his crush on Amy, a bartender at a local bar. So one night Joe went to hang out at the bar and brought his buddy Jeff. They were having drinks and Joe noticed that, while Amy was friendly, she was *really* flirting with Jeff. Jeff dug Amy too, but refused to make any kind of move. As Joe explains it, "I had already called dibs on her, and Jeff refused to break 'the bro code.'"

Kudos to you, Jeff, but luckily Joe is a man who is both practical *and* an opportunist. He still needed a QB, Jeff needed a TE, and Amy was getting annoyed that Jeff was ignoring her obvious flirting. Trade talks resumed and, when it was all said and done, "Matthew Stafford and Aaron Hernandez were traded for Jermichael Finley and dibs on Amy."

Now that's what you call a win-win-win trade.

"I wouldn't relinquish the rights to Amy until he accepted the trade. So, using our ESPN fantasy football mobile app, we completed the trade and he was free to flirt with Amy. He ended up getting her number that night, and I won my first championship thanks to Stafford."

Jeff and Amy ultimately didn't work as a couple, but I'm not surprised by the attempt. Romance and fantasy sports trades interact more often than you'd think.

Matt G. was a junior in college in 2007 when he had a shot at a fantasy football title. With surplus at running back, he needed a wideout and set his sights on Larry Fitzgerald, who had an easy schedule the rest of the way. One problem. Remembers Matt, "The guy who owned Fitz was an absentee owner who had checked out a few weeks into the season. It was tough to get him to remember his password, much less remember to set a lineup every week. I approached him with a few offers, but he couldn't be bothered."

But then, out of the blue, the Fitz owner went to Matt's room, sat down, and with no hesitation made an offer that has never before been uttered in fantasy football history.

"I'll give you Fitz if you let me borrow your video camera tonight so I can make a sex tape with my girlfriend."

Matt elaborates: "I was a video production major, so I had my own little handheld MiniDV for small projects. For a night's rental and MiniDV-to-DVD conversion services, Fitz was all mine. I shrugged off my fantasy football ethics concerns and shook his hand." Fitz crushed the rest of the way, and Matt won his league that year. Obviously, this was before flip cams and video recording on cell phones became prevalent. Turns out, it was reported as two junk players for Fitz, which caused some chirping, but not enough to overturn. In fact, the league never knew this story until Matt came clean in anticipation of this book being published. (Typical reaction: "This is absolutely hilarious and . . . you bastard. Sneaky sneaky bastard.")

As for the video itself, Matt *did* have to convert the MiniDV tape to a DVD, so keep that in mind. Do *you* want to see your good buddy and his longtime girl doing all sorts of freaky stuff? Exactly. Say what you want, but he *earned* that title.

And as crazy as that story is, it *isn't* the nuttiest fantasy sports–

related romantic triangle I've heard about. You see, Frank's fantasy football league has a rule: the owner who finishes last buys a lap dance for the winner. For you young writers out there, this is called "foreshadowing." Or, since it's a strip club I'm talking about, "pandering."

At the trade deadline in 2010, the top two teams in this league were Frank and another guy named Brad. As Frank describes it, "Brad has a smoking hot girlfriend." A hot girlfriend, it turns out, that another guy in the league named Steve had a crush on. Or, as I like to call him, "Out-of-Contention-with-Nothing-to-Play-For-and-Happens-to-Own-Michael-Vick Steve."

If you don't remember, Vick was in the middle of a ridiculous run in 2010. So Steve trades Vick to Brad for a bunch of scrubs, and Brad ends up winning the league. Which means Brad enjoyed the victor's lap dance. But then, about a week later, a picture of Brad getting the lap dance gets "accidentally" posted to Facebook. Suddenly Brad and his "smoking hot girlfriend" are no longer together. A week later, she's dating someone else. You guessed it: Steve. Or as he is now known, "Smarter-Than-You-Think Steve."

Luckily, turnabout is fair play, and the woman gets the last laugh in the next story, where Jameson Singer talks about the Fantasy Game of Thrones League, where his buddy Alex owned a team. As did Alex's girlfriend, Carly. Who wasn't happy when she found out Alex had cheated on her. I've heard of women getting revenge by dating another friend or dishing secrets, but Carly hit Alex where it really hurts: she traded Arian Foster to a guy in her ex's division for a backup. The happy recipient of Foster (the number one running back in fantasy at that point) ended up winning the division, the girl quit the league, and everyone learned a valuable lesson: hell hath no fury like a woman who owns Arian Foster scorned.

It's not just romance or avarice that fuels some trades. Sometimes it's a bet or just sheer boredom. In Will "Wild Bill" Finnegan's Steve

T DFL Fantasy League, need met bizarre opportunity. An expansion team was desperate for players, and his roommate's fish had died. The league bet him if he ate the dead fish, he'd get Jacoby Jones and Jacob Hester.

So basically, he got screwed twice.

But apparently that was business as usual for Will's league. They are a goofy, trading bunch of fools.

One time they took all their kickers, wrote their names down on separate pieces of paper, and put them in the blender. "We put the blender on without the lid, and whoever popped out when it was your turn, that was your kicker." They also did something similar with their worst wideouts and a microwave. Kickers in a blender, wideouts in a microwave? Get out of the kitchen, guys. Go watch some football.

Speaking of the kitchen, that's exactly where Myles Pappadato's Papalino's Alumni League started eight years ago. A 10-team baseball keeper league comprising guys who used to work at a pizza place, they were all at a poker game in April of 2012. Myles remembers that, "after some adult beverages," they got the idea that the poker winner could trade *for* anyone he wanted who was selected after the fifth round from one of the losing teams.

Team Bandits prevailed and selected Tigers pitcher Doug Fister from Team Bad News Bears. But how many times do we have to warn of messing with the fantasy gods? The next morning, "Team Bandits posted a victory rant on our league message board and demanded the trading of Fister to his roster." When reminded he had to send someone back for Fister, "the Bandits quickly replied that they knew exactly who to send back to the losing team, 'that scrub from the Mets, R. A. Dickey.'"

Final stats for Doug Fister in 2012: 10 wins, 137 strikeouts, 3.45 ERA, 1.19 WHIP, 162.2 innings.

And for that "scrub" R. A. Dickey? 20 wins, 230 strikeouts, 2.73 ERA, 1.05 WHIP, 233.2 innings. He won the Cy Young Award that year.

Chalk up another "w" for fantasy karma, as that was obviously not what Team Bandits had in mind. A feeling I could relate to as I tried to launch RotoPass.com. What was supposed to be a quick way to make a little money proved to be much more challenging. (Always the case, right?) Since fantasy sports is seasonal and many of the premier websites in the industry have very different price points, it took a while to figure out the exact business model: Do we charge by sport or by month? How much do we charge? One site costs $100 and another costs $20—how do we provide access to both sites so each website owner feels like he's getting proper value with his cut of the total price? What do we do with existing customers of the sites if they upgrade to a RotoPass? And then how do we track them? The whole thing was a nightmare to figure out, especially since I was still doing my day job of writing movie scripts.

Once I had a workable business plan, it took even longer to convince all the established websites to go along with an unproven idea run by an unproven guy. I went through many, many proposals, phone calls, and meetings with designers, lawyers, tech guys, and, of course, the other fantasy sports website owners.

Took me over a year, but eventually it all got done, and it launched in June of 2004 while I was still writing for Rotoworld.com.

Well, until I was fired.

Trade Advice from My Late, Great Uncle Lester

"Maaaaaaaaaaaatthewwwwwwwww."

Even though my name is only two syllables, he always stretched it out so that it sounded like four, in that unmistakable drawl.

"Maaaaaaaaaaaatthewwwwwwwww," he would say as he chomped on his cigar and adjusted his trademark 10-gallon hat. "Come philosophize with your old uncle." And with a huge smile on my face, I would bound into his office and do just that.

My great-uncle Lester Gold was 88 years old when he passed away February 28, 2011, and many of you reading this didn't realize it at the time, but the world became a much lesser place that day. It's rare, of course, that you have a close relationship with your great-uncle, but Lester was a rare man. It was impossible not to have a close relationship with him.

My father, no slouch in his own right, gives Lester much of the credit for his focus, ambition, and success. Much of my drive, ambition, and focus comes from my father and my Uncle Lester, so, really, it all comes from him when you get down to it.

I don't know that there is any definitive way to judge whether a man had a successful life, but whatever metric you wanna use, Uncle Lester blew it out of the water. A self-made and self-taught man, Lester grew up the son of poor immigrants. When he was 13, his mother passed away, so he had to start working to help support the family. "I'm a peddler," he would always say. "Just a peddler." But Lester wasn't "just" anything. He started with junk, biking back and forth between junkyards in Denver. Soon he had scraped together enough to buy his first car for $5. And then he promptly sold it for $10.

He took that $10 and bought another car and sold that one and kept buying and selling cars and eventually was able to open his first used-car dealership. He was 18 years old.

That year was a good one for my uncle. Because that was also the year he got together with my Aunt Cookie. They've been together for 70 years now, and nothing as simple as death is going to keep them apart. Their souls are together for eternity.

My Uncle Lester was fantastically successful in business, opening up a chain of car dealerships and then getting into oil for a long time and then land development. I couldn't possibly tell you how many millions of dollars the man was worth because he never flaunted his wealth. The only time it ever came up was to either donate it (he was very generous) or spend it on family.

So many memories. Once, when I was 14 or so, I was having lunch with Lester and Cookie, and I asked him naively, "Uncle, you're so successful. How do you do it? What's the secret?"

"Maaaaaaaaaaaatthewwwwwwwww," he said, "it's very simple. I figured out a long time ago it was just easier to make more money than it was to stop your Aunt Cookie from spending it."

My aunt cackled in that great laugh of hers and nodded. "He's right. I grew up on a farm. And we had work horses and show horses. I told your uncle on our first date . . . I'm a show horse." And they both laughed together. They did that a lot.

As you might imagine from a man who started working at 13, served our country overseas in World War II, and was a self-made millionaire with the same girlfriend—as he always referred to Cookie—for seven decades, my uncle had a lot of strong opinions backed up by a wealth of life experience.

He not only had a specific point of view on everything, he had a colorful phrase to describe it. We called them "Lesterisms," and when I would go to Denver and "philosophize with my old uncle," he would share them with me.

I have found that Lesterisms are helpful in life and in fantasy sports. And before you flip to the next chapter because you think you know everything you need to about winning at fantasy—or life—consider my uncle, who always felt that we should never stop learning.

As a man dedicated to the Jewish faith, he started a weekly Talmud study group with a local rabbi. When he was 64. And studied it for the 24 years up until his death. If Lester was still learning at 88, you can take a few moments to let my uncle help you the next time you are doing a fantasy trade. Here are some of my favorite Lesterisms.

"Don't make a decision until you have to." Too many times I see players panic and make a deal because "this guy is coming back from injury," or "I don't have a quarterback for my bye week in three weeks." Fantasy value changes all the time. Don't make a deal or a decision on a player until you absolutely must. This is

especially true in keeper leagues. I turn in my keepers at the very last possible minute. He can be a star one minute and sitting on the bench the next for a variety of reasons. Don't make a decision until you have to.

"Don't risk what you cannot afford to lose." A deal is not just about the upside but also about the downside. If this deal goes completely south, can your team still compete? People always look at the upside of the deal, but having a low downside is just as important. Understanding both potential outcomes of the deal will help you evaluate it better.

"In the old used-car sales days, if a guy was trying to trade in one car for another and asked if the car leaked oil, that meant his car leaked oil." It's not just about what you are saying in the negotiation, it's about what the other party is saying. Listening is much more important than talking when making a deal. Which is why talking in person or on the phone is much better than just emailing the guy a trade offer out of the blue. You want to get the most out of the deal? Talk. And *listen.*

"If you're in a poker game with five guys and each guy has $100 and you've won $400, it's time to leave. You've already won most of the money." . . . *"If you can get 80 percent of what you want in a deal, take it. Most guys screw it up trying to get the last 20 percent."* . . . *"It's a good deal only if both sides are satisfied."* These three pieces of advice all tie together. The idea is to improve your team. Making it a superpower is great, but unrealistic in leagues where people know what they are doing. Don't be greedy. Get a deal done that helps you, not a deal that kills the other guy. You'll want to trade with him or her again, and setting fire to the earth doesn't do that. Nor does gloating about the trade afterward to the league.

"Don't trade something you need for something you don't."

Seems simple, but you'd be amazed how many people get enamored with big-name players and superstars without considering whether their team actually *needs* that big-name player. Always think about what your starting lineup will be once this deal is done, and whether that lineup is better than what you have. Tom Brady is great, but if you have to bench Drew Brees to play Brady, that's not really a great trade for you since I'm sure you had to give up a stud RB or WR for Brady.

"The best way to double your money is to fold it up and put it in your pocket." Sometimes the best trades you make are the ones you don't. It's not always necessary to make a deal. Always be willing to walk away.

"You don't need to tell a man what he already knows." Part of the art of negotiation. Tell him something he doesn't know. He's aware that his point guard can't shoot or that his quarterback is a bum. Talk up your players. Tell him something to give him hope, not make him feel worse.

"Do not presume an outcome before it occurs; more times than not you will be wrong." Put yourself in a position to have the best possible chance at success, but understand it is just a chance. No deal is a slam-dunk. Nothing is guaranteed, so don't treat any player or situation as such.

"When a mouse is caught in a trap, he's not thinking of the cheese, he's thinking of how to get out. But once he's out, he's thinking about the cheese again." This is about understanding that a deal is not just about what *you* get. It's also about what the other guy gets. Understand the point of view of your opponent (and if you don't know his or her point of view, *listen*) and realize that his point of view may very well change after the deal is done (or not). Tread carefully before, during, and after the negotiations.

And my favorite . . .

"Never chase a woman, a streetcar, or a deal."

My Uncle Lester preached being conservative in business (*"Lucky is a bad business plan"*) but being adventurous in life (*"You never know how big of a ditch you can jump over until you fall in"*).

He had a million of them. *"If you tell a lie, you better have a really good memory." "Borrow money when you can get it, not when you need it."* And *"Anyone can get along with easy people. A great executive can get along with difficult people."*

But the one he used the most was the answer to a question. Every time I saw my uncle, I'd ask him how he was doing. He answered the same every time.

"Still climbing that mountain, Maaaaathewwww. Still climbing that mountain."

He was never satisfied. He felt there was always something he could improve on and do better.

As the *Intermountain Jewish News* wrote about him, "The word 'colorful' was invented for Lester Gold. We might call Gold, who died this week, a philanthropist, an astute businessman, a behind-the-scenes leader who made things happen. We might say all this, and even add that he was an extraordinarily devoted husband and father and grandfather. We may say all this, and be right, and still fail to capture him."

By his example, Lester set high expectations for anyone in his orbit. He and Aunt Cookie had three daughters. Those three daughters had seven kids. Those seven grandkids have 14 children of their own, with another on the way. They all live in Denver, very close to their Poppy and Gammy. I can still see my uncle now, sitting in his white recliner, a huge grin on his face, as any number of kids or grandkids or great-grandkids ran around with shrieks of joy.

I know I'm not anywhere near the kind of man my uncle was, and I can't imagine how I could ever be. But it's a worthy goal to shoot for. So I'm still climbing that mountain.

8.

Not All Trades Go Smoothly

––––––––––––––––– *or* –––––––––––––––––

"We Created a Second Hakeem"

They weren't the only things in life Josh G. cherished. But they were up there.

One was Josh's best friend of 18 years. Another was being commissioner of their fantasy basketball league, Pimps Don't Cry, a job he took seriously. And those two items were now conflicting.

It was a few months into the season, and "Dan" (the friend) wanted a rule change. By having unlimited transactions in their head-to-head league, it "was punishing him for having a good draft," Dan argued, "as he couldn't drop his good players to fill in on off-days, the way others could." Josh understood where he was coming from, but "I told Dan I was uncomfortable changing any rule after the season had started, especially since this was a money league."

Back and forth they went, with Dan pressuring Josh and Josh holding firm. And so, unable to get his way on the rule change, Dan used the fantasy trade, often a beautiful thing, for less than beautiful purposes. Dan and his brother dumped their entire teams in one-sided trades to try and destroy the league. They then both quit the league. Josh tried to make peace, asking the guys to stay and see if they could work something out. "It's too late for that" Josh was told.

As Josh let me know, "A few hours later, Dan texted me and told me that he had replaced me as a groomsman in his wedding." Insane, right? Josh adds, "He was kind of known for throwing temper tantrums like an eight-year-old. While it sucks to lose a friend, I had been getting tired of his self-centeredness for years."

Still . . . 18 years of friendship is a long time. It's been two years, and they haven't spoken since. Someone who was supposed to be in his wedding. Over fantasy basketball. No one takes fantasy more seriously than I do, and even I will tell you it is not worth ruining relationships over, let alone with your best friend for almost two decades.

Listen, you didn't read this book for me to lecture you about the importance of relationships. Or even fairness. But the fantasy trade? That's my wheelhouse.

I hate *hate HATE* the veto. It's the coward's way out. If I were suddenly made the ruler of all things fantasy, there would never be a veto except in cases of obvious, provable collusion. And in that instance, only the commissioner or host website for the league should veto.

They say there are only three things in this world you can truly count on: death, taxes, and that when you make a fantasy trade, someone will bitch about it. Which is a shame because people should almost never complain about a trade.

Understand these two key things:

First, the art of negotiating is a skill in fantasy. That's part of being a general manager. A huge part, in fact. It's a skill that is admired and sought after in real-life general managers. Why should it be any different in fantasy? Second, it is *not* your job to coach someone else's team. If you think that tight end isn't nearly enough for that quarterback and running back combo, it doesn't matter. The only thing that matters is that the guy getting the tight end thinks so. Everyone should be allowed—encouraged, in fact—to coach his or her own team. Even if it's stupidly.

Because I got news for you. No one ever knows. I remember one of the first email flame wars I got into about a trade. In the Doug Logan League from chapter 2 (a dynasty fantasy football league), I traded a package of players for, in essence, Brett Favre, then one of the best quarterbacks in fantasy. It was a depth-for-a-superstar deal, perfectly legit. But the league went nuts because the only quarterback the guy was getting back was a recently promoted backup who got the job only because the starter had been injured in preseason. I argued that the point of the deal was to give him depth at RB and WR, which is what the guy said he wanted, and the backup was better than they realized. He was happy, I was happy, what's the issue? On and on they bitched. Until about week three or four, when they realized the backup QB I had dealt—Kurt Warner, in his 1999 "greatest show on turf" season— was better than Favre would ever be.

No one has complained about a trade in that league since. (And despite dealing Warner, I still managed to win the league that year, thank goodness. Otherwise I'd still be in therapy over it.)

I'll say it again. As long as both teams feel the deal helps their team, regardless of whether you agree, it *must go through*. I especially can't stand the people who block a trade just because it doesn't involve them or because it's part of their "strategy" to block other teams from improving. That's the coward's way out, and you're a scummy, spineless punk if you do that.

Win on the virtual field, not in the bureaucracy.

If every person adopted this attitude, you wouldn't have crazy email flame wars or message boards blowing up, you wouldn't have hurt feelings or worse, and you wouldn't see stories like Joshua's where you just shake your head.

In the spring of 2004, I had a similar "what the hell just happened here?" falling-out related to fantasy when I was fired from Rotoworld.com.

Starting in 1999, I was a three-sport guy for them, writing my "Talented Mr. Roto" column once a week during the season for fantasy football, fantasy basketball, and fantasy baseball. Apparently, the readers must have thought I knew what I was talking about, because early on the owners told me the column had become the most popular on the site in terms of traffic. They eventually gave it prominent placement and called me their senior writer. I was doing national weekly radio hits promoting Rotoworld on Fox Sports Radio. I contributed to their draft kits and magazines. I represented them at industry trade shows and public appearances. I had started working for them for free but for all that I was now up to the princely sum of $100 a week. But I was doing it because I truly loved it.

Now, at that time the dot-com bubble had burst, Internet advertising wasn't prevalent, and people were still figuring out exactly how to make money online. As a result, Rotoworld wanted to cut some costs, so I got a call. They wanted to pay me $25 a week or let me go.

Actual conversation:

ME: Wait, after writing for you for four and a half years, you want to cut my pay 300 percent?
BOSS: Well, when you say it that way it sounds bad.

Sigh.

Throughout my life I have tended to react very poorly when I think I'm being treated unfairly. I am a very black-and-white kind of guy, and for whatever reason, fairness is a huge issue with me. The majority of problems I've had with authority figures, from childhood to twenty minutes before I wrote this, stem from something happening to me that I deem to be unjust or unfair.

So it's pretty surprising that I didn't just scream at the guy for 10 minutes, burn the bridge, and never speak to him again. It's not that $25 or $100 made that much of a difference in my life. I obviously did this job for the joy of it, not the money. But it was the principle. I had done really good, high-quality work for them, built an audience, promoted them on radio, never missed a deadline, and now this? I was pissed. Really pissed.

But for once, I bit my tongue and did something smart. I said . . . Let me think about it.

I then quickly started up a Yahoo interest group. I made mine a "fan group." It's an online community that anyone can create—they are free, down, and dirty. But the key is that to join the group you need to give an active email address. In creating the group, my whole goal was to suck as many email addresses out of Rotoworld as I could before I left. This was before the days of Facebook or Twitter, so I had no real way of telling people where I might be going next unless I had an email address. And while my bosses thought I was "thinking" about their pay cut, I was actually putting a link to this Yahoo group into my columns. That way, when I went to a new website (or if I wanted to try and sell them a RotoPass), I'd have some emails to tell fans where to find me. I started talking to other popular websites about writing for them, and I came close to joining my friends at Rotowire.com.

But before I decided what website I would start working for, the Yahoo group exploded. I had over 6,000 members in two weeks and a very active message board, which in those days in the fantasy sports universe was a really good number.

As all this was going on, Rotoworld's owners eventually discovered the link and fired me outright. And I was sad. I had loved writing for

Rotoworld, loved most of the people I worked with, and frankly, was kinda bummed it took them so long to discover what I was doing. Didn't anyone there read my column?

During this time the Yahoo group kept growing. People would leave messages and questions for me, and before I could answer, other people would answer them and then post their own questions to me. It quickly developed into a fantasy sports community, and its fast growth led me to think, *Hey, instead of joining another site, why don't I just start my own?*

I quickly developed a plan. My cumbersome nickname proved to be lucky again. The URL for TalentedMrRoto.com was available. So I grabbed that, hired a cheap designer, and threw up a down and dirty website.

If I am being honest, my thinking at the time was this: I didn't care if the site was any good, I just needed some sort of content. My grand plan was that the TMR site, as it came to be known, would be one huge advertisement for RotoPass. I would get them to the TMR site with my writing and radio appearances, but then I would try to upsell folks to buy a RotoPass. That was the entirety of my genius business plan for TMR.

So I went to the Yahoo message board and looked for guys who were responding to posts in an intelligent manner. When I found one, I would send him a note saying I couldn't pay him anything, but would he like to write for me as a "fantasy expert"? I also asked a few Hollywood writer friends who played fantasy if they wanted to do something on the side, and voilà, I had a writing staff. I created a content plan, taught the writers how to post their columns, slapped a message board up there, and bingo, bango, on March 19, 2004, the site was live.

I then spent all my energy on getting RotoPass off the ground, promoting it and improving it, and basically left TMR to its own devices for a while. My management style has always been to hire good people and get out of their way. The TMR site was no exception.

After about three months, the TMR site was actually . . . not terrible.

Very not terrible, in fact. TalentedMrRoto.com, the "throwaway" site, was producing some great content.

Many of the writers I hired over the years would ultimately become some of the best-known names in the fantasy industry, including some of the stars of Yahoo, CBS, NBA.com, SI.com, AOL, and, of course, ESPN. We were drawing more and more fans, and suddenly I was spending just as much time on TMR as I was on RotoPass. Even though it had taken almost a year of work, it still seemed very quick. By the summer of 2004, I was no longer a guy who took a couple of hours a week to write a fantasy column—I was the CEO of two burgeoning websites.

I had traded a small job at a big website to be my own big fish. And I started trading off more and more of my movie-writing duties to my partner to concentrate on the two sites—thinking about how we could improve the sites, fixing things, calling or emailing people, and trying to negotiate deals with bigger sites. Things were changing very quickly.

Which shouldn't have been a surprise. Fantasy players are *always* looking to trade. My "career" at Rotoworld, such as it was, hadn't turned out like I had hoped. So I was doing what came naturally. I traded. One site for another, one disappointment for a new challenge, one focus for two more.

It was a heady, confusing time, and I was excited about the path I was on, even if I had no idea where it led.

Trying to make the best decision when there is no clear-cut answer is exactly what Curtis Black found himself facing. Curtis is an original member of the 23-year-old Fantasy Basketball League ("the FBL, no points for creativity").

It was the 1994–95 season, and one of their owners (who insisted on being called J-Smooth) owned Houston Rockets superstar center Hakeem Olajuwon. Back in 1995, you had to pay for email, and the league was filled with poor college kids, spread out all over the country. As a result, "most of the league business was done over voice-mails and through actual mail. In order for a trade to be legit, both owners involved had to phone 'The Ern' [the commish] with the details of the trade," Curtis explains.

So J-Smooth was working the phones, trying to deal Hakeem, leaving voice-mail offers for the UCSB Slackers and the Atlanta Dixie-Rebels. Curtis continues: "This was all done over winter break. Winter break left some of us away from our college voice-mail." And as the story goes, J-Smooth later left a message with the commish something to the effect of "I traded Hakeem tonight, the deal is legit."

Here's where the problems start. After the J-Smooth confirmation, *both* other owners called in to confirm their deals for Hakeem. Basically, J-Smooth had offered Hakeem, over voice-mail, to two different owners. Both agreed to the deal and called the commish to confirm. J-Smooth, obviously, had not been specific in his voice-mail about which team he was trading Hakeem to.

Adding to it all is that they played two games after the trades, and since the commish had not called to deny the deal to either party (he was also away from his voice-mail over winter break), both teams were counting Hakeem's stats in these games. "In January, when we all returned to school—there was chaos."

Both teams insisted they had been offered—and accepted—Hakeem in a trade and had made other moves based on having Hakeem. As a result, there was lots of discussion about what to do. Could it be erased? Reversed? Who would get Hakeem and who wouldn't? What do you do with the team's lineup that didn't get Hakeem?

Nobody, it seemed, was worried that J-Smooth (a perennial bottom-dweller) had gotten two sets of players for Hakeem. Each owner was screaming that Hakeem was his, so in its infinite wisdom, the FBL did what they thought was fair. "We created a second Hakeem."

So they let both owners use Olajuwon's stats for the rest of the year, and I've decided that, if I ever start an indie rock band, I'm calling it The Second Hakeem.

The two Hakeems gave new meaning to the term "Twin Towers," but the idea of dual athletes in a fantasy league reminds me of Maurice Jones-Drew. As many people know, Maurice is not just a star running back for the Jacksonville Jaguars and a perennial first-round pick, but he is also an avid fantasy football player himself, hosting his own fantasy football radio show on SiriusXM. MJD is the first active NFL player to be both an athlete and a huge advocate for fantasy.

So the fact that he plays in a lot of fantasy leagues and, as an athlete, is a first-round pick has led to situations where, because of where he's picking, he doesn't have the chance to draft himself. Normally, people in the league are understanding and let MJD draft himself. But not always.

One year, in order to promote fantasy, the NFL Players Association had a fantasy league with a bunch of NFL players, including MJD and Chicago Bears running back Matt Forte. And who did Forte select with his first-round pick that year? Maurice Jones-Drew.

It was a good pick, as MJD was going in the top three in fantasy drafts across the country and Maurice had a low draft pick in the first round. Naturally, he tried to trade for himself. And Matt Forte was having none of it.

As the season went on, MJD put up monster numbers, making his fantasy owners happy. And making it impossible to get himself back in a trade. "Come on," Maurice texted Forte one week. "You gotta trade me to me."

Forte texted back. "Hell no. I'm gonna beat you with you."

Speaking of texting trade offers, "Chris in Indy" is in the same ESPN league with his wife, Jen, who has always loved Fred Jackson. But in 2011 Chris managed to draft Jackson before she did. "All she could talk about is how she wanted Jackson on her team. Meanwhile, she was sick of having an injured Arian Foster sitting on her bench."

It was week three of the 2011 season, and while Jackson was going off for 21 points, Arian Foster was inactive, as his preseason hamstring injury had acted up. So sitting downstairs in his "man cave" watching football, Chris texted his wife, who was one floor above him in the kitchen.

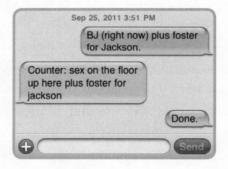

Sep 25, 2011 3:51 PM

BJ (right now) plus foster for Jackson.

Counter: sex on the floor up here plus foster for jackson

Done.

"Needless to say, Fred Jackson wasn't the only one who scored that day. Arian Foster resumed being himself in week four, and I'd consider this the best trade I ever made."

Lorne Bilesky's AFLB League is based in Spokane, Washington, and has been around since 1983. They've shared in births and deaths, marriages, divorces—and now most of them are grandfathers. And in the almost 30 years they've been together, one trade stands out more than any other.

In 1998 the league was taking its annual road trip to a Seahawks game, crammed into a van and drinking heavily, when Jim, owner of FUBAR, started trade negotiations with Tim, owner of the Brain Dead

Dick Heads. Both were complaining about how bad their teams were, and they started tossing around names.

Lorne remembers, "They could never agree on which two players to trade, so it began to escalate to include more and more player combinations. Finally, very late in the night, Jim said, 'What the hell, let's just trade teams.' Tim agreed, and it was the source of high comedy for the rest of the night."

After a night of heavy drinking, it's perfectly normal to regret decisions you've made, and apparently Jim was no different. The team he had dealt included Dan Marino, who had gotten off to a slow start (for him). Jim's fears were well founded: "A couple weeks later, Marino erupted for five TDs," Lorne tells me. "The rest of the squad started playing to their expectations, and this vaulted Tim to the top of the standings, while Jim and his new squad languished near the cellar."

Tim won the league that year and has won four other titles since. And since that night, Jim has never known what it is like to be champion of the AFLB.

Jim's last title was 1984. I'm pretty sure that's a fantasy football record. Can someone send a shaman to Seattle? Or at least bury a Dan Marino action figure with some beads and a quick chant for Jim?

While it is usually not to the extent of Jim's regret, having post–fantasy trade remorse is as old as Jim's winless streak. You know how they say, "Every time you hear a bell, an angel gets its wings?" Well, every time you see a player get injured or lose his starting job, realize that someone, somewhere just traded for him.

Among the events that got mentioned the most were trading for Manny Ramirez just before his (totally unexpected) 50-game suspension, trading for Priest Holmes the day before he (again, unexpectedly) retired midseason, and trading for Plaxico Burress just before he (hopefully unexpectedly) shot himself in the leg at a nightclub.

In 1997 I was flying across the country on trade deadline day in my fantasy hoops league. I should have just left well enough alone. But instead I spent $90 on an airphone to try and win a league with a $50 prize. The centerpiece of the deal was David Robinson, who had missed a good chunk of the start of the season and had only recently come back to play six games. The day after our deal, my first with The Admiral, he reinjured himself and missed the rest of the year. Good times. But here's the thing. Spending an entire flight getting dirty looks from fellow passengers and spending almost twice as much money as I could win just to do a fantasy basketball trade might seem over the top, but that's nothing.

From stories like Josh G.'s to smaller ones where people dropped all the players on their team in protest of a bad trade (to try and screw the whole league up), to getting the host website to block someone's IP address (essentially locking them out), or to one time when I got a phone call at 3:00 AM from someone screaming at a trade I had pulled off . . . I've heard every extreme trade story.

And while I don't agree with it at all, I get it. Because fantasy sports is more than a hobby. It's more than a friendly pastime. It's an *obsession*.

PART FIVE

BECOMING OBSESSED

9.

Going Above and Beyond to Play

or

"This Is Our Third Kid. I Only Have One Title."

We have all been there.

We have a good team.

What we don't have, however, is a great team.

We study rosters. We scour the waiver wire. We mull over a million different moves. All we need is one more stud for the stretch run. Just one. Getting him, however, isn't always easy.

In 2011, Troy M. was in just such a situation in his Melbourne, Australia–based 12-team keeper league, The Inner Circle. Even better, his buddy Marc was in a rebuilding year. Even better than that, Marc had an unkeepable Calvin Johnson, the number one WR in fantasy that year, and he was ready to deal.

So the week of the trade deadline, Troy offered all sorts of deals. Back and forth they went, but they still hadn't been able to work something out. So desperate was Troy that he had even spent a good portion of his buddy's bachelor party on the phone, but nothing got done.

And so, on the final deadline day, Troy went to the wedding with the sad knowledge that his deal was dead. Troy remembers, "It was a traditional church service, and so it was reaaaaaally long. But about halfway through the service, my iPhone vibrates in my pocket. So . . . as carefully as decorum would allow, I snuck it out." It was a message from Marc! The text read: "Stafford, Cruz and 4th next year for Megatron. Final Offer." Excited trade talks were back on! Troy countered: "Cruz fine. Staff No. Cam and 2nd?" And incredibly, the iPhone vibrated again. "Okay. I'll go offer."

Troy can't believe it! A week of negotiations later, Calvin Johnson was his! "I rushed to accept on my iPhone app before Marc changed his mind," when suddenly Troy felt an elbow in his ribs.

And noticed the entire church staring at him.

Because *he was the best man.*

And the priest had asked him, *YET AGAIN, if he had the ring!*

Troy then pulled off a move that has never been done before or since in fantasy history. "I reached into my pocket to pull out the ring with one hand while accepting the trade with the other."

Troy would like me to refer to his friend who got married with the fake name "Lawrence" because, frankly, "it's still a sore point with him."

I'm amazed he still talks to you. Troy understands the disbelief. "I had held up the entire wedding, but . . . I did get Megatron, and a couple of months later I had the league title."

Being distracted from something important by fantasy sports is nothing new. In my world, it had been going on a long time. Going back to early 2005, I had a big problem. Two, in fact. The first I had been dealing with in therapy, specifically, the guilt I felt that I was blowing off my wife, my movie-writing career, and everything else to focus on two websites that weren't even profitable.

My other big problem was the two websites. Specifically, they were creating a real conflict. Back in the summer of 2002, a guy named Steve Mason had contacted me. He hosted a national sports talk show on the Fox Sports Radio Network and was a fan of my column. Would I want to call in and do a segment on fantasy football? And once again I somehow managed to ask a smart question.

ME: Wouldn't you rather I come in?
PRODUCER: What?
ME: Don't interviews sound better in person?
PRODUCER: Well, yeah . . .
ME: I live like five minutes away. I can just come in instead of calling in. I don't mind.
PRODUCER: Uh, sure, I guess. Okay.

No one had ever offered to drive to the studio before, especially for a five-minute segment. But sure, if you want to, knock yourself out, he said.

Here's why I did that, and it goes back to a Lesterism. *"Face to face is always better."* It wasn't until very late in life that my Uncle Lester ever started doing contracts, and only then because other companies insisted on it. For him, a handshake was always enough. His attitude was, a man's word should mean something. And it's also why Lester didn't believe in email.

We see this in fantasy leagues all the time. Email or text trade offers that arrive out of the blue get turned down just as quickly. With technology today, it's too easy to get lost, to be just a name at the end of an email. Whether it's romance, business, friendship, or fantasy sports, *evrything* comes back to relationships. Which is why I wanted to come in.

I didn't care about the clarity of the audio. I wanted it to be as good a segment as it could be, of course, but more important, I wanted to meet them. Once I met them, I wasn't just some voice at the end of a phone. Now I'm a guy they've shaken hands with. BS-ed with before and after the segment. Now I have a relationship with these guys, as opposed to being some faceless email saying, "Hey, how about next week?"

The first segment went well, the guys were all nice, and I was invited back for the following week. And the week after. Steve eventually asked me to do two segments, which eventually turned into doing an hour and then guest hosting over the holidays to all the way to (after lots of meetings and proposals to the Fox Sports Radio bosses) a job in 2004 and 2005, when I became the official Fox Sports Radio fantasy "expert," doing hits on the air throughout the week and doing fantasy updates every hour on NFL Sundays.

I bring this whole look back/sidebar up for a few reasons. First, it's as good a fantasy (and life) lesson as there is. Talk to people. Face-to-face. Whenever possible. And second, because it illustrates the issue I was having with the two websites.

Every time I'd do a radio hit, Steve would say, "And here to talk fantasy football, the Talented Mr. Roto, Matthew Berry, from RotoPass .com." A nightmare. Too many names, too hard to remember, and even when I asked them not to use my TMR nickname, the biggest issue was still there.

If someone enjoyed my radio segment and wanted to read me, they'd go to RotoPass.com and find . . . not me. Same problem with the link in my Rotoworld column.

I know what you're saying. Wait, didn't they fire you last chapter? Yes, they did. But as they told me in a follow-up phone call a few weeks later, they didn't really mean it. After the quick growth of the Yahoo group, Rotoworld didn't want to lose me. "Why don't you come back, we'll start a message board on Rotoworld, and you can tell all your followers to start posting messages here," they helpfully suggested.

But at that point plans were already under way for TalentedMrRoto .com to launch soon, and RotoPass.com was up and running, so I politely declined. But I did make them a counteroffer. Let me come back and write for you . . . for free. All you have to do is let me link back to RotoPass.

Seems insane nowadays, since the traffic they would send me would ultimately be many times more valuable than the $100 a week (or even $25!) they were trying to save, but they really wanted to save that money. Also helping my cause was a guy named Rick Wolf, who was running Rotoworld for the owners. He liked me and fought for the deal with the owners. And so I returned to Rotoworld, without pay, but with the ability to promote and link my little heart out.

But again, same issue. You read my column, liked me, wanted to read more of me, so you clicked on the RotoPass.com link and found that it was just a portal site where you bought the subscription and got taken to a bunch of other fantasy sites, none of which I wrote for.

So it proved awkward to promote RotoPass in the column or on the radio. I had gotten all the established sites to join RotoPass in part because I had promised I was going to promote the RotoPass site all over, so even though TMR was growing, I really didn't want to focus on TMR that much. RotoPass was supposed to be the moneymaker. How could I get the word out about *that?*

Trying to solve that issue took up a lot of time in the summer of 2004, along with all the other issues that go with running two recently launched websites. Plus I had my day job, the movie writing, so I was really working like crazy. Lots of hours, long nights, and not a lot of attention paid to my wife. She understood and supported everything I was trying to do, but demanded that I relax and focus on us during a romantic, two-week vacation in Italy. I gave her my word. And it would be easy to turn my fantasy brain off.

Remember, in 2004, technology was very limited. Cell phones didn't have the Internet on them, you couldn't get email while mobile and we were in deep, remote, nothing-around-for-miles-except-beautiful-countryside Italy.

We were finishing up a long, leisurely lunch at a quaint Italian wine bistro when I went to the bathroom.

I passed by the bar, where they had one lone TV showing CNN International. As I was walking past, the ticker scrolled by. Carlos Beltran, then one of the best players in baseball, had been *traded*. From the American League. To the Houston Astros, then in the National League.

In my NL-only Fat Dog league, this was huge news. Players of this caliber rarely got traded into the league, and more than a month before the trade deadline too. I was in the hunt for the title that year . . . I *had* to make a bid. So, with my wife waiting in the other room to continue our romantic away-from-fantasy-sports vacation, I did what any self-respecting fantasy owner would do.

I bribed the bartender with $50 American to let me make an international call and talked my brother Jonathan through the process of putting in a bid on Beltran. When I finally returned, my wife was puzzled. "What took you so long?" I smiled at her, not wanting to lie. "I got really sick in there."

Hey, I said I didn't want to lie, not that I didn't lie. The white lie to escape someone (or something) for a fantasy move is a time-honored tradition. When you are obsessed with fantasy sports, it can consume your life. And when it consumes your life, you'll do fantasy wherever and whenever you need to.

"Lewis" had a draft during a wedding, but didn't want to use the frequent-trips-to-the-bathroom plan. You see, the reception was at the hotel. So a few hours into the party, he snuck away and did the draft in his room before rejoining the party later. When asked where he was all that time, Lewis told everyone that he hooked up with a girl from the wedding. But "she left for the night because she got sick from the booze."

And that, my friends, tells you everything you need to know. Fantasy owners would rather be thought of as a guy who left his cousin's wedding to hook up with a girl so drunk she had to leave soon after than say he was doing a fantasy draft. Not sure what it says about Lewis, but apparently everyone bought the story with no questions asked.

Speaking of no questions asked, remember Don Carlson from chapter 1? He's a firefighter, playing in the 10-team Fire Station 1 League out of Los Angeles. "One year, before smartphones, etc., we had a brushfire in Malibu. Sometimes, during brushfires, a crew can be very busy. Constantly moving to new places and fighting fires with little time to rest. But other times there is a lot of down time, especially when you set up to protect a certain area.

"And what I had been thinking for the last 24 hours while on this brushfire was, *If this is gonna last another 48 hours, I'm not going to be able to set my lineup.*"

The fire did rage on, but during a patrol Don found a family standing outside their house. So Don approached them, wearing his fireman's uniform, badge prominently displayed. Then, in his most official-sounding voice, said he needed access to their computer. "Of course, officer! Anything to help with the fire!" Request granted, lineup set, and the family never knew. Until now.

Luckily for Don, he was able to make his moves in private. Tyler was not as lucky. One Sunday morning he realized he had forgotten to put Adrian Peterson and Brett Favre back in his starting lineup off a bye. No big deal. It happens. So he took out his iPhone to make the change. Only problem?

"I was taking my SATs."

It's been a while since I took my SATs, Tyler, but they frown upon that, right?

"I got caught. I had to go before a group of people to prove I wasn't cheating. My explanation was that I was editing my fantasy football lineup. They just laughed at me."

I would love to have been in that "hearing."

"My father understood why I did it because he's in the league and a serious player. My mother, on the other hand, thought I was an idiot."

Kinda see both sides here, my friend.

Tyler continued: "In addition, I wasn't able to get the lineup change in. I ended up losing that week and missed the playoffs by one game."

There is one silver lining, though. Tell 'em, Tyler.

"They knew I wasn't cheating because I did so poorly on my SATs."

Tyler's mother is a teacher in the county, and the school board tells the story to this day.

You know, when I'm asked about fantasy, I always say it's like a Springsteen concert. Like, you know Bruce Springsteen is popular and maybe you'll even turn up the radio when a song of his comes on. But once you see him in concert, you finally understand the fanaticism, the devotion, the crazy obsession. Same with fantasy sports. Once you try it, you get it. And stories like this don't surprise you. In fact, you have some of your own.

Mark Halpern's wife went into labor on a Friday. "Our Football for Fools league has a weekly free agent auction, and bids are due by noon on Friday," Mark says. "As commish, I need to manually process the bids." There was also a Saturday game that week, so the bids needed to be done ASAP so teams could set lineups, etc. Mark had his laptop, ran the auction, and made the moves *for every single team* from the delivery room. While his wife was sitting there. *Screaming in pain.*

"My mistake was not waiting until she had the epidural." Good hint for you future father/commish combos out there. Is Mark's obsession extreme? Yes. But, as Mark points out, "This is our third kid. I only have one title."

From being in the hospital to on his way to one, David Harris wasn't going to let something silly like excruciating pain and insane injury stand in the way of fantasy.

In 2007, on the morning of his fantasy football draft, David was in what can only be described as a horrific motorcycle accident. With a broken pelvis and two broken hips, David was in the ambulance racing to the ER when he called his mom to ask her to pick up a few things for him on her way to the hospital. "One of those items was my handwritten player rankings. She arrived at the hospital with them at 11:00 AM, and my draft was scheduled for noon."

In case the whole "worrying about his fantasy draft after a motorcycle accident with a broken pelvis and two broken hips" thing didn't tell you he was hard-core, the "handwritten player rankings" should have sealed it.

David continues: "I was able to get admitted to the hospital and get nice and doped up on morphine about 10 minutes before the draft started. I used my cell phone to call in to the draft."

Totally drugged? How'd that go?

"Apparently, I continually sang 'Black Betty' by Ram Jam during any free moment."

A very underrated song, incidentally.

"My friends tell me that it was very funny. When you are in an accident like that, they put you on a self-controlled morphine drip, which allows you to hit a button every few minutes to get another shot through an IV. When I would first hit the button, I would go extremely incoherent for the first 30 to 45 seconds, and then would be good again until the next push of morphine. During those times, I would start to sing, or be distant."

His friends would alternate between annoyed and worried, which is what friends at a fantasy draft with one guy on the phone singing "Black Betty" should be. And let David's story be a lesson to all you drafters out there.

"After talking with my buddies for some reminders on that draft, I am proud to say that not once did I attempt to pick a player who had already been drafted."

Nice! You see that, people? There's no excuse.

"In the end, I limp a little bit, and am in pain every now and again with certain things that I just can't do anymore. But I won the second of back-to-back championships that season, and I am thankful and lucky to be alive."

Amen, David.

"And now, when someone tries to reschedule the draft due to a last-minute obligation, we remind him that I did the draft on morphine, lying in a hospital bed."

Damn right you did. And I hereby grant everyone reading this the right to use David's story as well. The next time someone in your league is talking about flaking on the draft, you tell them the story of David Harris, who drafted hours after an accident with a broken pelvis, two broken hips, and just one handwritten cheat sheet.

TIME-OUT:

Different Kinds of Fantasy

When someone gets obsessed with something, they want to do more of it. They join multiple leagues, they play multiple sports, and sometimes they invent new ways to play. I've always said, if you can find a way to keep score, you can play a fantasy version of *anything*. For years my friends have played fantasy summer movie league (at www.summermovieleague.com). You have a "fantasy studio," and you win by how much money your movies make at the box office.

Fantasy football, fantasy basketball, and fantasy baseball are the most popular fantasy games, of course, but pretty much every sport has a fantasy game. From fantasy NASCAR, fantasy golf, and fantasy college football to things like fantasy bass fishing, it runs the gamut. Daily fantasy games like DraftStreet.com, where you draft your team and win or lose in the same day, have become popular recently. Here at ESPN, many of the *SportsCenter* anchors do a fantasy umpire league, where they get points for ejections. And no pun intended, fantasy sumo wrestling is huge in Japan. There's even reverse twists on sports, like Grantland's Bad Quarterback League, where you play fantasy football but with terrible NFL QBs. The worse they do for their real NFL teams, the better they do for you.

Frankly, I consider things like Super Bowl squares, NCAA basketball brackets, and office pool pick 'ems to also be fantasy. Anytime you are selecting something, get some sort of reward for the performance of whatever you selected, and are competing with others, that's fantasy. And the concept has been taken and molded into almost everything you can imagine. Here are some of the more, shall we say, offbeat fantasy leagues.

Fantasy Congress: You pick both representatives and senators, and you get points when they introduce bills, have bills pass out of committee, and get bills passed in each of the houses of Congress. Extra points if the president signs the bill into law!

Fantasy Supreme Court: Similar, but different. Predict how each of the nine justices will rule on each case: affirm, reverse, or *recuse*!

Fantasy *Top Chef,* fantasy *Survivor,* fantasy *American Idol,* fantasy *Big Brother,* fantasy *Bachelor,* RuPaul's Fantasy Drag Race: Pretty much every reality and elimination show has a fantasy game you can play where you select contestants and get points on how long they last or things they do in the show. And of course, there is Grantland's Fantasy Reality League, a combination of many of these shows.

Fantasy rodeo: Draft a fantasy team that will win the most money throughout the entire rodeo. Pick one header and one heeler in the team roping. Giddyup.

PhantasyTour.com: A set-list prediction game about the band Phish. It's a great community, and hey, (puff) if you don't win, that's (puff) um, it's really o—— (puff), I'm sorry, what was the question again?

Fantasy Wall Street: You buy and sell real stocks with fake money. Obviously, there's no real consequences for mistakes. So you know, pretty much like the real thing.

Fantasy weather: After being given a location on a map of the United States, you forecast high and low temps for the next five days, wind direction, speeds, and the always tricky precipitation amounts. Fantasy Snowfall is similar but simpler: Submit the four cities you think will get the most inches of snow during a given week. Having spent four years there, I can assure you Syracuse is always a safe pick.

Fantasy spelling bee: Always popular. You pick kids for the National Spelling Bee, which ESPN broadcasts every year, with points for how long your kid lasts. I always go for the kid with the longest last name.

Fantasy World Series of Poker, fantasy WWE wrestling, fantasy X-games, fantasy Street League (skaters), fantasy beer pong (yes, there is a World Series of Beer Pong), fantasy Tour de France, fantasy Iditarod, and fantasy Corn Hole (based on players in the Midwest): These are among the sports versions of fantasy that showed up more than I would have thought.

Lent Madness: A faith-based learning game in which 32 saints are placed in a tournament-like single elimination bracket. Each pairing remains open for a set period of time, and people vote for their favorite saint. Sixteen saints make it to the Round of the Saintly Sixteen; eight advance to the Round of the Elate Eight; four make it to the Faithful Four;

two to the Championship; and the winner is awarded the coveted Golden Halo. I wonder if the "12 seeds always beat a 5" thing holds true here too?

Celebrity death pool: Many people are in on this one. Too depressing for me, though.

Fantasy TV: Pick TV shows, with standings based on ratings.

Fantasy fashion: Draft designers of things like runway shows, handbags, jewelry, and get points for magazine and online press.

Celebrity fantasy: Same idea—you choose celebs and get points based on press mentions of breakups, rehab, babies, being part of a celeb couple, etc.

And of course, Oscar pick 'em pools: Among the more popular ones from pop culture that aren't based on a specific show.

Fantasy executive: Participants can pick their teams from more than 90 of the world's top executives representing nine different corporate functions. In this fantasy game launched by *Fortune* magazine, you earn points by how closely your team ends up matching the teams formed by top execs, headhunters, and management professors. Now you can complain "they picked the wrong guy for the job!" in real life *and* in fantasy.

10.

Innocent People Get Sucked Into Fantasy Madness

or

"How the #!&$ Did You Get My Number?"

Sunday mornings during football season, Texas A&M University student Adam has a very simple ritual. It starts with a nice bowl of Cheerios, continues with a comfortable couch, and finishes with fixing his fantasy roster about an hour before kickoff.

In the semifinals of his league's playoffs in 2011, he's just about to start when he gets what can only be described as a very disturbing text from his resident adviser.

"We are having some difficulties with our Internet services. Internet will be down until further notice."

And with a hurt Ahmad Bradshaw needing to be replaced, Adam freaked. Using the app on his iPhone is not an option—he dropped the phone two weeks prior, and college budgets being what they are, Adam can't afford to fix the screen. All his apps have been rendered useless.

There's no point in going to a neighbor's place—they are all without

Internet as well. And on a Sunday morning after a party-filled Saturday night, he's not about to knock on college kids' doors asking if they have a smartphone with the fantasy app. He also can't drive to somewhere with Internet because he doesn't have a car. And he doesn't live within walking distance of somewhere that might have Internet either.

But, my friends, if there is one benefit to being a broke college student, it's that you become pretty damn resourceful. No car. No smartphone. No Internet. But what does he have?

A bus. That's right. Adam's dorm is on a bus route. A bus route that goes by the library. A library . . . that has *Internet*!

Adam runs outside and hops on the campus bus. By this time, he's got 30 minutes until kickoff, and the bus, not surprisingly, is moving fairly slow. There's five more stops until the library, and Adam is getting antsy. So he walks up to the bus driver and tells him the situation. Adam relays, "He simply laughed at me."

DRIVER: We'll get there when we get there.

But desperate measures call for desperate times. So, broke or not, Adam whips out his wallet.

ADAM: I got 20 bucks. What can you do?
DRIVER: I see a 50.

Now this is all the money Adam has in his wallet right now, $70 is a lot to him, but it's the playoffs, time is ticking away, and he's come this far.

ADAM: Fine. Here's 70 bucks. But you skip the rest of the stops and head straight for the bus stop at the library.

The driver takes one look at Adam.

DRIVER: Deal.

And the driver does just that! Blowing by five different bus stops, passing by waiting students, he drops Adam off with time to spare. Adam gets into the library, puts Brandon Jacobs in for the now-ruled-out Ahmad Bradshaw . . . Jacobs winds up with double-digit points and Adam wins his matchup by 10 points, a game he would have lost if he'd left Bradshaw in.

So all's well that ends well until a few days later, when he gets a call from the dean. The dean, well, he'd like a word.

The next day Adam walks into the dean's office only to find his bus driver from Sunday already sitting there. The dean wastes no time. "Did you pay our driver $70 to ignore his route so you could fix your fantasy football roster?"

"Yes, sir. I'm truly sorry—"

That was all he needed to hear. The driver, sadly, was let go. Adam was fined $100 and had his bus-riding privileges suspended for the rest of the year.

But Adam got to stay in school, and as he was walking out of the office the dean addresses him. "Young man. Consider yourself lucky." Adam turns and looks back at him. "I drafted Vick and Charles this year."

Back in 2005, I didn't need to bribe a bus driver, but in many ways I was in a very similar situation as Adam. Like Adam, I was very limited in my budget, and I had a big problem with no obvious solution and not a lot of time left to fix it.

RotoPass.

The charter websites that made up RotoPass were starting to get antsy. They had all signed on with my fledgling little website, but in order to get these established companies to go along with unproven me, I had given them all nonbinding contracts. "Hey," I said, "if you don't want to be in it, I don't want to force you. Join up, and if you hate it, leave whenever you want."

So not only had the "how can I start promoting this?" issue *not* been solved, there was now mounting pressure to do so. Because if one site left, they all would.

Back at another lunch with my Internet-savvy friend, the same guy who had told me about the adult age check site, I asked him to help me brainstorm ways to get the word out.

Especially since I had no clue about any of those Internet tricks. Search engine optimi-what? Really? Meta-tags? What's a meta-tag? Uh, no, I don't have a link exchange program on the site. Do you need one? Seriously, I had no technical background, no Internet experience; I only had enough smarts to hire people who knew what they were doing and get out of their way. Beyond some simple Internet tricks, we were spitballing ideas on how best to promote the site. He suggested getting an athlete or coach to endorse it, but I didn't think it would work. The professional leagues and their athletes have gotten the message now, but back then most professional athletes hated fantasy and fantasy players. Getting one of them to promote would come off as phony, especially because it's not like I could have afforded a really famous athlete. I didn't think "Hi, for RotoPass.com, I'm F. P. Santangelo" was gonna move the needle.

Plus, real fantasy players knew that professional athletes looked down on fantasy and had no expertise when it came to playing it. So I posed the question differently. How could I get the word out on a budget?

Then my friend, who was very smart in lots of areas but knew nothing about fantasy sports, asked a very simple and obvious question. One that, frankly, had never occurred to me.

He said, "Well, who is The Guy?" When I looked at him quizzically, he explained further. "Who is the, you know . . ." (searching for a name), "'Martha Stewart' of fantasy sports? The one person that when you say fantasy sports everyone thinks of? Who is most associated with it? See if you can get that person to endorse it."

And I said, well . . . no one.

There were a couple of guys who were known to longtime fantasy players. . . . Brandon Funston, first of ESPN and then Yahoo, Eric Karabell of ESPN, and Ron Shandler of BaseballHQ.com were the first folks who popped into my mind, all of them good friends.

But, much as I like and respect them personally, I didn't think any of them had popped in a way that when you thought of fantasy sports you immediately thought of *that person*, the way you think of Mel Kiper Jr. when someone mentions NFL draft day.

With no one obvious to hire to help promote the website, my buddy suggested I do it. Why didn't I become my own spokesperson?

ME: Me?

HIM: You've played long enough, right?

ME: Yeah, since 1984.

HIM: And how long have you been writing about fantasy sports for a website?

ME: Since late '99.

HIM: And doing national radio?

ME: Since '02.

HIM: So you've got credibility. And the nickname . . .

ME: Talented Mr. Roto?

HIM: Yeah, I like that. It's memorable. Good brand name. You could build that up.

Hmmmm.

TalentedMrRoto.com was growing faster than RotoPass, and thanks to all my radio experience plus years of pitch meetings in Hollywood, I was comfortable speaking in front of a microphone or to large groups of strangers. If I could develop more of my personality and make myself more of a brand name, well . . . then . . . hell, maybe I *could* be my own spokesman for RotoPass. That was the idea at any rate. When you want to be successful, a good place to start is to find a very successful person you admire and try to emulate them. Which is exactly what I did. But for someone who was trying to make it in the fantasy sports business, you might be surprised to learn that I chose Howard Stern.

I am a huge Stern fan and a listener of more than 20 years. But even if you are not a fan of his edgy brand of humor, he is an unbelievably smart businessman and a pioneer. The number of things that he created or was the first to accomplish is staggering and too long to list here, but he's among the most influential and creative minds in the history of entertainment. But even with that, you might think what Howard did would not be relatable to me.

But I disagree. One thing that often gets overlooked about Howard is that, among all the things he's done, he redefined what it means to be a morning DJ. Because he is now the "King of All Media," people forget that, before the books, movie, TV shows, celebrity friends, and huge national radio show, he was, like thousands of others, just a local morning DJ. Playing songs, introducing traffic and weather, reacting to the day's news. A morning DJ. There's a million of them.

But Howard said, I don't care what everyone else says a morning DJ is supposed to be, I'm gonna do it how I want. And the way Howard did it was by, among other things, being totally honest and making everything he could all about himself. Brilliantly.

The fans of Howard's—and there are many millions—are not just fans of Howard. They are *passionate* fans. Because they feel like they know *him*. It's not just that he's funny or smart or is a good interviewer or says outrageous things. When you listen to him, you feel as if you know *him*. Better than you know some of your closest friends.

So if Howard could do it, why did *I* have to be like every other fantasy sports analyst? There were many good analysts out there, but there's only so many ways you can say, "Start this guy, sit that guy," you know? At the time, every writer I was aware of was fairly serious, used tons of statistics, and kept it all about the advice.

I'm pretty good with stats, but I'm not Bill James. And I've watched tons of sports over my lifetime, but I never played professionally and was never a professional scout or anything, so there are people who can watch game tape with a more experienced eye than me. But the one thing I know I can do better than any person in the world?

Talk about me.

So in addition to the analysis, I wrote about my life, my friends, my wife, my brother, my leagues . . . everything was fair game. I didn't want to be a stereotypical fantasy nerd. So I talked about all the things guys like—pop culture, movies, and hot girls—and I wrote long egocentric stories that seemed random but ended up being a lesson about fantasy analysis.

Instead of three long, stat-filled paragraphs about one player, I tried to keep it quick, make my point, make it funny, and move on. I tried to always give readers "an actionable item." In other words, instead of saying "Well, if this happens, then maybe this will happen, but if it doesn't, you don't want him," I'd say "I would trade for this guy, I would drop that guy, I like this player more than that one." Too many analysts wavered, I felt. So I would be strong in my opinions and I told the columnists that wrote for me the same thing. "Hey, predicting the future is impossible," I would say. So say what you think will happen, say what an owner should specifically do with that information, and have a good, well-researched reason behind the analysis. You'll get some right and you'll get some wrong, but as long as you have a valid reason for feeling the way you do and you communicate that research, that's all that matters. Ultimately, it's on the readers to decide if they agree with you.

Back then, the unwritten rule of fantasy was to only print email praising you and your correct predictions. I decided to go the other way and printed all the angry hate mail that came in. I pointed out my mistakes and my wrong predictions. I was as open and honest as I could be with everything in my life, good and bad. In addition to my weekly columns and radio hits, I started a blog called "The TRUM (Thoughts, Ramblings, Useless info, and Musings)," which I wrote almost every day and emailed to every single member. A mixture of fantasy sports observations and whatever else was going on in my mind.

As you might imagine, my self-centered, strong-willed, and different approach would rub a lot of folks the wrong way (and still does!). Back in the day, Rotoworld had a distribution deal with FoxSports.com to run all of its fantasy content. Mine was the only column they refused to run.

But I loved the scene in the movie *Private Parts* where the disbelieving program director, "Pig Vomit," is being told by a researcher that Howard Stern has hit number one in the ratings.

> RESEARCHER: The average radio listener listens for 18 minutes. The average Howard Stern fan listens for—are you ready for this?—an hour and 20 minutes.
>
> PIG VOMIT: How can that be?
>
> RESEARCHER: Answer most commonly given? "I want to see what he'll say next."
>
> PIG VOMIT: Okay, fine. But what about the people who hate Stern?
>
> RESEARCHER: Good point. The average Stern hater listens for two and a half hours a day.

PIG VOMIT: But . . . if they hate him, why do they listen?

RESEARCHER: Most common answer? "I want to see what he'll say next."

There were a lot of lessons in that little scene. And it gave me the confidence to hang tough as many other people in the fantasy sports industry had no idea what to make of me. Howard's struggles were something I clung to tightly as I would lie awake at night and doubt myself. I had no idea if I had the talent, the appeal, the luck, the ability, and everything else that goes into making it full-time in this or any other industry. And in the dark places of my mind, the small crevices of my psyche that I held tight and never let anyone see, my honest feeling was . . . no way.

Other people had been in the business longer, had more of a track record, had more successful websites, had more of a head start. I wasn't a terrible writer, and I had some solid predictions. That was pretty much it. It couldn't possibly be enough, right?

I realized there was a very good chance I was going to fail. But I knew that the one thing I could control—frankly, the only thing—was work. I vowed to myself that no one was going to outwork me. I might fall flat on my face, but it damn sure wasn't going to be because I was lazy.

If I was ignoring my wife, my writing career, and my friends before, now it was like I had never met them.

Every night, while my wife was asleep, I was writing "The TRUM." And chatting on the site. And posting on the message board. I was promoting the TMR site at every opportunity. In short, by the end of 2005 nothing else mattered.

If I may throw out a generic stereotype about fantasy players here, it's that this behavior isn't unique. Or at least, my approach to the issue wasn't unique. Because, as a whole, we are an obsessive group. Poring over stats and box scores, studying the waiver wire so much we can recite it from memory, and, if one Internet study is to be believed, thinking about our fantasy team more often than sex.

I hear more tales of fantasy obsession than any other category. And when you think about it, almost every story in this book is, in some way, about obsession. Whether it's throwing yourself into a brand-new website with a few thousand members instead of your well-paying actual career, being a pastor who cheats, or bribing a bus driver with your last $70, there is no end to the lengths people will go to for fantasy glory. And these are the people who go above and beyond the people who go above and beyond.

Like Cousin Sal from *The Jimmy Kimmel Show*. Sal was running two fantasy leagues in the early '90s, and with no Internet to compile the stats, he had to gather stats manually through newspapers. If you lived on the East Coast, the box score for the Monday night game wouldn't even appear until Wednesday morning, an excruciatingly long time to wait, especially if it was a close game. Sal remembers, "I'd typically phone sports editors from various newspapers for stats. I annoyed them all so much. Eventually none of them would take my calls. Somehow I got the *New York Daily News* sports editor's home number, and in efforts to get stats to determine a hotly contested fantasy game, I called him. It was a Tuesday about 7:00 AM."

SAL: I'm sorry to bug you at home, but I really just need to know about one player.

EDITOR: How the fuck did you get my number?

SAL: I don't know, really. I just got it.

EDITOR (sensing Sal was crazy): Well, what do you need?

SAL: Haywood Jeffires. I know he had six catches—was it for more than 75 yards?

EDITOR: Six for 77. Don't ever call this number again.

SAL: Thanks . . . wait. He didn't run the ball at all, did he?

CLICK.

While I am sure the editor was confused, I totally get Sal's laserlike focus on trying to find info. When fantasy is at stake, people can't be deterred. They forget whatever else they are doing and have their sights set only on the fantasy task at hand, no matter how it effects other people.

On July 17, 2009, Brandon Treadway had his Houston, Texas–based league over to his house to pick the draft order. "As with anything fantasy football–related, beer was also involved," Brandon remembers.

Which explains why Brandon didn't realize his girlfriend was calling; he was on the phone with the nonpresent league members to tell them what pick they had.

And why was the girlfriend calling?

Because it was Brandon's wedding day.

AND BRANDON WAS LATE TO HIS OWN WEDDING.

The guys in his league were also Brandon's groomsmen and had actually stopped by the house to put on tuxes, but then they started talking about the upcoming draft, and then they were picking names out of a hat and calling nonpresent team members, and, well . . . yeah. Late. To his own wedding.

As Brandon notes, he loves his wife, but "she has the remarkable ability to remind me of this incident every time an argument about my insensitivity arises."

Listen, Brandon, your wife experienced what most of our friends and significant others do—they get sucked into our fantasy madness. And it's not just wives and friends who get sucked in. Sometimes it's . . . innocent kids?

Cameron Hefner was a student teacher who, thanks to the teacher's (misplaced?) trust, more or less totally oversaw a fifth-grade class. As Cameron says, "I loved the kids, and I loved what I did, but unfortunately it was fantasy draft season."

So Cameron's obsession leaked into his lesson planning. "I did many a math problem for the kids using fantasy stats: 'If the league awards 1 point per reception, 1 point per 10 yards rushing, 1 point per 10 yards receiving, and 6 points for a touchdown, how many points would Adrian Peterson have if he rushed for 90 yards and had 4 receptions for 20 yards and 1 touchdown?'"

Twenty-one points! I don't want to brag, but I knew that on the first try. Oh yeah. I *am* smarter than a fifth-grader.

"I finished up my student teaching, graduated, and got my teaching license. I am not, however, currently teaching, but decided to follow another passion and became a youth pastor. Still working with kids. Still playing fantasy football. Still mediocre at both."

I'm sure you're great, Cameron. And seriously, don't sweat it. Your story is nothing compared to Mark 's story. Mark was in college in 2010, and while he played in a few fantasy leagues, his roommate Charlie was on a different level. "Charlie was basically eating and breathing fantasy football 24/7," Mark explains.

One night Mark and his girlfriend Anna are back at his apartment having sex when suddenly, Charlie *walks in the room,* looking for Mark's computer!

The girlfriend is, ahem, at an angle where she doesn't see him come in and, Mark says, "I didn't want to draw any attention to the situation and make her uncomfortable, so I just kept going." Charlie is aware of what's going on in the room, but as Mark and his girl continue on, Charlie just says, "I need the computer," finally finds it, and then leaves, thankfully closing the door behind him. Later that night, the girlfriend is asleep, and Mark confronts Charlie. "What the hell?"

Well, apparently, while Charlie was out he got a text that Adrian Peterson was on the trading block, so he *had* to act quickly. No apology, no embarrassment, just a simple "I needed to make an offer."

Mark continues: "Stunned, I had nothing to say and went back to my room. The worst part is, he didn't even get Peterson."

First the "borrow your camera for Larry Fitzgerald" story and now these guys? If I've learned anything in doing this book, it's that a lot of college kids are having to watch their friends have sex in the name of fantasy football.

But it's not just college kids who ignore everything else around them for fantasy . . . Rock-and-roll icon and Rush frontman Geddy Lee is so into fantasy baseball, he always looks at his team's live box scores during the band's intermission. Many years ago, sportscaster Dan Patrick left a hospital early after knee surgery to make his fantasy draft, and then, when he realized he still wouldn't make it in time, stopped on the side of the road and used a pay phone while *standing up* for an hour and a half to do his draft. And while Grantland.com's Bill Simmons was walking the red carpet at the 2004 ESPYs, he was on his BlackBerry trying to swing a trade for Ichiro Suzuki. "It was one of the five most ridiculous moments of my life and couldn't possibly be explained to any foreigner."

Steve Straub's story is tough to explain no matter where you live. He is a member of the Erie, Pennsylvania–based Chauncey Billups Fantasy Football League. And Steve was stationed at Bagram Airfield in Afghanistan when he was having his online draft with his buddies back home. Time differences being what they are, it was the middle of the night while Steve drafted. But of course, that wasn't the only thing that made Steve's draft different from yours or mine. "It was about 1:00 AM local time when rockets began to hit our base," Steve recalls.

Wait. Hold on. Rockets?

"Yeah, the rockets landed about 50 yards away, and three or four of them landed in my general vicinity in a period of about 10 minutes. They are deafening when they land, and they are usually 107mm rockets."

And you didn't get the hell out of there?!!?

"Well, no shrapnel or dirt or anything was sent in my direction, and I couldn't go anywhere else or I would have lost my Internet signal. The Internet here is poor at best."

You know what else is poor at best? Surviving rockets.

According to Steve, "Security officials began walking around in battle gear as they ordered me to the bunkers. I told them that I couldn't go at this time because it was a crucial point in the draft. They could see the frustration on my face, as I saw on theirs, and they insisted, 'Sir, you need to get to the bunkers.' I replied, 'No, I need to find a good running back for my flex position. Have you been listening to anything I've been saying?' They became irritated and then finally walked away."

That's right. They walked away. And Steve *kept drafting through a bombing*. I take it back about Sal. *THIS* is laserlike focus.

"I finished the draft with no more issues, and right now, I am getting the last laugh, as I am tied for first place," Steve says.

Well, I'd argue you got the last laugh by cheating death, but tomato, tomahto. Incidentally, Steve also sent along the Associated Press article about this particular bombing of the Bagram Airfield. They destroyed a NATO helicopter. Steve tells me his team name is A Doctor Without Borders, since he has been in a different country for every fantasy draft the league has had. Which maybe explains why Steve didn't understand what the big deal was. "Security was disgruntled with my reaction, but I was just as perplexed with their reaction. Fantasy football doesn't seem to take its toll on their lives as it does mine."

Hard to top that, but I will say Keith Clark has a story that epitomizes fantasy sports obsession better than any I've ever heard.

In 2006 Keith's best friend (and league-mate) Chuck Cope suffered a collapsed lung and was rushed to the emergency room. Chuck was in an induced coma for a couple of days as his family and Keith waited hopefully at the hospital.

It was 50/50 as to whether Chuck would even make it.

Eventually . . . a break! Chuck had awoken. He was barely clinging to life, but at least he was alive. Chuck's wife hurried their son and Keith into the ICU, where Chuck was. Still intubated, Chuck couldn't speak, so he had a piece of paper and pencil. And very shakily, he scratched out his first words after this near-death experience.

"Did I get Romo?"

PART SIX

THE MIDSEASON REFLECTION

11.

When Death Impacts Fantasy

or

"This Little Society That We Construct in the Ether Has Real-World Implications and I Am Grateful for It"

"Because I'm miserable."

She stares at me blankly. I have been in therapy for all of 30 seconds, and the first question my therapist asks me, of course, is why I am here.

And after I answer, I get no reaction. She's just staring at me. Not judging, not encouraging, not anything.

Just staring.

A million thoughts race through my mind. Is this what therapy is? We just look at each other? What the hell am I supposed to do now? Keep talking? Is she trying to "break" me? This is weird, right? It's weird.

I stare back. I can actually hear the old-fashioned clock on her desk ticking as the second hand moves slowly. Finally, she breaks the silence.

"Why?"

"Why what?"

"Why are you miserable?"

"If I knew, I wouldn't need you, now would I?" I joke.

Again she stares. Tough crowd. Apparently, I'm gonna have to do all the talking.

I plow ahead. "My career as a screenwriter is going well. I have good friends. I'm healthy. I'm winning my fantasy leagues. I have parents who love me, a younger brother I'm close to, and I'm happily married to a nice Jewish girl. I even have an adorable puppy. On paper, my life is perfect.

"So why the hell," I ask my therapist, "am I miserable?"

I should have been thrilled with my life. Fulfilled. Grateful. Looking at my situation objectively, I knew I was beyond lucky.

So why didn't I feel like it?

All the personal stuff I was dealing with was affecting every aspect of my life. Especially fantasy sports. I was getting in fights and email wars with people in my leagues. I was getting super-upset when I didn't win. What the hell kind of pressure was I putting on a fantasy sports league?

There's not much positive I can say about it except this: I was *only* putting pressure on myself, not on anyone else. Something that Ryan's father *can't* say.

Ryan grew up in Dallas in the early '90s in a house full of die-hard Cowboys fans. When Ryan was eight years old, he was in a simple, six-member, touchdown-only fantasy league with his family, including his previously mentioned dad and his Grandpa Jack. League rules were basic: You played one QB, one RB, one WR. No pickups or trades during the season, and each year you could keep one player.

It was that age-old "who to keep" question that had eight-year-old Ryan racking his brain heading into the 1997 season. He was the defending champ, and now Ryan had to choose among these 1996 fantasy stars:

QB Brett Favre (39 TDs)
RB Terry Allen (21 TDs)
WR Cris Carter (10 TDs)

Ryan's dad is a competitive guy. Like, competitive competitive. The kind of man "whose antics force you to stuff all your Monopoly money into your pockets as you run to the bathroom at 2:00 AM during an eight-hour game." Dad had been pressuring Ryan during the off-season, telling him that Redskins RB Terry Allen was the enemy. That a real Cowboys fan would cut him. "So, I reluctantly kept Brett Favre," Ryan remembers, "and a few minutes later, when my Dad selected Terry Allen with the first pick, I knew I had made a mistake."

Ryan continues: "I am not ashamed to say I cried at the realization of this deception. Cried. Like a baby."

Ryan, dude, you were eight. I don't blame you. Kinda awful your dad would do that. That any dad would do that.

"My Grandpa Jack consoled me, telling me, 'Your dad is a damn fool to take Allen first; he won't have another year like last season again.'" And Grandpa Jack was right. Terry Allen finished with just five scores in 1997 and never had another season with more than eight.

So Ryan's dad got what he deserved. Sadly, Grandpa Jack did not.

"Two days later, Grandpa Jack announced he had lung cancer," Ryan said. "A lifelong smoker. It was a painful process to witness. But by the following February, he had reached a sort of calm clear-mindedness and seemed content. Then the day came, February 3, 1998. Everyone knew it would be soon, so we were all given alone time with Grandpa Jack. My dad told me to talk to him normally, as if nothing were wrong.

Grandpa Jack did not like giving an appearance of weakness, a true Texas Cowboy at heart."

Ryan continues: "When my turn came, he seemed happy but very sick. We talked Cowboys, Ranger baseball, school, and a myriad of other topics for about 30 minutes. The only thing I truly remember is the very last thing he said to me. . . . As I rose from the chair next to his bed, he gave me a big smile and said, 'Ryan, don't let that cheating dad of yours steal Emmitt Smith off my team. I left him to you in my will.'"

"I managed to chuckle out a 'Thanks, Grandpa,' and left as he took a long drag on his cigarette. He died a few hours later."

Ryan remembers that, after Grandpa Jack's funeral and wake, when the dust settled, "my dad comes to me after the reading of the will. 'How did you get Emmitt Smith? All I got was Isaac Bruce.'"

The two of them honored Grandpa Jack's wishes by each keeping the player they were left. The following 1998 season, Emmitt Smith had 15 total touchdowns. Isaac Bruce had one. Why do I think Grandpa Jack was laughing his ass off in heaven that year?

In addition to exchanging emails, I've met Ryan and I have to tell you, he's perfectly normal. It's amazing that he's not screwed up with that family dynamic. Guessing Ryan has Grandpa Jack to thank for that. Because personally, I'd have been very angry if my dad had manipulated me at eight years old to try and win a family fantasy league. Of course, had that been the case, it would have taken me forever to realize I was, in fact, angry at my dad.

You see, as I continued in therapy, I realized I'd been angry for a long time but had just pushed it all down, pretending everything was fine and then taking it out on something dumb, like the drive-thru getting my order wrong. Or, you know, a fantasy game not going the way I wanted.

I wasn't angry at my dad or mom, but lots of other stuff? Man . . . I had a lot of deep-seated resentment that I never knew existed. I won't bore you with everything I learned in therapy, but suffice it to say I've got a lot of issues.

Like that I moved around a lot as a kid and had trouble fitting in, which led to me somehow associating success with being liked and included, which then made me put way too much pressure on myself to be successful, to seek out recognition only to feel better about myself. Like that when you do that, there's no such thing as enough success to make you happy. It *has* to come from within.

Among my issues was a struggle to reconcile the fact that I am an extreme personality but I also have a desire to be liked by everyone. I feel strongly about certain things (like fairness and bullies—I will always stand up and help those I can), and I'm not shy about voicing my opinion, even if it's unpopular. But, of course, that sometimes rubs people the wrong way.

As I was finding out, being extreme can be helpful—it certainly gets you noticed—and it means that while there will be some passionate fans, there will also be some very strong opposition to you. And that was something I could understand logically but had trouble feeling emotionally. One of my biggest issues was how I focused on the negative. Like, I could write something and show it to 10 people, have nine people love it and one guy think it's okay, and all I would do was obsess on the one guy and not get pleasure from the nine who loved it. Most folks accept all the praise and none of the criticism—I actually did the reverse.

Told you. Me = screwed up.

It was something, I told my therapist, I was going to need to work on. You know, for as long as I can remember, people have used sports as a metaphor for life. So if sports is life, and fantasy is sports, it should come as no surprise that between all the crazy stories and wacky hijinks, between the wins and losses, life and death make their way into fantasy sports. Reality has an unfortunate way of interfering with fantasy. . . .

At the 2008 trade deadline for the Steelers Fan's Keeper League out of Pittsburgh, Dan was trying to make a move. In heavy negotiations with his buddy Dave "Tij" Armitage, Dan was trying to acquire LaDainian Tomlinson. Multiple offers went back and forth between the two friends, but in the end Dan came up just short. Tij told Dan he was going with what his brother-in-law Jason had offered. "In addition to draft picks, Jason offered to work on Tij's kitchen for free!"

I know what you're thinking: hey, Berry, we already read about this guy in chapter 7. That's true. But there's more to the story. I just wanted to save it until now.

Anyway, Tij got a new kitchen, Jason got Tomlinson and the title that season, while all Dan got, frankly, was some frustration. But as it turns out, Tij wasn't just a guy who didn't have to pay for renovations; he was also a wheeler-dealer and a truly fantastic guy.

How fantastic? When Dan complained about being aced out of LT for a new kitchen, Tij offered to make amends. And make amends he did. He traded Aaron Rodgers to Dan for below market value.

Not surprisingly, Dan won the championship the next two years in a row. "Do I owe it to Tij's kitchen and good graces?" Dan wonders. "Probably more than I want to admit."

And after the Rodgers trade, Dan hooked Tij up in return, sending Calvin Johnson to Tij for a below-market-value draft pick.

Truthfully, and this is the key to the story, whether he was getting a new kitchen or not, Tij just loved to trade; he was constantly wheeling and dealing. "Every year," Dan tells me, "Tij would either be a buyer or a seller, always planning for current or future domination."

In a heartbreaking turn of events, Dave "Tij" Armitage is no longer with us, having lost his battle with cancer on New Year's Eve 2011.

He was 33 years old.

Dan tells me, "He leaves an infant son, Kingston; his wonderful wife, Lauren; his mother, father, and sister. Besides his friends, family, and his teaching career, I can't think of anything more important to Tij than fantasy sports. He was *the* guy when it came to blockbuster trades."

And so, two months before his death, Tij took his close friends to dinner. "We talked fantasy for hours." One last negotiation, one last deal with each of his best friends, a wheeler-dealer to the very end. By the end of the evening, Tij had traded his entire team (except Megatron) to different people in his league and amassed an absurd number of picks for the upcoming year, "virtually guaranteeing Tij's first championship."

Tij's team is run by a close friend of his who carries on his legacy and passion for fantasy football. "Now the rest of us are playing catch-up, just the way Tij would have wanted it." The team ended up in second overall in 2012 and is set up for a run of domination. As for Dan, he'll have Aaron Rodgers on his team forever. Not just because he's awesome, of course. "But also because I never want to forget just how I ended up with him. Miss you, bud."

Heartbreaking as that story is, I love the league gathering for one final dinner/massive trade session for a guy who loved to deal. I love leagues that find all sorts of ways, big and small, to honor those who have passed away.

Zach Miller tells me about the Flop Dong Fantasy Baseball League and its commissioner, Brian Rose. Brian's father, Fred Rose, passed away after a long battle with cancer. On the day of his funeral, June 15, 2012, everyone in their league benched all their players for a day of silence to honor Fred. As Zach says, "In our league, we are a family, and we need to support our members."

John Raymond agrees. John has been in a fantasy football league with the same people since 1993. As John says, "To be honest, we are not the best of friends. We just happened to have converged early in the rise of fantasy. I haven't seen most of the people in the league for at least 10 years."

Heart-wrenching is the only way to describe October of the 2009 season, as John's nine-year-old son Carson got sick suddenly and passed away a week later. "The rest of the year was a hazy fog. I know there were several times when I neglected to set a lineup only to find on Sunday that someone had done it for me, replacing a bye week or someone who was injured with an active player. Despite the kindness and assistance of my competitors, I crawled to an 8–8 finish."

Later that year, John and his wife started the Carson Raymond Foundation in honor of their son. And the league? "Without provocation, every weekly winner, the Super Bowl champion, and runner-up donated all their winnings to the foundation. This little society that we construct in the ether has real-world implications and I am grateful for it."

Carson's favorite sport was baseball, so as a result, the Carson Raymond Foundation provides opportunities for children who normally couldn't afford it to play ball. In the past two-plus years, the foundation has built three baseball fields, provided equipment and scholarships to hundreds of kids, and run baseball camps for about 500 elementary-age children in the Charlottesville, Virginia, area.

As for the league? It continues on and, John says, "slowly the usual array of snide comments, cheap shots, and disparaging Photo-Shopped pictures have reemerged."

Adrian Orona wrote me to tell me about his fantasy football league, now in its fifth year. Just after Thanksgiving, one of the members, Richard Ortiz, passed away from a heart attack. After finding out the news, the rest of the league decided to leave all of their lineups untouched. And Richard's team, which had two losses at the time of his passing . . . just kept winning. "Week after week until, finally, Richard made the finals for the very first time!" Adrian tells me.

So what happened in the finals???

"Well, Tony Romo happened."

I remember. Week 15 of the 2011 season, Romo hurt his hand and finished 0-for-2 with 0 yards. I assume Romo was Richard's quarterback?

"Yep. Richard ended up losing by 11 points. Even in death, you can't count on Tony Romo."

The league has renamed their league and trophy after Richard's screen name as a way to honor and remember their friend. "While it didn't end the way we had hoped, he will always be a champion in our books."

Oddly, I ended up getting a lot more stories about guys dying midseason than I would have thought. But this next one is one of the most shake-your-head-and-say-damn stories I've heard.

About a decade ago, Brent Adamo remembers, the Weese Football League in Phoenix needed another member. One of the guys in the league, Chris Campeau, invited a coworker named Jim. A huge football fan, Jim had never played fantasy before but was very interested. And, apparently, very good at it. The first eight weeks Jim's team went 8–0.

"Every Tuesday he'd always say, 'Rookie ball coach . . . knows what he's doing.' Drove me nuts."

And then, Brent tells me, without warning, Jim fell off the face of the earth. No one has heard from him. "We determine we will just set his best possible lineup based on the website's projected points."

And the team kept winning, reeling off three straight. That's when they finally found out why no one had heard from Jim. He had been found murdered, the victim of a robbery.

Speechless.

But in the middle of all this horrific darkness, there was one cool little moment: Jim's team kept winning and it *never lost*. That's right. Start to finish, no trades or pickups, just the league setting the projected best lineup . . . Jim's team ran the table and won the championship.

In the history of the Weese Football League, Sean says "this is the first and only team to ever go undefeated. We sent the winnings check to his sister."

Chris adds, "The perpetrators were later arrested. One of them died in a shootout with police. At the funeral for Jim, I had let Jim's relatives know he was doing rather well in our fantasy league and that we would be donating all the winnings to the family. I remember receiving a thank-you card from the family with Jim's photo in it."

I can't prove it. I realize it sounds crazy at worst or hopelessly naive at best. But I believe there is a reason Jim's team won that league. Small and dumb as it may be, given the atrocities he and his family suffered, there is something mystical and magical about fantasy that goes beyond what we understand.

There are a million things in this world that make no logical sense. Every day we see and hear stories, big and small, for which there is no explanation or a tenuous one at best. The cynic would say it's just luck, and they might be right. But, and maybe it's the child in me, I still like to believe that there are forces greater than us working here on Earth. And that sometimes something doesn't happen because it is supposed to, but rather, it happens because it should.

TIME-OUT:

The Best Fantasy Team Names

From death to birth. Specifically, the birth of fantasy sports. When you talk about the start of it all, the thing that always gets overlooked is the book. They'll occasionally mention Bill Gamson, Robert Sklar, and the Baseball Seminar. They'll sometimes talk about Bill Winkenbach and Andy Mousalimas and the GOPPPL, the first fantasy football league, created in 1963 and played in the Oakland bar King's X. They usually discuss Strat-O-Matic, APBA, Bill James, and they will always speak lovingly (and deservedly) of Daniel Okrent, the creator of Rotisserie League Baseball. They mention the impressive résumés of that initial league, they bring up the now defunct restaurant they all gathered at, they remark ironically that the founding fathers never made money off this insanely popular game they created, and they always throw in the fact that Okrent has never won the game he created.

But they rarely mention the book. And the book is key. Had *Rotisserie League Baseball*, the little green book that introduced the world to the game, been boring or written poorly, who knows where we are or if it ever catches on? But luckily, it wasn't. It was smart and clever and funny and it just seemed like the founding fathers were having such a blast playing this game that I (and everyone else) desperately wanted to find a league. From their individual "team media guides," complete with details about "promotional days" at their "home stadiums" to the trash talk to mocking of athletes, even the way they wrote the rules . . . the book was inviting and fun, opening up a whole new world that people had never considered.

And for me, I loved the team name. In the book, they made a big deal about the team name, declaring that all team names should be some sort of play on the owner's name. That's why you saw among the first-ever fantasy baseball names Daniel Okrent's Okrent Fenokees, Bob Sklar's Sklar Gazers, Valerie Salembier's Salembier Flambes, Peter Gethers and Glen Waggoner's Gether-swag Goners, Lee Eisenberg's Eisenberg Furriers, Corlies Smith and the Smith Corons, Bruce McCall's McCall Collects, Michael Pollet's Pollet Burros, Tom Guinzburg and the Guinzburg Burghers, Steve Wulf's Wulf Gang, Rob Fleder's Fleder Mice, and more.

More recently, team names are not just a play on an owner's name but plays on athletes' names, plays on pop culture, inside jokes within the league, or just plain filthy. They reflect the personality of the owner, the personality of the league, and they are crucial. Personally, I like having the same team name year after year after year. Builds a sense of history. I tend to use names that have meaning to me. The Fightin' Rabbis has been a longtime favorite and the Hollywood Phonies (based on my previous career) is the Fat Dog entry. Podcast fans will not be shocked to learn my team in the league that I lost Mike Trout in is The Bitter Berries. My love of Jimmy Buffet is the inspiration behind my Doug Logan team name, the Parrotheads, and my unhealthy obsession with *Beverly Hills, 90210* shows up as I am often the West Beverly Wildcats. (I know. Nothing crazy there. I've just had them for years. I'm sentimental.)

Others change it up, sometimes as often as every few weeks or at least once a season. They are very different, but the one thing they have in common is they are almost always hilarious. For years I have printed the best ones (that I can print, it is a family website, after all) in the preseason of both baseball and football.

So here's a sampling of the best and/or most popular fantasy team names I've heard over the years. In no particular order . . .

Football

1. Breesus Is My Homeboy!
2. Yippy Ki Yay, Marshall Faulker
3. Multiple Scoregasms
4. Run, Forsett, Run
5. The Chronicles of Favria
6. The House [Why? Because the House always wins!]
7. Pimpin' Ain't Brees-y
8. Kibbles and Vicks
9. It's on Like Ndamukong
10. I'm Bringing Hasselbeck
11. Snakes on Reggie Wayne
12. Brady Gaga
13. Gronk if You're Horny
14. Belicheck Yourself Before You Rex Yourself
15. Wilfork for Food
16. Pete Carroll-ine [Bum Bum Bum]
17. Moons over My Tamme
18. Luck Be a Brady Tonight
19. Gronky Punch
20. Learning from My Vickstakes
21. Hakeema Matata
22. Teenage Newton Ninja Turtles

23. That's What She Bid

24. Whoa Whoa Whoa, Stop the Gronk

25. Off in a Corner [because no one beats . . .]

26. Somebody That I Used Tebow

27. Luck, Beat Tom Brady Tonight

28. My Delhomme Is My Cassel

29. A perennial . . . Somewhere over Dwayne Bowe. Or Double Dwayne Bowe.

30. 4th and Drunk

31. 2 Mannings, 1 Cup

32. Ed Hochuli's Gun Show

33. Suggs to be You

34. Romosexuals

35. Cut That Meat!

36. She Hate Me

37. Darth Waivers

38. Boy Named Suh

39. Orakophobia

40. Praters Gonna Prate

Baseball

1. My Dinner with Andrus

2. Openly Bay

3. Hameltime!

4. Tabata Bing!

5. FIP 2 Be Square

6. To Kila Marlon Byrd

7. 902Cano

8. Sipping on Gin & Youk

9. Dexy's Midnight RISP

10. The Duda Abides
11. Baby Got Bacne
12. A Priest Walks into Aybar
13. Bryce Bryce Baby
14. Lady Galarraga
15. I Shin Soo Choose You
16. Blue-Va-Ja-Jays
17. Aroldis and Kumar
18. New Kids on the Knoblauch
19. Attack of the Chones
20. Personal DeJesus
21. Angels in the Troutfield
22. Longorious Basterds
23. Call Me Mabry
24. Twisted Fister
25. A perennial . . . Honey Nut Ichiros
26. The Kempire Strikes Back
27. Another perennial . . . Carry on My Heyward Son
28. Dropping Gloads
29. R. A. Dickulous
30. 99 Problems but a Pitch Ain't 1

Of course, some people go meta.
[Insert Terrible Pun Here.]

And, when all else fails there's always . . .
I Blame Matthew Berry.

12.

Fantasy Sports Saves Lives

_or_

"I Used to Think He'd Be Dead by 50. Now I Think He'll Outlive Us All."

I am a big believer of moments in time. That life is comprised of them and that they are fleeting. And when one such a moment happens, they are to be grabbed on to, held tightly, and shared.

Jeremy Carroll's fantasy football league, Ten Yard Fight, formed in 2002 with 12 best friends from Clawson, Michigan, experienced that moment. Jeremy explains: "Our founder and first commissioner, Christian Davis, is a great guy, but he has never been the best fantasy player."

Christian confirms this: "Over the first 11 years of the league, I only made the playoffs four times, and I never won a playoff game. In the other years, I was always near the bottom, and in fact, I once had back-to-back seasons of 1–12."

Christian is an only child, and tragedy struck in February of 2011 when his mother, Susan, suddenly passed away. "It broke my heart. My dad Richard suffered through chronic arthritis, a quadruple bypass, and many other issues, so when my mom passed first, it was a very sad shock. To be honest, with all of my dad's health issues, I felt like if he went first, Mom wouldn't have to stress out all the time and could focus on herself. So when it happened to her, there was almost more of a sadness to it. I don't mean it to sound like my dad and I had a bad relationship. I loved him very much, but I don't think I told him that as often as I told my mom."

Soon after, Christian's father would succumb to his failing health: just five months after his mom passed away, Christian's father died too. "At 31, Christian was suddenly without any immediate family," Jeremy says.

Christian's father's funeral was just a week before the draft, and naturally, between his dad's last days and all the arrangements, Christian had had no time to prepare. Jeremy is blunt. "His draft was terrible. But he did unveil a new team name and logo."

Christian says: "Knowing that it was hard to tell my dad exactly how much I appreciated him, I came up with a way to honor him. Before his health failed him, my dad was actually part of a skydiving club called the Thunder Chickens. So in my silly attempt to make things better, I promised myself I would add that to my team name."

And so, with the most career losses in league history, a terrible team, and a heavy heart, Christian Davis began the 2011 fantasy football season.

After an 0–2 start, it was looking like another typical season for Christian, who had made only one significant change: switching his team name to Team Super Punch and the Thunder Chickens. Then, out of nowhere, "Christian starts making some smart moves, buys low on Arian Foster, etc., and suddenly . . . his team starts winning!"

Did it ever. He went 9–2 the rest of the way, winning his division and his semifinal matchup. For the first time in the history of the league, he was playing in the finals. Against Team Jellyfish, his archrival, a team that had already beaten him twice that season and owned him every other year.

The championship game came down to the Monday night game and the whole league got together to watch the game. The Jellyfish had a lead heading into Monday night, and combined with Roddy White's 127 yards, Christian was still losing with less than five minutes to play in the game. Their matchup should have been over at that point because the Saints were beating the Falcons handily. But Christian's QB Drew Brees stayed in anyways and, with 2:51 left in the game, threw a touchdown pass to Darren Sproles . . . clinching Christian's first-ever title by a slim margin!

Christian remembers, "I know it's fantasy football, and Drew Brees finding the open man has nothing to do with my parents and me, but that night it was hard not to feel that maybe, just maybe, there was something bigger than us at work. I like to think of myself as a man of faith, but it's been hard at times to imagine heaven. Still, that night, I snuck away, looked to the stars, and literally said thank-you to my parents."

Jeremy adds: "It was an incredible moment, brought to us by fantasy sports. For the first time in nearly a year, I saw him truly happy. The tears of pain were gone, replaced by tears of joy." Christian agrees. "Obviously it was a tough year, but the way the season unfolded definitely made me smile. Not sure I've truly stopped since."

The league has a trophy with each winner and the year engraved on it. Listed on the side for 2011 is TEAM SUPER PUNCH AND THE THUNDER CHICKENS. "An entry that, no matter how bad my lifetime record is or how many terrible trades I make, will always be there."

Christian changed his team name back to Team Super Punch for the 2012 season. He kept the logo from the Thunder Chicken season,

but he didn't want to use the name. "I wanted to keep that season perfect forever."

I too embrace the healing power of fantasy sports. As I was continu-
ing my therapy, I was unearthing an amazing amount about myself,
including this realization: It wasn't just that I loved fantasy sports. It
was that I hated a lot of other parts of my life.

It seems obvious now, but it definitely wasn't then. It never occurred
to me that I could actually hate show business. I had worked so hard to
break in and stay in. It was glamorous. When I would talk to friends
from back home, they were always jealous. And I knew how many people desperately wanted to make their living in it. What's the old joke?
Stand on the corner of Hollywood and Vine and ask strangers, "How's
your screenplay?" Eight out of 10 will have an answer. The other two
are actors.

So how could I hate it, right? Maybe I didn't hate show business;
maybe I just hated how my career had gone. That had to be it. As I
mentioned before, I'd always felt that "if we could just get on a hit show,"
I'd be happy. But then, as we started to work in movies and actually do
decently, my feelings didn't change.

I was never a huge success, but I was a working screenwriter with a
healthy pay quote. And no matter what job we got, no matter how much
success we had, there was always someone I was jealous of. I hated how
I would see people (including myself) get screwed over by those more
powerful and there were no repercussions. In fact, often that terrible
behavior was rewarded. I hated the phoniness of show business. I hated
how insecure and petty it made me feel as I read *Variety* every day and
got bitter about other people's success. It wasn't my nature to root
against people, and yet show business made me feel that way.

I hated the lack of any fundamental structure for success. If you
want to be a doctor, there are certain steps to take, and if you accom-

plish them, you're a doctor. That's not true in screenwriting, where everything is so subjective and talent often goes unrewarded while social skills—who you know, how comfortable you are grabbing beers with a producer or executive—are overvalued. I realized in therapy that none of it was healthy and all of it had to change to keep me sane and give me a shot at happiness. That's why I was obsessed with my two little fantasy sports sites and was blowing everything else off. It was all that made me happy.

By 2005 I had been doing so much work in therapy that I finally had the guts to do what I should have done long before. I quit show business. The thing I had been working on nonstop since I graduated college in 1992 I was now going to completely throw away.

I gave my writing partner Eric one year's notice. We would do one last project together, earn a little money, and then I was done. I told him I'd probably fall on my face and make about a tenth of the money I did as a screenwriter, but I couldn't do this anymore. I was gonna take my little, unprofitable, fewer-than-2,000-paying-members-at-the-time websites and try to make a full-time career out of fantasy sports, one way or the other.

Another change that had to be made was my marriage. We had tried counseling, and by the end of it, it was clear we just wanted different things. No drama, no third person, just two people who got married young and had since grown into two different people. So, it was sad but mutually agreed upon. At the end of 2005, we officially split up for good. Friends of ours say it remains the most peaceful, amicable split they've ever seen. She was and remains a terrific person. She was very supportive of me when I was starting all this fantasy sports stuff, much more so than many wives would have been. She's the one who first suggested I go to therapy. She just wanted me to be happy. And vice versa. She has since happily remarried, and we are friends to this day.

But as the calendar turned to 2006, there I was. For better or worse, I had thrown away everything I had pursued for 12 years to try to change my life.

I had lost the wife, the writing partner, the career. All I had left was the dog, the websites, and a half-empty living room.

I was starting completely over with no clear way to support myself, and I was fairly alone.

I was 36 years old.

And all I wanted was to be happy.

I didn't know it then, but fantasy sports was about to save my life.

If that sounds a bit melodramatic, that's fair. But when I was a 10-year-old kid and had just been crushed in one of my first tennis matches, I remember a coach telling me this Vince Lombardi quote: "It's not whether you get knocked down; it's whether you get up." Among my favorite quotes of all time, and one I had to keep reminding myself of as I started out on my own. As former NFL head coach Dick Vermeil once said: "If you don't invest very much, then defeat doesn't hurt very much and winning is not very exciting."

It is because of the horrible lows that we can appreciate the terrific highs. And while you may think it's hyperbole to say fantasy sports was about to save my life, it is not so in the case of Doug Selmont.

In the spring of 2008, Doug was a high-level athlete, training for his first marathon. He had a girlfriend of a year. And then he was diagnosed with an incredibly rare, dangerous form of appendix cancer called pseudomyxoma peritonei, or PMP for short.

At age 25.

Late that August, Doug's longtime Orange, Connecticut–based fantasy football league held its draft. After the draft, he said good-bye to his friends. "One week later, I headed to Baltimore for a radical surgery with curative intent for my disease."

The operation lasted a grueling 14 hours. Doug had 30 pounds of tumor removed from his abdomen. He lost every non-essential organ he had. "This cost me many of my life's goals, including the Hartford marathon I was training for."

In recovery in the hospital, Doug was not doing well. In fact, for the first weekend of fantasy, he couldn't even set his own lineup, so his girlfriend Lindsey had to do it for him.

But then . . . a small bright spot. Doug won his first game. "The next day I had several tubes and drains removed. It was my first victory coupled with a fantasy victory."

As Doug remembers, "The next week, I won again in fantasy and was released to go home soon thereafter. I don't know if it was fighting spirit, but somehow each victory in fantasy football brought about a victory in life."

Heading home, Doug faced his biggest challenge: six months of chemotherapy. "My lack of real-life competition was replaced by a competition that had terrible effects on my body. But I did it. And while recovering from the infusions, I started to read a lot of articles on fantasy sports. Like, every single one I could get my hands on."

Instead of focusing on his chemo, Doug focused on his league, his team, and the deals he could make. After studying matchups and schedule, Doug traded for Chargers QB Philip Rivers, who he believed was due for a big finish.

Doug made the playoffs, and during that three-game stretch Rivers averaged over 280 passing yards and three touchdowns a game. Doug cruised to the title and, most important, won his battle against cancer.

"As for the girl that set my lineup? She is now my wife. And we couldn't be happier together. . . . Maybe the point is that when I needed it the most, when I needed to see victory in something minor to motivate myself for victory in something major, it happened. I may not ever get to run the Hartford marathon. I may not be able to play on a flag football team anymore. But I will always have that fantasy championship. Most people would laugh at this idea that a fantasy sports team can be important, but I hope people can see how positively it has affected me."

Magic. Fantasy makes a difference in people's lives. Sometimes it's emotional, like in Christian's story. Sometimes it's mental, like Doug's story. And sometimes it's even physical.

Every year Richard Karp made a bet with his best friend Brian Naftly on their fantasy football matchup in the Maryland Football League, or MFL. "Started out as a few bucks, upped to league fees, then to maid service for the season, and eventually escalated to the point where I suggested that the loser can't eat fast food for an entire year," Richard explains.

Here's why that last bet was important. Brian is five-two and weighed closed to 300 pounds. "To be polite, he was massive!"

Richard didn't think Brian would take the bet. At the time Brian was early twenties, single, and had zero idea how to cook. But he took the bet, and even better? He lost. "My buddy didn't just give up fast food for a year," Richard says. "He's a very dedicated guy, so in addition to that he started working out, eating healthy, training, jogging, boxing, and more. He lost weight. A lot of weight. He now travels all over the country to run marathons. The guy is in better shape than just about anyone I know. I used to think he'd be dead by 50. Now I think he'll outlive us all. All thanks to a fantasy football game."

Derrell Wright is another guy who saw the bright light of fantasy at the end of a dark tunnel. "I've been suffering from depression for a few years now and I'm finally getting the help I need through medication, therapy and, strangely enough, fantasy football."

After three years of marriage and two kids, Derrell and his wife separated. He says, "The roller coaster of emotions I ride on a daily basis is often suffocating. The thing that's helped me is my overwhelming focus on fantasy football. Honestly, it's an obsession, but in this case it's actually helping my mental health. Every time I find myself slipping into a sad state and thinking about my wife or the fact that I'm not with my kids, I log on to ESPN and bone up on the latest injury news and sleeper pickups. The result? I'm in first place in both of my money leagues. More important, I'm not wasting my time trying to change things I have no control over. Instead I'm wasting it playing fantasy football!

Seriously, though, I'm connected to the guys in the league, most of whom are my support system during this tough time, and without the league we wouldn't all be in such regular communication. So, while I'm not sure where life is heading all the time, I know, for the first time in a while, that things will be okay."

Thanks for sharing that, Derrell. Damn cute kids. And, as I was finishing up the book, Derrell told me, "Kelly and I reconciled and have been going to counseling for the last six months. Things are up and down, but we're working on it and feeling better each day. We're together and still fighting for our marriage, which is all I can ask for sometimes."

Well said, Derrell. The thing I love about your story is that we all know people need distractions from their demons. Fantasy sports is as great a distraction as was ever invented.

Up until 14 years ago this past April, Wally Spurlin spent a lot of time at bars. *A lot.* "I had tried a certain program involving steps and found it did not work for me at all. For many addicts, a big part of maintaining a sober life is finding ways to occupy all the hours we spent drunk, high, or chasing women who also like to get drunk and high. Without interests or activities to pull us forward in sobriety, it becomes very likely that addicts will slip back into the easy, comfortable, albeit self-destructive lifestyle."

Luckily for Wally, he was asked to join the Purple Helmet league out of Troy, Michigan, in 1999. He remembers, "Something clicked inside me as I began to research what I could online and in magazines. Jake Plummer will always hold a special place in my heart, as he was my number one pick that year. Nine TDs and 24 INTs later, I learned that:

(a) It's best to go RBs early.
(b) Jake Plummer sucks."

Both good lessons, Wally. But they're not the only ones he learned. "Over the years I found the time I spent researching off-season free-agency moves and the offensive schemes of coordinators was much better than trying to remember where my wallet or car was. I just want to acknowledge the role fantasy football has played in my personal recovery. It provides people like myself a haven from a pretty dark reality and a different path to some light. That is something very special and something I am thankful for every day of my life. Since getting sober, I have turned my life around, gotten married this fall, and am a stepfather to a nine-year-old daughter. So feel free to add 'lifesaver' to fantasy's ever-expanding résumé. In my eyes, it applies completely."

Congratulations on overcoming your demons. And Jake Plummer.

Both difficult challenges. And while you never want to say one person's demons or physical issues are harder or tougher than someone else's, I think we can all agree that Chris Leeuw's story is up there.

On August 8, 2010, Chris went kayaking with a few buddies. Midday, they took a break. Chris remembers, "I wanted to cool off and have some fun, so I climbed up to the top of a 50-foot bridge and jumped off into the water. Unfortunately, some dude I didn't know jumped at the same time and landed exactly on top of me. Instantly, two vertebrae were shattered, and there I floated, paralyzed from the neck down.

"Life can change in an instant."

Doctors gave Chris little hope of ever regaining significant movement.

Now, to say Chris is a fantasy football fanatic is the undersell of the century. His Bradyback Mountain team has been in the Pirates of the Taconibbean League with buddies from around the country since 2005. Every summer they rent a lake house for a weekend and party, relax, hang out, and pick their draft order. That year the draft-order weekend was a week after Chris's accident. He didn't make the weekend, of course, but "I let them know there was no way in hell I was dropping out of the league . . . and I'd be taking their money with weekly beat-downs. Paralyzed or not."

After a week, Chris got moved from the ICU to a new rehabilitation hospital. He had gained some sensation back and even had some movement in his toe, which were good signs. Draft day was approaching, and Chris wasn't going to miss it.

"We had it planned out perfectly. A buddy who wasn't in the league was going to be in my room with the computer at my eye level, so I could tell him my choices. We made sure we had the wireless passcode and everything," Chris relays.

Unfortunately, the day before the draft, Chris took a turn for the worse. "After a spinal cord injury, your entire body and central nervous system are out of whack. It wreaks havoc on everything early on."

He had developed a huge fever, was battling multiple infections, and when he was being showered, Chris lost consciousness. Fearing a seizure, the rehab staff put Chris in an ambulance and sent him back to the ICU.

On draft day, Chris was doing a little better, but frankly, he was still a mess. He had a high fever, he was hooked up to IVs, he had a blood clot in his lungs, he was in the ICU, and, oh yeah, he was *completely paralyzed*.

I speak for everyone when I say, if Chris had missed the draft, we all would have given him a pass. Dude, you're paralyzed. Get better. We'll see you next year.

But Chris would have none of that. "It seems crazy to write, but in the pathetic state my life had turned . . . football was just about the only thing I had to look forward to. I knew from everything I had to deal with, at least I could have a semblance of a respite on Sundays. I wasn't missing the draft."

When draft day came, however, there was a problem. A big problem. "In the new hospital we couldn't access the wireless code, and none of the nurses knew how to sign in. I was pissed."

But again . . . Chris *wasn't missing the draft*.

So they call one of Chris's buddies back home and have *that* guy log on to his computer as Chris. "There we were: me, talking to my buddy at the hospital, talking to my other friend 1,000 miles away, asking who was still available, trying to convey who to take, etc."

Wow.

"Yeah, it was a confusing mess, drafting almost blindly, but it worked. I'd yell, 'Who's the best player available? Scan by receiver! . . . How many TDs did he have last year again?'"

And get this for dedication . . . on all fronts.

"At one point, a nurse even had to drain my bladder with a catheter . . . but the draft went on! (Kudos to my buddy who remained there through the procedure)."

Kudos indeed. And to the nurse. But a huge round of applause to you, Chris. (*You* ever try to draft on a phone while someone is sticking a catheter in???)

And thank goodness Chris was able to do it. "The new football season became one of my only outlets. It was one of the things that helped pass the time and drive my mind away from my predicament. I always found time during my six months in the hospital, even at night when visitors left, to have aides read me your articles and tweets and adjust my lineup. After about four months, I gradually regained the use of my hand and could use a phone and jump on a computer myself. That was an awesome moment."

I can only imagine.

"Now, more than a year later, I'm still in therapy, working out four hours a day, but you'll be happy to know I've relearned how to walk, have the use of most of my right arm again, and can even drive a car. I have a long way to go, but here I sit—typing this message."

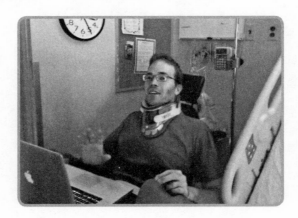

This might be my favorite story in the book. Awesome.

"I guess this falls under the 'obsession' category—not missing my draft while clinging to life in the ICU—but looking back, it's more an example of how sports can provide an outlet to help navigate the worst of life's tribulations. It's funny how seemingly meaningless sports can be so much more if you think about it."

I think about this story and the others in this section all the time.

Every moment is precious. Because they are fleeting. And we're damned lucky to have the ones we get.

PART SEVEN

THE STRETCH RUN—TIME TO GET TO WORK

13.

The Challenges of Playing Fantasy at Work

_or_

"I Should Have Fired Him by Week Four"

The conference room table.

What I remember most was the conference room table.

It was big, made of rich mahogany, and seemed to stretch forever. I was dressed up and shaved, a rarity for me in those days, and as I was shown in I hoped they would tell me where to sit. I had never had a meeting as big as this, so I was nervous. What do I do? Sit close so they can hear? Farther away to show respect? Do I take the drink offered or not? Okay, they just brought me the drink. No coaster? I'm gonna leave a mark. I can't leave a mark, right? I'll just use my notes. I remember my last thought before it started: _Please don't throw up._

He was impressive in person. He was in charge of one of the biggest sports media companies in the world. I was passionate. I had ideas. I pitched my little heart out.

"Fantasy sports are more than a fad. This space is going to explode. You have a real opportunity here. I think I can help."

He looked at me as he considered my whole presentation. He seemed to be thinking but gave away nothing. He thanked me for my time and the thought I had given this. He said he'd be in touch.

A week later, I got the call: they were passing, but they wished me luck.

Now completely out of show business, I was pitching to whoever would listen. Different media companies, TV stations, cable channels, websites, radio stations; if they had an audience, I gave them a full-blown presentation. PowerPoints and press clippings and stats and research with passion.

And none of it mattered.

They were passing, but they wished me luck.

I'm pretty sure I lead the world in luck wished during those years.

Having just quit Hollywood and gone through a divorce, I wasn't exactly flush with money. I wasn't broke, but what I did have I wanted to save. Who knew when (or even if) I'd make a living from these websites, so the only way to promote them was with, gulp, me.

So after every rejection, it was back to the phones, emails, brainstorming.

And I kept the faith.

I'm a never-say-die guy. Sometimes stupidly, often stubbornly, but I am, to my core, a never-ever-say-die guy. The best way to get me to do something is to tell me I can't. I didn't get into many of the colleges I applied to and shouldn't have been admitted to Syracuse. Only a bunch of videos I'd made as a high school kid got me past my unimpressive high school résumé.

I was fired as the host of a college TV talk show because they felt I was too uncomfortable on TV. I was forced to quit writing for my college newspaper. I was fired from my first production assistant job in

Hollywood. I was fired a week into my first professional TV writing job. In show business, I was turned down for representation 14 different times, including twice by 3 Arts Entertainment, which ended up representing this book.

But I kept the faith.

I wrote for years in Hollywood, and the only movie that ever got made from one of my scripts was the worst one my writing partner and I ever wrote. We got screwed over by studio execs, movie producers, and other writers. I tried to get a side job for fun writing fantasy at two different websites before catching on at Rotoworld. And I was eventually fired from there.

And I kept the faith.

Which I would have to continue to do because what other choice did I have? I was unemployed, approaching middle age, and suddenly single. And I wanted fantasy sports to become my work.

Pipe dream.

Frankly, it's a dream I've heard from a lot of people over the years. Not just because they love it, but because if fantasy sports *is* their work, then they won't get into trouble when they do fantasy *at* work.

Yes, despite growing in popularity, fantasy sports still hadn't become mainstream. No major media companies were committing to them at the time, and even "normal" companies frowned upon their employees playing them.

But that doesn't mean it doesn't happen. And just like I kept hearing "no" when I was trying to turn my hobby into work, when people combine fantasy sports and work, it often doesn't go well.

Isaac Robinson is the commissioner (and, he'd like you to know, 2012 league champion) of the Hopeful Chiefs Fan League out of Chanute, Kansas. In the league, they have a trophy for the guy who wins, of course, but also one for whoever comes in last.

"It's called the You Suck Balls Award," Isaac explains, "and it's made of a block of wood. Affixed to the top of the wood block is an athletic cup, the whole thing is spray-painted gold, and the team names of the 'winners' are engraved on the side."

In this league, Royce, owner of Raider Nation, has "won" the loser's award for two years running. Now, it's normally awarded during the following year's draft, but Royce was working then and it could not be presented to him in person. So, on August 18, the trophy was delivered to Royce's porch.

And that's where the trouble begins. You see, the job that caused Royce to miss the draft? It was working for a congressman. A controversial one. One who had been getting death threats. So when Royce comes home to find a ratty cardboard box sealed with duct tape and a scrawled note saying, "Special delivery for Royce," what does he do?

Exactly. DEA, ATF, bomb squad, FBI agents are *all* dispatched to his house. "The neighborhood was evacuated," Isaac remembers. "The roads were all closed. TV reporters and vans were covering it."

While this is going on, the FBI tries to contact the congressman to make sure he is okay. He's actually on a plane and unreachable (the FBI doesn't know this yet), so they rush to his house. Naturally, the congressman's wife is freaked out by men in black clothes shining flashlights in her windows, so she calls the police. Now there's a showdown at the house between the local cops and the FBI!

Meanwhile, back at Royce's house, the bomb squad has brought in . . . wait for it . . . the bomb squad robot.

So, hidden behind protective shields, with all the FBI, ATF, and bomb squad department people nervously watching, the technician is using the robot to remotely scan the mysterious box to find . . . the words YOU SUCK BALLS staring back at them!

Isaac spends the next hour patiently trying to explain to the FBI that no, he does not mean any threat to the congressman, and that Royce does, in fact, suck balls at fantasy football.

Eventually, everything is figured out and Royce confirms the trophy is part of his league.

The final tally, Isaac?

"My league's trophy is now in Washington, DC, in the possession of the ATF, and still has to be analyzed for terror. I believe I am now on some FBI watch lists, and my league cost our government *millions of dollars and many hours of law enforcement manpower* . . . all because my friend had to work instead of coming to the draft."

And of course, because he sucks balls at fantasy.

I'm guessing Royce's boss wasn't too thrilled with him after that whole episode. By missing the draft, Royce accidentally caused disaster, but sometimes disaster happens *during* the draft because of work.

Dave Nardelli is in the "Crew League" with nine coworkers. He travels for work, so it's no surprise that during his draft in 2011 he was, once again, on the road. Specifically, he was in a hotel room, waiting to draft online, when his phone rang.

A coworker was on the business trip with Dave and was calling from the hospital. The coworker was actually supposed to be in the hospital overnight, but suddenly he had been released and needed to be picked up. And of course, Dave had the only rental car.

"I'm pissed . . . 10 minutes till draft time," Dave says. "But I get in the car and call my wife. 'Babe, you need to log on to ESPN for me and help me draft over the phone.'" With his wife, Dave made a few picks on the 30-minute drive to the hospital. He then pulled into the hospital parking lot.

"My coworker opens the passenger side door to get in, and as he's doing that . . . *he falls to the ground.* He is having a grand mal seizure."

Obviously, Dave instantly hung up the phone to help his coworker, leaving his wife to try and finish the draft on her own. "Just go down the rankings sheet!" he yelled, and hung up.

But fantasy karma had his back. By doing the right thing and blowing off his draft to help his coworker (who should never have been released from the hospital in the first place), Dave's wife ended up picking a helluva team. Percy Harvin, Jimmy Graham . . . Team SNards finishes in the money. So the story has a happy ending. Except for Dave's coworker. He's dead. Kidding. Maybe. I should check.

You can call me crazy, call me a dreamer, call me a hopeless romantic, but I'd like to think that, faced with helping a coworker who's having a seizure or finishing your fantasy draft, everyone would help the coworker. Or at least multitask. But sometimes the decisions about what to do when fantasy sports and work intersect are not so clear-cut.

"Since charges are still pending, I should probably just use my first name." That's Sam. Sam's story takes place at a TV news station. They had a work league that included everyone from the news director and anchors down to photographers and production assistants (PAs). The season was going along fine, and one of the guys in the league, we'll call him "Yancy," was on pace to make the playoffs. But while that was happening on the virtual field, suddenly things were amiss at work.

Due to the legal nature of the story, Sam can't give specifics, but the company launched an investigation with the local police, and came up with the perpetrator, who was let go. Exclaims Sam, "I would have never guessed in a million years who it turned out to be."

Yancy?

"Yancy!"

I guessed on the first try. Of course, I was only given two names, and it wasn't likely Sam would tell a story about himself getting fired, so not exactly Sherlock Holmes either.

Sam continues: "Needless to say, it was a surprise to everyone when the email came out about him being fired in connection with the investigation. And it seems weird, because this is a real-life situation where someone lost his job, but after the initial shock, the first question that came to mind was: how would this affect the league?"

I get it. Yancy didn't do anything wrong in the league itself, but all the league members were people from work. And he was fired from work with good reason. Why do I think Miss Manners never has to deal with this?

So what'd you guys do?

"Well, the commish immediately locked him out of his team. Someone would set his roster that week, but that didn't solve our long-term problem. Do we kick him out or let him finish the season? But if he wins it all, then what? Do we withhold the money? Roll it over to next season? I wrote in to your podcast, Matthew, and you suggested we kick him out."

That's right, I did!

"Your reasoning was, 'What's he gonna do, sue?'"

Well, did he?

"No."

Told you.

"Yep. And even though Yancy's team qualified for the playoffs, the team with the next-best record took his spot. I made it to the championship game, but ended up losing in the Super Bowl to . . . you guessed it . . . the team that only got in because we kicked Yancy out. That team ended up running the table. Stupid Drew Brees."

Yeah, that was the year that Drew Brees was trying hard to break Dan Marino's record, and the Saints kept pouring it on. I played Brees in a couple of finals that year myself. Stupid Drew Brees indeed. But even though it didn't go the way you wanted, Sam, your commish handled it perfectly.

There is no more thankless job in fantasy than the league commissioner. Coordinating draft times, chasing league dues, having to rule between friends, enforcing rules, everyone's always bitching at you (or about you). It just sucks.

Like being a boss in the workplace, where many of the same

issues often arise. You have to make tough decisions, people are never happy, and the pressure to get the job done is ultimately on you. It's a tough gig.

I've been a commish of many leagues and also a boss on multiple occasions, and it's no accident that I am no longer in charge of any leagues or any people.

So if doing either job is a bitch, what if you've got both jobs? And over the same group of people? That's the situation "Spencer Meteer" (not his real name) found himself in. He is the commissioner of a league that is the "Shangri-La of fantasy leagues."

It's a very involved league with off-season rules meetings, tons of trash talk, and a highly anticipated trophy presentation ceremony, complete with half-dressed trophy models.

The problem? The league consists of the CFO, CEO, two senior VPs, the controller, and a bunch of "worker bees" at a midsize, publicly traded company. Once you're in the league, you keep your franchise forever.

Unless you're fired.

Apparently, in 2010, there were some screwups in the internal reporting. The senior VP of finance blamed a worker bee, so the worker bee was fired and, more important, removed from the league. Nine months later, no more worker bee, but still the same issues with reporting. It's clear the problem is the senior VP of finance. And that leads to Spencer's dilemma.

"The hard part of the decision wasn't *whether* I should fire the guy . . . it was *when* I should fire the guy," Spencer explains. "I was having real internal struggles with my work/fantasy football life balance. He needed to go, but we also needed him in the league. He was the returning champion, in the playoff hunt, and a leading scorer. This would be an unprecedented decision and could send shock waves through the league! I should have fired him by week four, but since I didn't, I was stuck. Especially since it was getting late in the season, so I knew I couldn't hire a replacement for him in just two weeks. So, as boss first and commissioner second, there was only one correct decision to make. And that, very simply, was to keep him on and root like hell he didn't make the playoffs."

Let this be another lesson, kids. If you're gonna screw up your job, make sure you're doing well in the work fantasy league.

Well, fantasy karma once again smiled, this time on Spencer: the senior VP had the second-highest weekly score in week 13, but faced the highest-scoring team. The VP just missed the playoffs.

"Monday I go in and meet with HR and go through the formal process for termination. I call him into my office on Tuesday morning and let him know that I have to let him go. He sat stunned for a moment and asked why, and I explained why. He asked if there was anything he could do to change my mind, and it took everything not to say he should have been gone in week four!"

As the senior VP walked out of the meeting he said to Spencer, "I hope this doesn't mean I am out of the league."

Spencer was shocked. "A guy with a wife and four kids just loses his $180K job and is concerned about a $200 fantasy football league! I just replied, 'This is strictly professional.' He smiled and said 'Okay.' I'm just going to have to wait until the off-season to let him know he's out."

Or you could just give him a copy of this book. Highlight that last sentence and bookmark it. He'll get the hint. But, Spencer, I am amazed by the fact that you would keep a terrible employee who caused another employee to be fired just to preserve the sanctity and integrity of a fantasy league.

"Hey, that is what a commissioner does to protect his league."

Issues like that one didn't stop fantasy football from being played in a lot of workplaces back then, but they certainly didn't help. And I kept facing opposition in major media when I'd pitch my fantasy sports ideas

in those days because people had so many negative preconceived no-
tions about it.

No, it is *not* gambling.

No, it is *not* just for nerds.

No, it is *not* hard to play.

But maybe the biggest challenge was the belief that fantasy is detri-
mental to work. Many companies then had (and still have even now)
Internet firewalls blocking access to fantasy websites and content. And
many places had specific rules against playing, discussing, or even
emailing about fantasy football.

The fantasy sports goalies ("No fantasy is getting in here! Nothing
fun!") at work would base their policies in large part because of a study
done by the research firm of Challenger, Gray & Christmas. They would
read blaring headlines and hyperbole-filled articles, like this excerpt
from a site called Replicon.com.

Fantasy Football Sacks Office Productivity for $18.7 Billion—How Much Is It Costing Your Company?

Recent studies suggest that Fantasy Football players are
costing employers as much as $1.1 billion in lost productivity
every week of the 17-week National Football League season.

This study, conducted by Challenger, Gray & Christmas
Inc., took the estimated number of current fantasy football
participants and multiplied that number by their average
earnings every 10 minutes, about $6, resulting in a stagger-
ing weekly total of $1.1 billion.

Challenger's calculation assumes participants spend 10
minutes per day, or almost an hour a week, drafting players,
setting rosters and plotting strategy at the office. While another survey of 1,200 fantasy sports participants found that

60 percent spent more than an hour each day thinking about their fantasy teams.

I would fight the perception whenever I could. No one works eight hours straight. Whether it's Facebook, Twitter, texting, gossiping at the coffee machine, checking email, online games, whatever . . . everyone's brain needs a break.

During those years, it felt like every time fantasy sports took one step forward it would take two steps back. You'd hear something positive, like someone famous admitting he played fantasy. Then you'd hear something negative, like what happened to Cameron Pettigrew.

As a relationship manager for the private-client group at Fidelity Investments, Cameron understood the importance of camaraderie and relationships. So playing in a $20 fantasy football league made perfect sense.

Until, of course, he and three of his coworkers were fired.

For playing fantasy football.

Now, Fidelity did have a policy in place forbidding fantasy sports, even if it was poorly communicated and ignored by 10 different leagues that included managers and leaders at the company. But Cameron was very careful. He knew the policy, and he knew Fidelity had blocked the fantasy sports website his league used, so he couldn't have accessed it if he wanted. He never sent an email or did anything relating to fantasy sports. But on October 20, 2009, the fantasy sports goalies at Fidelity intercepted emails that were being exchanged in a *different* Fidelity office league. So they questioned the commissioner of *that* league. And it would seem as if the guy who ran that league threw Cameron under the bus, because Fidelity started looking hard at Cameron.

They couldn't find any emails, they couldn't find any Internet searching, but they did find *one* instant-messenger conversation between Cameron and a coworker that was sort of related to fantasy. "One of my buddies sent me something about how bad Trent Edwards was playing or something like that," Pettigrew says. "So they called me in and talked to me for about 90 minutes on everything I ever knew about fantasy football. They interrogated me as though I was some sort of international kingpin. The next day I get the call saying I had been terminated."

And yet Trent Edwards continued to keep his job of sucking for the Buffalo Bills. Doesn't seem fair.

Now, before you think Fidelity is way too harsh (they are, I just want you to hold off thinking that for a second), know that they are not alone in their attitude. Most companies don't take it to the extreme that Fidelity did, and this particular incident happened in 2009. But the attitude had been around a long time and didn't seem like it was changing.

It wasn't just that I had given up everything in my life to pursue a career that might not ever exist. It was that I was now pursuing a career based on an activity that was getting people fired.

What the hell was I thinking?

TIME-OUT:

Don't Be That Guy

Oftentimes in a workplace there is one person who just doesn't seem to get it and who makes the office atmosphere unpleasant. Unfortunately, I've also seen that behavior way too often in fantasy leagues. Too many leagues have one person who takes it way too seriously, who doesn't get that it's supposed to be fun first, who ruins it for everyone else. One person who is . . . *That Guy*.

That Guy shows up to your draft with an out-of-date magazine. Then he wants a do-over when he finds out the guy he just drafted is out for the year. Or worse, tries to bum your cheat sheet. Get your own sleepers, hoss.

That Guy doesn't read the league rules or emails, but then asks the commish 10 minutes before the draft, "Hey, how do I log in? And wait, is this a PPR league?"

That Guy pretends to draft T. J. Houshmandzadeh, mangles his name, and then says, "*Championship.*" It hasn't been funny in a long time, dude.

That Guy talks about how loaded his team is. In the third round. Or has a critique after every pick. If I wanted play-by-play, I'd have brought Mike Tirico. Settle down, sailor.

That Guy takes his full time on his very first draft pick. Or his last kicker pick. Scobee or Feely, man. It's not that hard.

That Guy is late on making good on his entry fee. Really, man? If you can't afford it, don't join. And if you can, don't make me chase you down.

That Guy is a sexist. He won't let a woman in his league, or thinks it's the end of the world when he loses to a woman. Some of the smartest sports people and best fantasy players are women. Everyone plays. Get used to it and get better.

Having said that, don't be That Guy who brings his nonplaying girlfriend or wife to the draft. If you're not in the league, you're not invited.

That Guy is an Internet tough guy who directs anger at an athlete or commentator about fantasy football. If you wouldn't say it in real life, don't say it behind a fake screen name, okay? It's a game played with an oblong-shaped leather ball. Stuff happens, and it's a game we play for fun. Calm the hell down.

That Guy needs to tell you about his team. You didn't ask about my team, why do you think I care about yours? Your fantasy team is the new golfing story or vacation pictures. No one cares.

That Guy is a rankings slave. I *do* rankings for a living, and I'm the first to admit it's a loose guideline to help with market evaluation. Think for yourself.

That Guy makes terrible trade offers. No, dude, I do not want to trade my superstar who had a bad week one for your scrub who just went off. Unless you'd honestly be willing to do the same trade in reverse, don't offer it.

That Guy won't respond to trade emails. Hey, you don't want to do the deal, fine, just say a quick "no thanks." Are you in this league or not? Oh, you are? Then respond to an inquiry like a civilized human being.

That Guy, however, won't take no for an answer. If you do get a response of "no," you're allowed to send a follow-up email saying, "Well, is there anything you'd consider for so-and-so?" But after that? Walk away, brother.

That Guy complains about what would have been. "If only I'd started [a scrub who went off] instead of [a star who underperformed], I'd have won!" Yeah, dude, because you're the only one who would have had a better lineup if you could see into the future. Just stop.

That Guy abuses the waiver wire, picking up players and immediately waiving them, and does this over and over to pollute the pool and make it so people can't grab free agents. That's not strategy, that's having no life. Win on the field, not in some sort of technology loophole, jerk.

But mostly, That Guy ruins your enjoyment of the greatest hobby ever invented. Don't be That Guy.

14.

The Benefits of Fantasy in the Workplace

or

"No One Seems to Realize That Adrian Peterson Isn't a Parishioner"

Father Blake is a recently ordained Episcopal priest.

But more important, he's the commissioner of the Episcopal Football League (EFL), started at the seminary he attended. He's dedicated to the Lord, of course, but he also loves him some fantasy sports.

And while I have no doubt he wrestles with the great theological issues of our day, in the spring of 2011 he had a much tougher conflict to confront.

"How do you tell a bunch of eighth- and ninth-graders that there is no youth group because April 1 is *always* fantasy baseball draft day and it's a Sunday this year?" Father Blake wondered.

I have no idea, Blake. No one is stupid enough to entrust me with teaching religion to children.

Eventually, after much reflection, the answer came to Blake: "You don't. You lie about it, and you get to your draft, because no one wants to be stuck with an auto-drafted team for six months . . . that is my version of hell."

Hmm. Maybe I'm not the only one who shouldn't be teaching Sunday school. But apparently, Sunday school is *not* Josh's biggest issue. "The biggest conflict of faith comes during the football season," Blake explains. "Why would God choose to schedule two of the best things in life on the same day? Service begins at noon and ends after kickoff, thus making last-minute roster moves impossible. I've never left a service early (yet), but I've frequently arrived a few minutes late after waiting on game-time decisions to be announced."

Luckily for Blake, his Boss is much more forgiving than the people at Fidelity. That's a good thing because, instead of choosing, Blake has found a way to work fantasy football into his job.

"My fantasy roster has made it onto the weekly prayer list more than a few times," Blake confesses.

The prayer list?

"It's an opportunity to offer up prayers for particular people as well as thanksgivings for the good things in life. During the week, people send in names of friends or family they want to be named specifically during the services on Sunday. Since I write up the bulletin, I will often add a few names to the list that I know need prayer. Usually those are parishioners. . . ."

Usually is the key word there.

"We pray for the nation, the Church, and then something along these lines is said . . . 'For the special needs and concerns of this congregation, we pray for the sick and suffering, especially Carl, father of Janet, for Ken, who is having surgery, for Ben, son of Jill and Steve, for Ryan Mathews and Adrian Peterson, who are day to day, for Angela Hock, Tony Romo, Mary Ann Hill. . . .'

"A short silence follows, and I say to the congregation, 'Hear us, Lord,' to which everyone responds, 'For your mercy is great.' Then we continue with the service. No one seems to realize that Adrian Peterson isn't a parishioner. It ends around one and I spend the next 30 minutes chatting with people and hoping that our prayers have paid off. That Tony's injured rib heals soon, and that Ryan Mathews's ankle isn't a big deal . . . because I need to win this week or I'm out of the playoffs."

I'm not surprised by your story at all, Blake. Just because there were places like Fidelity that believed and supported the claims of the Challenger, Gray & Christmas study didn't mean people stopped doing fantasy sports at work. Just the opposite, in fact.

Even though fantasy had managed to worm its way into churches and other workplaces, major media was still keeping it at arm's length, putting few resources into it. What little they did was often buried on the website and took a while to find. And no one I talked to seemed super-inclined to change that anytime soon.

So as I was getting rejected by major media company after major media company, I focused on making TalentedMrRoto.com the best site I could. I used the Matthew Pouliot style of hiring. If there was someone or something I liked, I gave the person a shot. The audience would tell us if they enjoyed reading them or if they didn't know what they were talking about. I grabbed more and more writers, people I saw on our message board with intelligent posts, Hollywood writer friends, and one guy who wrote me a two-page email giving ample statistical evidence why I was dead wrong about José Guillén. It was well written and smart, so I hired him. His name was Ken Daube, and he not only became one of our most popular columnists, he now writes for ESPN.

I knew nothing about running a website or even a business, so I just acted on instinct. I knew what I liked and what I would want in a fantasy sports website. Namely, answers to my questions.

So every columnist had "office hours" on our message board, and we had a rule: *no* post went unanswered. You posted a question, you got an answer. To encourage more participation, we had a "TMR Hall of Fame" where we retired your "number" for outstanding work on the message board. And the people who were the best on the message boards got hired as columnists or as DPs—designated posters. These posters had the TMR seal of approval. It created competition, loyalty, and repeated use of the message board. It made the site a community.

We had nightly chats and loads of personality. A sign on the front page blared, "It ain't braggin' if it's true!" with a list of our latest accomplishments in expert league play or industry competiton. Most important, we had great customer service. We promised the public that any email would get a response within 24 hours. Internally, the rule for our customer service people was within six hours, which worked great. People would send something in, expecting a response the next day. And when it came back a few hours later, they were thrilled.

Underpromise and overdeliver. Wise words my father, Dr. Leonard L. Berry (a customer service guru), taught me.

As the site started humming, I caught a break from an unlikely place: my sitcom and movie-writing agents. You know, from the career I had quit six months prior?

They called to tell me that members of the NBA, led by Adam Silver (soon to be the commissioner of the NBA), would be spending the day at the agency hearing pitches on potential movies, TV shows, and other entertainment ideas that would involve NBA players, teams, and locations.

"If you want," my agent said, "we'll put you in a room with these guys. You can pitch them a fantasy basketball show."

I loved fantasy hoops. The first fantasy column I ever wrote was a fantasy basketball column, and I'd been playing it for years. It's really a fantastic fantasy game, and we did lots of fantasy basketball at TMR.

So pitch them a show I did, but as we were discussing it they wanted to know how the show would go with all their current offerings on fantasy basketball. How to answer that? They *did* have a pretty good nightly fantasy basketball show on NBA-TV (shout-out to Rick Kamla!), at a time when no one else was doing fantasy on TV. But that was on late at night and was more highlights-of-the-night-driven than anything else. Rick wrote some for NBA.com, but other than that, no league management service, no other fantasy-only writers other than Rick, nothing to help support and promote their late-night show, not enough "small games," like pick-'ems or salary cap games. There was a lot that could be done.

I was nervous. Do I tell them what they have is great? Or am I honest and say they still have work to do? Maybe because I had been turned down so much by that point, I figured what was the worst that could happen? I get another rejection? Big deal. When was the next time I was going to be in a room with the people who ran all the business of the NBA? Besides, by that point I could have done my pitch in my sleep.

"Fantasy sports are more than a fad. This space is going to explode. You have a real opportunity here. I think I can help."

They didn't wish me luck. Instead, they said . . . "Go on."

So I did. Tons of studies have shown that the people who play fantasy spend more time watching, reading, discussing, purchasing, and doing every other kind of "-ing" you guys want than the people who are just fans. The more people play fantasy basketball, the more people will watch and care about the NBA. Fantasy hoops would drive traffic, drive longer engagement, and drive revenue. In addition, it would help serve NBA fans, and adding a league manager product on their site, combined with supporting content, would help give them something else to sell and package to their advertisers. There was a lot more detail than that, but that was the general gist.

Unlike many people I had met with, the NBA was already well aware of all this. Adam Silver, who is incredibly bright, said they had been wanting to add to their fantasy offerings but hadn't heard a plan they liked yet. Until mine. So two follow-up calls later, I was hired by the NBA to be a consultant to its fantasy business. In addition, they would use me on NBA-TV and NBA.com as a fantasy analyst. But most important, they hired TMR.com to provide the draft kit and all the fantasy basketball content to NBA.com, plus they would link back to TMR.com. We were suddenly in the black, on the map, and on our way.

I had kept the faith.

Remember the '80s movie *Can't Buy Me Love?* In it, a nerdy kid (played by Patrick Dempsey, who every girl I know thinks is the hottest guy ever, so whatever on "nerdy," but fine, we'll play along) hires the hottest girl in high school to date him for a month. The idea, he says, is that once one hot girl dates him, every girl will want him. It works in the movies, and frankly, it works a lot in real life too. One person takes a chance, and then everyone else is willing.

Now that the TMR site was dating the "beautiful woman" NBA, lots of places were willing to dance with us. By now, the *Sporting News* fantasy section was up and viable, so my old friends Mike Narhstedt and Brendan Roberts had me do columns with a link back to TMR. MLB.com hired me and the staff to do its official daily fantasy blog. James Quintong, who took over at SI.com, started running a bunch of our fantasy articles, all with links back. I did a few TV segments for NFL Network and had tons of different radio interviews. Along the way, our little site kept growing in traffic, subscriptions, and notoriety.

I always say, no journey is alone. And a journey that started with me, the dog, and a dream now had more than 50 columnists and designated posters on board—writing columns, hosting chats, posting on the message board, and so much more.

The list of people who helped out is in the acknowledgments section. It's way too long to put here, but I do have to mention Pierre and Janet

Becquey, who ran the site, edited everything, handled customer service, and were the heart and soul. Pierre was the first guy I "hired" off
the old Yahoo fan group, and he and his wife quickly became invalu-
able. Parents of four young kids, and yet every night they were writing,
posting, editing, replying. (Pierre, incidentally, now oversees fantasy
content for ESPN.com.)

It was an exciting time, and TMR seemed to get bigger and bigger
every month. The site crackled with energy, intelligence, humor, and,
even though none of us had met each other in person, friendship.

We were, as the kids once said, doin' work.

If the last chapter was stories about the challenges when fantasy
sports and work intersect, this chapter is about how much fantasy
sports *adds* to a workplace. Don't believe me? Will you take the word
of Challenger, Gray & Christmas?

You heard me. The same doomsayer consultancy firm that had
warned employers about how much money they were losing in productivity because of fantasy football *changed its tune!*

On September 30, 2010, new research from Challenger, Christmas
& Gray showed up on its corporate blog. Among the findings?

> In a survey by global outplacement consultancy firm Chal-
> lenger, Gray & Christmas, Inc., the majority of respondents
> said fantasy football had little to no impact on productivity.
> John A. Challenger, chief executive officer of Challenger,
> Gray & Christmas, said, in part, "An across-the-board ban
> on all fantasy football or sports websites could backfire in
> the form of reduced morale and loyalty. The result could be
> far worse than the loss of productivity caused by 10 to 20
> minutes of team management each day. . . . Companies that
> not only allow workers to indulge in fantasy football, but ac-
> tually encourage it by organizing company leagues, are

likely to see significant benefits in morale as well as productivity," Challenger said. "In the long run, this may lead to increased employee retention."

Exactly. The more fun people are having at work, the more they like and talk to their coworkers, the more productive they are. The more positive feelings employees have toward an employer, the more likely they are to work harder, stay later, and go the extra mile to get something done, and the less likely they are to leave or complain to others.

The report added:

> In a 2006 Ipsos Survey, 40 percent of respondents said fantasy sports participation was a positive influence in the workplace. Another 40 percent said it increases camaraderie among employees. One in five said their involvement in fantasy sports enabled them to make a valuable business contact.

They finally realized what many of us have known for a long time. Nothing brings people—and coworkers—together like fantasy.

Remember Cameron Pettigrew, the guy who was fired by Fidelity? He ended up being out of work for a year and a half! His firing made news in papers across the country, and he did a lot of TV interviews, including on ESPN. He said that while he didn't love being unemployed for that long, there were some definite positives that came from it. "I enjoyed my 15 minutes of fame. And it opened up a lot of dialogue. A friend who works at Chase Bank told me, 'We've been going through meetings because of you.' The incident spurred a lot of discussion on a real line in the sand about whether companies would allow fantasy football or not. And ultimately, that became a real positive for fantasy because, when companies started looking, they realized a lot of their best, most productive employees were also fantasy football players."

As a result, especially in the financial industry, many workplaces changed their policies. While there are still places that don't allow it, those are fewer and farther between. Cameron now works at a different financial firm, loves his new company much more than his previous one, and was able to complain to his coworkers without repercussion when Matthew Stafford's 2012 season went in the tank, taking Cameron's team along with him.

A great real-life example of how far fantasy has come in the office is Shaun Kernahan's Thousand Oaks, California–based work league. This company of 150 employees has divided the office into a 10-team league, with each team consisting of one department with a designated captain.

As Shaun says, "Every Tuesday morning the office is buzzing about who scored how many points for that week, and there is great friendly trash talk throughout the company. We have a large corkboard, covered in green construction paper and company logos, that tracks the progress of each team. Discussions over starters and waiver pickups build a comfort level for employees with their managers, making it much easier to go to a manager when they have a problem. And because everyone's playing, everyone's interacting with different departments. IT is talking trash to marketing. Underwriting's doing a trade with operations. It's helped us learn more about the company. The week before the Super Bowl, we have a chili cook-off where we present the winning teams with gift cards and a trophy."

In short, "it creates a 17-week company party that keeps morale up for everyone."

And every day more and more offices are like Shaun's. As well they should be.

Because fantasy helps people in their job. All the time.

Even if it's not immediately obvious how.

"Christina" is a perfect example. As she explains, "One of the most important aspects of being a sex worker is the ability to create intimacy, often in a relatively short period of time."

Wait. What? That's right. "Christina" is a webcam and fetish model.

And when you are a webcam model, the idea is to keep the guy online for as long as possible. "Talking about fantasy football is an easy way to do that, at least for me," Christina says. She's been in a 12-team league for three years now and loves it. "I've grown up a sports fan, and it's become an increasingly large part of my life throughout my adulthood. I'll have games on in the background, so while I'm dancing around, my eyes can be on the TV. Occasionally, I'll live-tweet a game that I'm watching to interact with my own fans while I'm away from the computer. Or be on webcam with the fantasy app open next to me so I don't miss anything. And everyone gets to share my happiness or frustration during the games."

But don't they just want you to, uh, just get naked?

"People confide in sex workers every day. In a lot of ways we're like friends and therapists as much as sex objects. They confide their most intimate secrets, fears, and loves. Particularly as I currently work in the fetish industry, I am privy to information that people are scared to even share with their spouses. So I've found that many of my clients can relate to fantasy football on some level. I don't just have the joy and heartbreak that comes with being a fan, I share it with my community. Whether that community is a group of other fans in a bar or strangers over the Internet, it's the sharing of the experience that counts."

If you're surprised that someone would do fantasy football while performing as a webcam model, you're not going to believe what other people do while they also play fantasy sports.

Matt Holliday, the St. Louis Cardinals All-Star outfielder, and I have a mutual friend. So when the friend said Matt wanted my number to occasionally ask fantasy football advice, I said sure. We text every once in a while, but there's one exchange in 2010 that I'll never forget. "I need to pick up a running back," Matt texted. "Which one of these guys do you like more?" And he listed three guys.

I texted back. "Dude, we're an hour away from Game 3 of the World Series!" Which, you know, Matt was *playing in.*

"Hey, it's how I relax," Matt said. "And I really need a running back. So who ya got?"

Speaking of playing fantasy sports as a way to relax before professional sports events, here's Dale Earnhardt Jr. "I'm in a fantasy football league with my NASCAR road crew, which consists of about 12 mechanics and engineers who work on my race car 38 weekends a year. We are a cohesive bunch, but during football season we get extremely competitive and rightly so. Winning our league comes with great reward—the opportunity to end any debate with 'Yeah, but I whipped your ass in fantasy.' To my knowledge, there's no good comeback for that. It's a discussion-ender. So with that at stake, we'll do anything to win. Me? I'm the guy who offers trade proposals the morning of a race—you know, the time when crew members are their busiest. You'd be surprised at the trades they'll accept during the hyper-intense moments on race day morning."

Sure, you may have checked on your fantasy team when stopped at a red light or something, but you ever discuss it while driving *200 miles an hour?*

Dale explains: "My spotter knows that there are two easy solutions to improving my attitude during a race should it go south. 'You're killin' 'em in the league today,' or 'The Skins are up big so far.' Those two comments, whether they are factual at the time or not, will light a fire under me any day."

The Big Hurt Fan Club league started in the Oakland A's front office in 2006 (when Frank "Big Hurt" Thomas joined the team), but General Manager Billy Beane didn't join until 2009. It's a 12-team auction league and you ready for this? Billy Beane, Mr. Moneyball himself, is actually a "stars and scrubs" guy when it comes to the auction.

"I like to blow my money on three studs early, talk a bunch of trash and then hand over the reins to my assistant coach Otto. Otto Draft."

Seems to work for Billy—he works the wire hard, he's (not surprisingly) a master at the trade and has finished second in the league for three straight seasons, each time losing in the Super Bowl. "I'm the Marv Levy of fantasy," says Billy ruefully.

They have some fun rules. There's no standard amount for the auction, as the budget amount is randomly generated just before the auction to throw off values (last year, they played with a $649 cap). And there's a punishment for doing poorly in the league—the bottom six have to be "Jamba Juice" slaves during the intense period leading up to and during draft week. Each of the top six finishers get one slave from the bottom six that has to take their specific Jamba Juice orders and go fetch them at all times throughout the week.

But most important, the league has proven to be a great source of bonding for the group. Lots of trash talk, between message board posts, emails, and the fact that one league member was portrayed in a movie by Brad Pitt. Billy dishes it out pretty hard but, Director of Baseball Operations Farhan Zaidi says, Billy takes more than his fair share of abuse, often in the form of cruelly photoshopped pictures. "The liability of having a bunch of different images pop up in Google search results." Which explains why the staff is so close. Nothing brings a group of co-workers together better than a digitally altered photo of the boss. . . .

Seriously, if your workplace doesn't let you play fantasy, show them this chapter. Because it's not just happening in cubicles across the country. It's professional athletes, it's priests, it's CEO's who do fantasy sports during work. It's . . . *candidates for president of the United States of America.*

In addition to serving in the US Senate for 12 years, plus running for president in 2012 as one of the leading candidates for the Republican nomination, Pennsylvania senator Rick Santorum is a hard-core fantasy baseball player, having been in the same 12-team AL-only keeper league since 1995. The Keystone League was formed when Rick first took office as a senator. "I didn't know what it was. Some guys in the office were forming a league, and I joined because I thought it would be good for camaraderie."

Was it ever. The senator got really into it. And has proven to be pretty good too, as his team, For the Glory, has won the title in 8 of the 18 years they've played. Many people with high-profile jobs will claim to play fantasy, but in reality they send a flunky to draft their team. Not the senator. Drafts have been rearranged according to the congressional calendar. They've drafted in his Capitol Hill office at *5:30 AM* so he could make both the draft and a congressional vote later that day.

How passionate is the senator about fantasy? Longtime Santorum staffer and Keystone League commissioner Jay French remembers a time in 2006 when Pittsburgh was hosting the MLB All-Star Game. Just before the game, the senator was to make a big public appearance at a fund-raiser with former New York mayor Rudy Giuliani. Santorum is a sitting senator at the time, running for reelection, and this is a big event. But Giuliani is running late. So people are running around, trying to rearrange everything, it's intense, and there's total chaos as the crowd is getting restless. When Jay approaches the senator, Santorum puts down his BlackBerry and has just one question: "How can you approve this trade?? Ichiro for DeRosa and draft picks? Terrible trade."

Oh yeah, he's a player all right. Jay explains: "I want to stress that at no point did public service ever take a backseat to fantasy. But this is his way of getting some normalcy during an intense campaign or the rigors of politics." And the next time you think you haven't had enough time to prep for a draft, consider the senator, who did his 2012 draft by phone, while being driven, just after *he had dropped out of the presidential race*!

The same day he announced he was dropping out of the race, he also had to do a deep, 12-team, AL-only keeper draft. Said the senator, "I'd been so focused on the campaign, I hadn't had much time to prep. It was the first time there were a few minor leaguers I hadn't heard of. To be honest, it sort of added to the misery of the day."

Now *that's* a tough draft day. To his credit, the senator battled back from a less than stellar draft to finish second in the league that year. Has fantasy helped his job? Absolutely, the senator says. In addition to bringing the staff closer together, "everyone always says in politics you don't want a staff of yes men. I've got no worries about that, they're all trying to pull outrageous trades on me!"

Finally, take "S.D.," who was transferred to Zurich, Switzerland, only a few days before his Ironman Fantasy Football League draft. Since he had just moved, he had no Internet at his home, and since the draft was at 2:00 AM Swiss time, there was no chance of finding an Internet café open.

So he decided to "work" late and draft from his office computer. Works like a charm, draft ends at 4:00 AM, and he decides to head home. Just one problem.

"Unbeknownst to me, my work badge was a temporary one and thus had very limited security clearance. I walked through the lobby and through two sliding-glass doors, which automatically closed behind me. However, when I attempted to open a second set of doors leading outside, they would not budge! And when I tried to walk back into the office, the sliding doors were locked as well!"

So S.D. was now stuck in this small glass entrance area. At his brand-new job. At 4:00 AM. In a foreign country where he knew no one. "It was not until 6:00 AM that a security guard spotted me. As I started to stammer in broken German, the CEO of the company came striding in to find his new American employee standing in a rumpled suit, conversing with security at six in the morning."

But by going to all that effort to make his draft, S.D. was rewarded with good fantasy karma, only the most powerful karma known to man. "The CEO decided the whole fiasco was caused by my incredible work ethic, burning the midnight oil late into the night."

S.D. smartly didn't correct him. S.D. discovered what a lot of people in business learn. That it's important to work hard and be good at what you do, but it also helps to be in the right place at the right time. A lesson I was about to learn.

PART EIGHT

THE PLAYOFFS

15.

The Five Biggest, Craziest, Most Game-Changing Plays in Fantasy Football History

or

"That Knee Cost Me $600,000"

"I've got the guy."

My old friend Steve Mason, from Fox Sports Radio, had since moved to 710 ESPN Radio in Los Angeles to do afternoon drive with his former radio cohost, John Ireland. And as the 2004 fantasy football season approached, Steve's then program director, Ray Kalusa, wanted to do a fantasy football show. Steve and I had stayed in touch, and Steve mentioned me as the man for the job.

When I was in college hoping to write for sitcoms, I managed to score a meeting with a big-time sitcom writer. He gave me some unexpected advice that was as good as any I've ever received.

He explained that there was no conspiracy to keep good people out. "When we open a script, we *want* it to be great. We are rooting for it. But most times it isn't. So we pass. And because we get so many submissions, we have limited time. So if I see another script from someone I've already read and passed on, I'm not reading a second one. Life's too short."

He continued with me. "Look, you'll get your shot. Everyone who's persistent enough always does. But when you get your shot, make sure you're ready. Because you only get one."

He offered to read a script of mine whenever I wanted. And of course, I was so excited I immediately ignored his advice and gave him my script. Which in retrospect wasn't anywhere close to being good enough to show. He passed, and I never heard from him again. I had my one shot. And I wasn't ready.

That advice has always stayed with me. Along with "face to face is always better," and "when a webcam model starts talking fantasy football, it's time to log off," it's as important a piece of advice as I can give. Most people are nice. Most people remember what it was like when they were starting out and how someone helped them along. So most people will give an aspiring person a shot. Not many shots. One.

So when Steve and I had lunch in the summer of '04 and he said he wanted to introduce me to Ray, I was ready. I had a CD "air check" of my best appearances, both with Steve and on other radio shows. I had copies of a few newspaper articles about me, research about the popularity of fantasy sports, and a professional bio about my two websites. When opportunity knocked, I not only opened the door, I was holding a plate of cookies.

I was hired to do *Fantasy Football Friday Night*, a two-hour weekly show from 10:00 PM to midnight during the football season. Second show was better than the first, third show was better than the second, and we grew. Fan reaction was good.

Getting into 710 ESPN was huge for me, because I wanted to be in at ESPN somewhere, somehow. And it was two hours, unlike my much shorter segments on Fox Sports Radio. I loved my time at 710 ESPN. But I didn't want to lose Fox, since that was also great promotion. So I convinced Fox Sports Radio to replace me with one of my Talented MrRoto.com columnists, a guy I'd discovered named Brad Evans. Brad did a good job for them, and now we got double promotion—on both ESPN in LA and Fox Sports nationally.

One of my best friends from college, Abbey Nayor, was working in sports publicity at the time. She suggested I hire a publicist. "But I'm not famous," I said. "That's why you need one," Abbey replied. She had heard good things about a guy named Doug Drotman, so after telling him my goals, we decided to work together. One of the first things Doug ever did for me was the most important.

Doug knew a producer at *Cold Pizza*, then ESPN2's version of *Good Morning America*. Doug got me a meeting with ESPN2's talent coordinator, a woman named Ivy Abrams. I pitched Ivy on doing a weekly segment on fantasy baseball, which at the time was in season. It was the lesson I learned with the NBA: no one wants to be the first to take a chance on you, but everyone wants to be the second. So I made sure to mention how much I was doing at 710 ESPN in every meeting I had. Not everyone at *Cold Pizza* was convinced fantasy would work on TV. But Ivy, bless her, fought for me, and Mike McQuade, a guy who is willing to take chances and was running the show, gave me a shot. Mc-Quade wanted to pair me with a baseball reporter they had found who was also just starting to do some TV. The reporter would give some baseball news, I'd give the fantasy spin to it, and they'd call it "Fantasy Meets Reality," which was at least semi-original back then. Who knew if it would be any good, but they'd try it out for a week or two and see. And I loved the new reporter they paired me with, a guy named Buster Olney.

Since I lived in Los Angeles and *Cold Pizza* was live, it meant I was waking up at 3:30 in the morning, driving 45 minutes to the studios, and putting on makeup just to talk fantasy baseball for three minutes. But I was thrilled to do it.

The first time I did live TV my heart was beating so fast I could barely breathe. The studio didn't have a monitor or a teleprompter, so I had all these stats I was trying to remember at five in the morning because not knowing when I was on-screen or not I couldn't look down. I'm sure my discomfort showed on TV. My most vivid memory is from my third-ever show. Remember now, it was 4:45 AM or so in Los Angeles, and I was still on a week-to-week basis with *Cold Pizza*. The studio was not a full-time facility. Meaning, it wasn't open 24 hours but opened when necessary to shoot stuff. It was also in a part of town that wasn't, shall we say, the safest.

So I get there, it's still dark out, and the door is locked. No lights, I'm wandering around, trying to find a way in, the hit is happening in like 15 minutes, and I'm freaking out. No one's here, I'm gonna miss it, I'm blowing my big shot, and it probably looks like I'm trying to break into this place. I decide I'd rather be arrested than miss the TV hit, so I start trying to break into the place. Seriously.

As I'm trying to pick the lock, my producer Gabe calls me, wonders why they haven't gotten a call from the studio for the uplink or anything. I explain the situation. Gabe says okay, hang tight, and now I'm just hanging out, feeling awkward, in this dark parking lot at four in the morning. Turns out the guy who was supposed to be there had overslept, *Cold Pizza* pushed the segment to the next hour, the guy showed up eventually, and all went well. But I'll never forget pulling on this locked door in a creepy parking lot, trying to remember how they show picking a lock on TV shows, panicked that I was gonna miss my hit.

The Gabe I'm referring to is Gabe Goodwin, or as he is known on Twitter and our podcast, "Gabe the WP," our angry, ranting friend. He was the first guy who helped shape all my segments and was among the guys who fought to keep me on the air.

Because when I wasn't having to break in, it was pretty much the same drill every week. The segment would end, I would drive home at 5:45 AM or so, watch back the tape, and notice all the things I could have done better.

Cold Pizza wasn't convinced they should even be doing fantasy, and if they should, was I really the best guy ? I had no guarantee. I was week-to-week.

It was my one big chance, and it could have easily gone either way.

That time in my life reminded me of *the* fantasy swing plays. You know the ones. Those insane, once-in-a-lifetime, what-the-hell-just-happened plays that swing thousands upon thousands of fantasy games one way or the other. They take on a greater magnitude because they usually happen during or leading up to the fantasy playoffs.

Here, in order, are the top five individual NFL plays that swung the most fantasy football leagues one way or the other:

5. **In week 13 of the 2009 season, New Orleans' Drew Brees threw an interception to Washington's Kareem Moore. On Moore's return, the Saints' Robert Meachem stripped Moore, recovered the ensuing fumble, and ran it in for a touchdown. There was much controversy about this play, as many folks wanted the TD to count for the Saints D/ST (since, technically, as soon as the Redskins had possession the Saints were "on defense"), but ultimately it was ruled a fumble recovery touchdown. Meachem was already having a huge game (142 yards and a receiving touchdown), so those who felt they had managed to survive the onslaught found out later in the week that there were six *more* points to Meachem's total, which caused a lot of wins to turn into losses. And vice versa.**

4. In week 10 of 2009, with the Jacksonville Jaguars trailing by two points with under a minute to play, Maurice Jones-Drew broke toward the end zone. But instead of scoring an easy touchdown, he took a knee on the 1-yard line so the Jags could run down the clock and kick a winning field goal. MJD, who plays fantasy himself, at least understood the implications. After the game, he said, "Sorry to my fantasy owners. They told me to get as close as I can and take a knee." On the plus side, MJD's fantasy opponents that week *loved* him. No apology needed.

3. You got victory wrapped up. You start talking trash, texting your opponent, declaring you *will* name your first child LeGarrette (or whoever just led you to victory). And then—at the last possible second—something unbelievable happens to snatch defeat from the jaws of victory. The premature celebration and awkward aftermath had its real-life version on *Monday Night Football* when, in week two of 2008, DeSean Jackson caught a 60-yard bomb from Donovan McNabb and flipped the ball away in celebration— a foot *before* he crossed the goal line. Brian Westbrook ultimately ran in for the score. Even though this was only week two, I'm putting it at number three because it was *Monday Night* and because it not only took six away from Jackson, but four points away from McNabb. Double crusher or double bonus, depending on your point of view.

2. In the 2010 season, Rashard Mendenhall was a star running back for not just the Pittsburgh Steelers but also fantasy owners. It was week 15, the semifinals of many leagues. And that week Mendenhall ran for a touchdown and 100 yards on the nose. But *five days later*, the Elias Sports Bureau (the official NFL statistician) ruled that he had only gained 99. That cost all Mendenhall

owners at least one point and, in some cases, multiple points if they got a bonus for 100 yards rushing. *Chaos.* Many teams that thought they were playing in their finals suddenly weren't, and teams that thought their season was over were now alive again. Adding to the issue was that many teams had already gone through waivers on Tuesday, prepping for week 16, so it caused even more problems. Beyond that, on ESPN we changed the scoring to what Elias officially ruled, but for people who ran their leagues on CBS, no such thing happened. CBS has a long-standing policy of not recognizing stat changes made by Elias after a Wednesday deadline. So you had ESPN showing Mendenhall with just 99 rush yards (the NFL's official stance) and CBS saying Mendenhall was locked at 100. *CHAOS.*

1. **The no-brainer: week 15, 2007.** With 2:19 left in a close game the Eagles are winning, Philadelphia running back Brian Westbrook takes off from the 25-yard line of Dallas, breaks free, and is heading for a touchdown when, suddenly, untouched, he *drops down on the 1-yard line and allows himself to be downed.* Ironically, it was a real smart football play, as the Eagles won the game. But fantasy owners went *nuts.*

More than 10,000 teams on ESPN were affected, winning or losing as a result of that one play, depending on where they were. Years after that, I met Brian at ESPN and asked him about it. He told me, "Not a day goes by that someone doesn't bring that play and fantasy football up."

Over the years, I've heard so many stories about that knee, each with one of two specific endings. The person was winning, the other team was down five when Westbrook broke for daylight, their season was over, and then . . . kneel-down. An improbable victory by the narrowest of margins. Or the flip side: someone was losing by five, they had a glimmer of hope, and then, just as jubilation was about to hit, their hopes were dashed at the last possible second with a then-unheard-of kneel-down with no defender near him.

But as bad as your most brutal loss may be, and I'm sure it's a doozy, there is a Wall Street league that puts yours to shame. The league (understandably) wishes to remain anonymous, but it's a 10-team league. With a $100,000 per team entry fee.

I was talking with a guy in that league who was in the semis. Down five. With only one player left playing . . . yep. "That knee cost me $600,000."

Brutal.

Of course, the other way to look at it: that knee *won* someone $600,000.

The slimmest of margins, the difference between winning and losing in those matchups, is razor-thin. And if the *Cold Pizza* segments had gone another way, who knows where my career would be? It was touch-and-go for what seemed like an eternity. But every week I'd hear from Gabe, and they'd say they wanted me back.

As the *Cold Pizza* segments got better and better, Mike Epstein, a producer at ESPNEWS, took notice. Football was starting up, and he wanted me to do a debate segment with Eric Karabell, ESPN's long-time fantasy analyst. That was the fall of 2005.

Then, the following February, at the NBA All-Star Game, I met an editor for *ESPN The Magazine*. So I trotted out a familiar refrain. "Hey, I'm already in the family, you know. Doing radio with 710, doing *Cold Pizza* and ESPNEWS. Why don't I write a fantasy column for you guys?"

He passed me on to Scott Burton, then the NFL editor for *ESPN The Magazine*. It turned out Scott was already a fan of my work, and so he said, yeah, let's try it. Once again, I had a shot. And was ready for it.

With the NBA deal, the ESPN exposure, and all the content TMR was doing for other websites, the two websites were profitable. No one was buying mansions, but both were in the black, as they say, and they were growing in revenue, traffic, and industry reputation.

Fantasy continued to grow, and I knew it was close. There had been a few smaller fantasy companies that had been bought, including Rotoworld, my first site. They had just been bought by NBC Sports and I could feel a boom coming on.

And then luckily, those magic words were spoken again.

"I've got the guy."

My boss at the NBA, a woman named Brenda Spoonemore, was having a discussion with her former ESPN coworker, a guy named Geoff Reiss. Geoff was doing a fantasy football show for ESPN2. Ron Jaworski, "Jaws" himself, would be the X's and O's football guy, and they were looking for who the fantasy football guy next to Jaws would be.

And Brenda said, "You should meet our guy. He's great."

So at the same NBA All-Star Game where I had spoken to the *ESPN The Magazine* editor, I had a drink with Geoff, who described what he was looking for. And I was ready once again, now with a CD of my best TV appearances from *Cold Pizza*, ESPNEWS, and elsewhere.

Later, Geoff brought me in for an interview with senior management folks like John Walsh, all the other producers, like Jamie Horowitz and Chantre Camack, and a consultant to the project, Bill Simmons. I found out later that Bill was a big champion of mine behind the scenes to upper management, and after a while, thanks to all of their support, I got the gig.

During this time when I was interviewing for *The Fantasy Show* as an on-air contributor, I had also been having some business meetings with John Kosner, who ran digital media at ESPN. Randomly, a very funny friend I wrote with on the sitcom *Conrad Bloom*, Les Firestein, had gone to college with John and was good friends with him. When

Les heard of my interest in fantasy sports, he offered to set me up to meet John. John had an opening to help run the fantasy sports business at ESPN.com and was looking to do something outside the box.

As you may have guessed, when I met John, I was ready. He told me his ideas, and many matched up with mine. I had met with John for the first time before I interviewed for *The Fantasy Show* and I found out later that John had already been talking me up internally. His support had helped get me the on-air job with *The Fantasy Show*. Now, as we continued to talk, John introduced me around ESPN, and after lots of meetings, phone calls, and discussions, plus the NBA very graciously allowing me to get out of my contract (I am forever indebted to Adam Silver and the NBA), I ended up selling TalentedMrRoto.com to ESPN and officially joined the Worldwide Leader in Sports as its senior director of fantasy sports. It was the fall of 2006.

A year later, Bill King wrote about the whole thing much more eloquently than I could for the *Sports Business Journal*, the noted trade publication. Here's an excerpt from the piece, "How Mr. Roto Came to Live a Life of Fantasy":

> . . . Landed a meeting for Berry with John Kosner, senior vice president and general manager of ESPN digital media.
>
> "When I first met Matthew, he was a ball of fire," Kosner said. "I was mesmerized by his passion for fantasy."
>
> Kosner wanted to hear more. He suggested Berry commit his ideas to paper. When they next met, Berry showed up with a binder that Kosner likened to a Bill Walsh playbook. ESPN would buy his site, make his the face of fantasy sports across all its platforms, and give him a role as an executive overseeing its fantasy games.
>
> "He came in with a plan," Kosner said. "Some of that was moving more fantasy content out from behind the pay

wall. But more broadly, it was about his making fantasy mainstream.

"There are some people who never thought we'd have fantasy on 'SportsCenter,' 'NFL Countdown,' and so forth. But he was absolutely tireless making the point about how important fantasy is to so many of our fans."

Berry would not disclose the terms of his deal with ESPN, but estimated that his salary and the purchase price, spread out over time, leave him ahead of where he was as a screenwriter.

"But I'm so much happier doing what I do now than I was in Hollywood that it's apples and oranges," Berry said. "Don't tell Kosner that. I like my salary. But I'd do it for free."

Every movie gets a tag line, something catchy to run across the top of the poster, and then on the DVD cover. "The Talented Mr. Ripley" had this: "How far would you go to become someone else?"

Each Sunday morning, during the "NFL Countdown" pregame show, Berry advises fantasy players on whom to start or sit.

"My dad still says to me, 'Every Sunday, it blows my mind,'" Berry said. "'What's Boomer doing talking to my kid?'

"It's bizarre. . . . I mean, it's like, nuts."

At the time, I had played in hundreds of fantasy leagues for 22 years. I had won a decent amount of the leagues, but you know what I found?

No fantasy title compared to this. Selling the site to ESPN, landing this job, getting to do what I loved for a living? Greatest win of all time.

I still play fantasy. I still love it. I still get upset when I lose and still enjoy when I win. But if I'm being truthful, it all pales in comparison with that moment.

When I watch football on Sundays, I'm rooting for my Redskins, I'm rooting for my fantasy teams, but mostly I'm rooting for my picks. If I said I liked Matt Schaub that week, I'm rooting for him to go off, even if I am playing against him in three leagues. Because I'd rather be right on the pick and lose all three games than the other way around.

Turns out the "league" I wanted to win the most was the one where I was competing with myself to make a career of this. The one that proved I wasn't crazy to leave show business. The one that got me closer to the end of my journey toward happiness.

Fantasy changed for me the day I got the job at ESPN. It's hard to explain other than to say . . . when you have the biggest win of your life, you don't sweat the others.

The Best Individual Days in Fantasy Football History

We all play fantasy to hang with our buddies, to keep in touch with people, to give us a rooting interest in games we wouldn't otherwise care about, and ultimately we play because it's fun. But the truth is: it's a lot more fun to win. A lot.

And there's no easier way to win than when you have a guy on your team who absolutely *crushes*. My ESPN colleague Tristan Cockcroft is amazing with this sort of thing (frankly, he's amazing with a lot of things, but also this), so I asked him: what would be the 20 greatest fantasy football days of all-time in the NFL?

The Twenty Greatest Individual Fantasy Days of All-Time (ESPN standard scoring)

1. 55 points: Dub Jones, RB, Browns, November 25, 1951: 116 rushing yards, 4 rushing TDs, 3 receptions for 80 receiving yards, and 2 receiving TDs.

T-1. 55 points: Gale Sayers, RB, Bears, December 12, 1965: 113 rushing yards, 4 rushing TDs, 2 receptions for 89 receiving yards, and 1 receiving TD.

3. 54 points: Clinton Portis, RB, Broncos, December 7, 2003: 218 rushing yards, 5 rushing TDs, and 2 receptions for 36 receiving yards.

T-3. 54 points: Cloyce Box, TE, Lions, December 3, 1950: 12 receptions, 302 receiving yards, and 4 TDs.

5. 52 points: Shaun Alexander, RB, Seahawks, September 29, 2002: 139 rushing yards, 4 TDs, 3 receptions for 92 yards, and 1 receiving TD.

T-5. 52 points: Jerry Rice, WR, 49ers, October 14, 1990: 13 receptions for 225 yards and 5 TDs.

T-5. 52 points: Jim Brown, RB, Browns, November 19, 1961: 237 rushing yards, 4 TDs, and 3 receptions for 52 yards.

8. 51 points: Corey Dillon, RB, Bengals, December 4, 1997: 246 rushing yards, 4 TDs, and 2 receptions for 30 yards.

T-8. 51 points: Doug Martin, RB, Buccaneers, November 4, 2012: 251 rushing yards, 4 TDs, and 4 receptions for 21 yards.

10. 50 points: Jerry Butler, WR, Bills, September 23, 1979: 12 rushing yards, 10 receptions for 255 receiving yards, and 4 TDs.

11. 49 points: Mike Anderson, RB, Broncos, December 3, 2000: 251 rushing yards, 4 TDs, 1 reception for 5 yards.

T-11. 49 points: Larry Brown, RB, Redskins, December 16, 1973: 150 rushing yards, 1 TD, 3 receptions for 105 yards, and 3 receiving TDs.

T-11. 49 points: Barry Sanders, RB, Lions, November 24, 1991: 22 rushing yards, 4 TDs, and 4 receptions for 31 yards.

T-11. 49 points: Michael Vick, QB, Eagles, November 15, 2010: 333 passing yards, 4 passing TDs, 80 rushing yards, and 2 rushing TDs.

T-11. 49 points: Jim Brown, RB, Browns, November 24, 1957: 237 rushing yards, 4 TDs, and 3 receptions for 21 yards.

16. 48 points: Priest Holmes, RB, Chiefs, November 24, 2002: 197 yards rushing, 2 TDs, 7 receptions for 110 yards, and 1 receiving TD.

T-16. 48 points: Fred Taylor, RB, Jaguars, November 19, 2000: 234 yards rushing, 3 TDs, 3 receptions for 14 yards, and 1 receiving TD.

18. 47 points: Marshall Faulk, RB, Rams, October 20, 2002: 183 yards rushing, 3 TDs, 7 receptions for 52 yards, and 1 receiving TD.

T-18. 47 points: Jerome Harrison, RB, Browns, December 20, 2009: 286 yards rushing, 3 TDs, and 2 receptions for 12 receiving yards.

T-18. 47 points: Jimmy Smith, WR, Jaguars, September 10, 2000: 15 receptions for 291 receiving yards and 3 receiving TDs.

If you had one of those guys that day, you won. That simple. Of course, if you played against one of those guys, chances are you lost. And it's weird. When I talk to people, the brutal or tough losses come up a lot more than the miracle wins. By a landslide, the *most* common story I hear is a "bad beat" story.

Luckily, other people's misery is hugely entertaining.

16.

The Top 20 Most Soul-Crushing Ways to Lose: Numbers 20–11

or

"So Then Chris Johnson DMed Me and Said, 'Don't Worry, I Got You'"

Like a train wreck, we can't help but look. And nod. Because we've all been there. If you've never played fantasy, there's no other way to describe a heartbreaking fantasy loss other than it kills your soul. *Kills*. It keeps you up at night as you thrash about angrily. You grind your teeth, you replay what-if scenarios over and over in your head, you're in a surly mood for a week (and if it cost you a title, likely forever).

You're short with coworkers, your significant other might as well be a ghost, and the only thing you enjoy more than brooding is brooding to anyone who will listen. You have something called "impotent rage" because there's nothing you can do to fix it, so you just have to sit there and stew. In your own loser-ness.

It eats away at you in a way that only those of us who have been there can truly fathom.

And as I started to get into this section, that quickly became an issue. Because the problem with a bad beat story is, well, the bad beat. You already know the ending, never an ideal way to tell a story.

But a book on fantasy *has* to include bad losses. They're as big a part of the fabric of fantasy sports, especially fantasy football, as anything. So here's what I decided: We know the story ends with a loser. The only thing that's up to chance?

Just how cruel the fantasy gods will be with us as it happens.

I realized what I needed to do was rank *the way* you lose. Here are the Top 20 Most Soul-Crushing Ways to Lose at Fantasy, Numbers 20 to 11.

Number 20: **The Bad Schedule**

You score the second-highest points of the week, absolutely dominating. Any team you play would lose to you. Any team . . . except one. The team you're playing, of course. All your studs go off, your sleepers pan out, your waiver-wire picks step up, and it's *all* for naught . . . because you're playing the highest-scoring team that week. It's like rain on your wedding day. It's a free ride when you've already paid. It's the good advice that you just didn't take. . . . Err. Had the '90s channel on. Sorry, Alanis. Switching now.

The only thing worse than playing the highest-scoring team is doing it for an *entire season*.

You have one of the highest-scoring teams in the league, but every week you play the *one* team that can beat you. I've been the highest-scoring team in a league and missed the playoffs before, and I've seen it a lot. You have a great team, you know you drafted and traded well, and yet you're sitting at home during the playoffs just like the guy who hasn't made a move since week two. Ugh.

Number 19: Really?!? *Him?!?!*

It's the sinking feeling. The slow realization that you're playing against someone who is completely going off. Like Michael Vick on *Monday Night* and other players on the list earlier of unreal performances. But even worse is when the crazy monster day comes from someone who never does that well, like when Jerome Harrison ran for 286 yards and three touchdowns. Or the famous Joe Horn "cell-phone" game, where he scored four times with 133 yards. Joe Horn cost me and a lot of others playoff games that year. But the most painful example of this of all time?

In week 14 of the 2010 season, the first round of playoffs for most folks, the Arizona Cardinals put up 43 points on the Denver Broncos. Which included five field goals from kicker Jay Feely, a 55- and a 49-yarder among them. Plus four extra points. But the play that seemed to push a bunch of folks out of the playoffs was early in the first quarter when, on fourth down, the Cardinals lined up for a field goal. And on the snap, holder Ben Graham pulled the ball up, flipped it to Feely, and the kicker *outran the defenders to the end zone*. That's right. A rushing touchdown. 28 total points. For a *kicker*.

Number 18: The Vulture

Your running back moves the chains, gets the ball down to the 1-yard line, and what happens? They bring in the "goal-line back" to take the easy touchdown. Or instead of giving it to your running back, the QB runs a sneak. Maybe you don't have the running back. Maybe you have the stud wide receiver or big red zone tight end. The QB goes back to pass . . . and throws it to a fifth-string wide receiver. Or a blocking full-back no one would ever own. Or a linebacker. Seriously. Did you know linebacker Mike Vrabel has 10 career receiving touchdowns? Ten! Really?! Really.

There's a million different vultures out there and they all have two things in common: they took a touchdown away that was rightfully your player's and they are frequent enemies of fantasy owners.

Number 17: The Fantasy Goat

Not GOAT as in the "Greatest Of All Time." No, I mean "goat." It's a term we use on our podcast. This is when an NFL team goes crazy and puts up something like 45 points, and every single fantasy-relevant player on the team has a great day. Everyone, that is, except one guy. The guy *you* own. Like the 2009 game where Drew Brees threw 358 yards and six touchdowns against the Lions. Starting running back Mike Bell had 143 yards rushing. Marques Colston, Jeremy Shockey, Devery Henderson, and Robert Meachem all scored touchdowns and had good days. But wide receiver Lance Moore? Two receptions for 38 yards. And that's why you lost. Brutal.

Number 16: Who to Blame? Look in the Mirror

Oh, you could have won. You had the right players. Just not in your starting lineup. Seeing a guy go off while sitting on your bench and the bum you started is doing nothing? Another level of cruel. Because you realize it's not the players' fault, it's *yours*. And the difference be-tween your benched guy and your starter is *always* the difference between winning and losing. But at least the guy is still on your team.

The next level version of the self-inflicted wound is when you've been carrying a sleeper all year, a guy you know will be great if his NFL team would just give him a shot. But because of bye weeks or injuries, you can't wait anymore and you cut him. And your opponent picks him up. And starts him. Against you. And that's why you lose. Of course this is the week the player finally gets a shot and goes off on you.

The unrealized potential of what might have been by either playing your benched guy or having the new stud keeps you up at night. It's the kind of cruel that keeps on giving, as it also makes you question yourself going forward, second-guessing lineup moves with the players in question as you chase the right guy to start the rest of the season.

But next time you cost yourself the victory, remember this story. In 2008 I wrote an article for *ESPN The Magazine*'s 10th anniversary issue, covering the previous 10 years of fantasy sports. And for that article, I interviewed Chris Cooley, then a tight end for the Redskins and an avid fantasy player. Chris had been playing fantasy since high school and was in a league with a bunch of close friends. He had also never won this league, but in 2005 he had a great shot.

"Week 15, and I was in the semis," Chris remembers. It was potentially a great week for Chris. On the NFL field, he helped the Redskins defeat their bitter rivals the Cowboys with 71 receiving yards and three, count 'em, *three* touchdowns. Only problem? The guy Chris was playing had, as his fantasy tight end . . . Chris Cooley. "So basically, yeah, I knocked myself out of the playoffs."

Number 15: It's Not Over Until Elias Says It's Over

In week 15 of 2009, Kurt Warner threw a short five-yard pass to Anquan Boldin for a touchdown. Much later that week, after official review, the NFL changed the pass to a lateral, taking away a touchdown pass from Warner. As a result of the scoring change, many "victorious" owners were then booted from the playoffs.

It's so cruel. You think you've won, you've celebrated, and then? The exact opposite. Kevin Wilson's Teflon United team has a painful one. In 2008, after the *Monday Night* game, he had a victory over his good friend Ben by the slimmest of margins, 80.2 to 79.6. On Thursday the NFL ruled that a 39-yard David Akers field goal was misrecorded by the stat keeper and the real distance was 40 yards. By making it 40 yards, the field goal was now worth four points instead of three, giving Ben the victory. A stat correction on field goal distance?!!!? And Kevin missed the playoffs that year by one game to Ben, his loss being the tiebreaker. Had he made the playoffs, he would have won it all.

Number 14: But Taking a Knee Means You Won, Right, Honey?

QB kneel-downs are killers. At the end of a game, if a team is winning, a QB will often kneel down to run out the clock. And because most fantasy leagues count quarterback rushing, those few negative yards on rushing are often the difference between winning and losing. Here are two examples that people tweeted at me:

> @blairCmcdonald: 103.40–103.15 in Week 4 [of 2011]. Eli Manning takes a knee 3 times in final minutes in win versus Arizona. Lose .3 and the matchup

> @majorleaguenerd: Week 3 SNF, Ben kneels to set up field goal. Minus-2 rush yards. League scores to 2 decimal places. Lost by 0.08. Missed playoffs by 1 game.

Losing by tenths of a point because your QB took a knee? Crushing.

Number 13: They Called What?!?

We've all heard the phrase "You never want to see the refs decide the game." There might not be any place where that's more true than in fantasy. Penalties on your player are hurtful, but even worse? Penalties on *other* players. How many times have you seen your player score an amazing touchdown only to be called back by a holding penalty? Or some completely unnecessary block in the back on the other side of the field? It drives you up a wall, especially when it's the margin between a W and an L.

What about when it's a flag that should *not* have been thrown? Or a missed call entirely that would have put you over the top?

I liked Robin Ljunglof's story for a few reasons. First, he plays with a group of friends in Sweden. Sweden represent! Second, the dumb simplicity of the call. It's week 16 of the 2011 season, Robin is in the semis and up six going into *Monday Night*. He's done, his opponent has Jeremy Maclin of the Eagles. Maclin is held in check by Minnesota, and late in the fourth Robin is *still in the lead*. But at the end of the game, Maclin makes what appears to be a 15-yard grab, pushing his total to seven points, making Robin a loser. But wait!

Replays show Maclin was *clearly* out of bounds, it's *not* a catch. Vikings coach Leslie Frazier throws a challenge flag. Robin's gonna win! But then . . . *nothing happens.* "The ref *doesn't see the flag,* the Eagles snap the ball, and I lose my game on that missed flag," laments Robin. Two bad calls in a row, first ruling it was a catch, then missing the challenge flag, cost Robin the finals, where had he played in it, he would have won easily the next week.

That's when you need multiple challenge flags. One for the play, the other to throw at your TV, your window, your computer . . .

Number 12: Whew . . . We Survived. Wait! What's He Doing in There?!

Jason C. of the Louisville, Kentucky–based Cactus League was playing for the division lead in week six of the 2010 season. He reflects, "If you recall, the Titans were winning 23–3 in the *Monday Night* game with less than two minutes to play in the fourth quarter, and they had the ball, fourth down-and-5, at the Jaguars' 35-yard line."

At that moment, Jason was up 12, he was done, and his opponent had the Titans' star running back, Chris Johnson. "At that point in the game, Johnson had 76 yards rushing and two catches for 20 yards, a measly 11 points."

The Jags had stopped Johnson on third down. So again, the Titans are up 20, there's less than two minutes to go, it's fourth-and-5, they are in field goal range, and the Titans . . . *"inexplicably hand the ball off to Chris Johnson, who then takes the ball 35 yards for a TD!* Game over, and I lose by three."

It's a common situation. You have a lead, but you are done while your opponent still has a stud to play. All you can do is hope for a bad game. But the frustrating part is when the guy has a great game but so far you've survived and you're still winning. By all real football logic, the NFL players should be done with their game, but for some reason they are still out there for no apparent reason other than beating you.

As a Chris Johnson owner in 2010, I was acutely aware of this game—it clinched a win for me that week. And because Johnson was a first-round pick that year and it was a *Monday Night* game, many people remember this play.

But I included this story mostly because of what my friend Adam Schefter told me. As viewers of ESPN well know, "Schefty" is one of the most plugged-in people in the NFL, the ultimate insider and reporter, often scooping everyone on the latest NFL news. He's also an avid fantasy football player. And that year he too was a Chris Johnson owner. Now, Chris and Adam follow each other on Twitter. And Adam remembers that heading into the game that night, he was down and only had CJ left. So the afternoon before the game, while he and Chris were "DMing" back and forth, Adam jokingly mentioned that he needed a big game from Chris that night, as he was down big in fantasy. And Johnson sent a DM back. "Don't worry. I got you."

As Adam watched Johnson inexplicably re-enter the game and scamper for a touchdown, he did wonder a little bit. "I don't know if my DM had anything to do with it, all I know is he said 'I got you' and sure enough, he got me. I squeaked by with a win that week."

Number 11: Come On! Even I Could Make That Play!

You're watching the game. Your player breaks free. Daylight ahead! This is it. You're gonna win! And . . . *WHAT. THE. HELL????* By week 12 of the 2010 season, wide receiver Steve Johnson of the Buffalo Bills had emerged as a fantasy darling, with nine touchdowns in the previous 10 games. But, wide open in the waning minutes of that week's game against Pittsburgh, Stevie *dropped* a perfect touchdown throw. Fantasy owners went from celebrating to crying. And then, in one of the weirdest tweets in history, Johnson ended up blaming God for the drop. It cost the Bills a huge upset and, more important, a lot of fantasy owners a win. Why so serious, Stevie? Because you just cost us a W, that's why.

If you think these are bad, wait until you read the top 10 ways to lose. But don't get depressed. I have a gift for you. The greatest fantasy loss story ever. It'll *definitely* make you feel better the next time you lose in a cruel way.

TIME-OUT:

The Matt Hasselbeck Story

Running back Maurice Jones-Drew is best known for playing fantasy football while also being an actual NFL player, but there are others, including quarterback Matt Hasselbeck. Matt plays in a league with a bunch of college buddies and his brother Tim Hasselbeck, who is an NFL analyst for ESPN and is also my co-analyst every Sunday morning on ESPN2's *Fantasy Football Now*.

In 2009, Matt went QB-heavy with his fantasy team. That year he was the starting quarterback for the Seattle Seahawks, so not surprisingly, he drafted himself and also his former teammate Brett Favre, who was then in his first year as the quarterback for the Minnesota Vikings.

It proved to be a smart draft pick. Entering week five that year, Brett Favre had become one of the league leaders in fantasy. Coming off a red-hot appearance on *Monday Night Football*, Favre had seven touchdowns in his past three games and was facing the Rams. Hasselbeck himself had thrown three touchdowns against St. Louis in week one of that year, so Matt knew firsthand that the Rams had one of the worst pass defenses in the league.

Hasselbeck, meanwhile, hadn't played for the two games leading up to week five because of a back injury, and the Seahawks were playing Jacksonville, who had a two-game win streak heading into the matchup.

So, as he was setting his fantasy lineup for the week five games, Matt Hasselbeck decided to . . . bench himself. For Brett Favre.

The Vikings got up big early, ran the ball a lot, and Brett Favre threw for just 232 yards and one touchdown plus an interception. He finished with just 11 fantasy points in ESPN standard scoring. *Sixteen* different quarterbacks finished with more points than Brett that week.

Meanwhile, Matt Hasselbeck ended up throwing four touchdowns against the Jaguars and finished with 27 fantasy points, more than Tom Brady, Drew Brees, Aaron Rodgers, Peyton Manning, or *any other quarterback* that week.

Think about that.

Matt had spent the entire week watching film of the Jaguars. He *knew* the game plan and exactly how they would attack the Jags. Matt was calling the plays in the huddle and could be audible at any time. He had *as much control* over an NFL game as any fantasy football player *ever,* and he wound up as the *highest-scoring player* at his position in the league.

And he was sitting on his own bench.

I like to think about that story from time to time during a fantasy season. And you should as well. Because over the course of your fantasy sports career many things won't work out the way they should, including you just making the wrong decision. Just like Matt Hasselbeck did in week five of the 2009 season. It's the nature of the game. All you can do is make the best possible choice, taking every factor into account and letting the game unfold. Matt was worried about his back acting up and figured Brett would remain hot against a terrible pass defense. It makes complete and total sense. But sometimes it just doesn't play out the way you expect.

It's like when you're sitting at a blackjack table. Some drunk girl is sitting on an 18, and the dealer is showing 10. So the drunk girl (or stupid dude, seen it both ways) says, "Hit me." The table rolls their eyes in disgust, and then the dealer throws down a three. The drunk girl is all proud. "I knew it! I had a feeling!"

And I'm like . . . No! That was dumb! Just because it worked out doesn't mean it was a good decision, you idiot. You just happened to get lucky. Had you stayed on 18 and the dealer revealed his 20, you would have lost. But it would have been the right move.

Because it's not about that one hand. It's about the whole time you're at the table. And not just that one night but every time you play. Because odds are, most times you bust when you pull a card while you are showing 18. And over the long haul—a night of playing cards or a season of playing fantasy sports—playing the odds will work in your favor many more times than not.

Once more: Matt Hasselbeck *knew* the game plan, he had *as much control* over an NFL game as any fantasy player could ever have, he wound up as the *highest-scoring player* at his position in the league . . . and he was *sitting on his own bench.*

If Matt couldn't nail it, what the hell chance do any of us have? The answer is that it's a very tough challenge, predicting the future. So this is as good a piece of fantasy advice as you'll ever hear: ask yourself what is most likely to happen, play the odds that give yourself the most likely chance to win, and let the chips fall where they may. All you can do. It's that simple.

17.

The Top 20 Most Soul-Crushing Ways to Lose: Numbers 10-1

or

"I've Hated Kris Benson Ever Since"

I don't know that anything tops the Matt Hasselbeck story for ways to lose, but then again, I don't know many fantasy football players who are also playing in the NFL. So for the rest of us mortals, here are the definitive top 10 most soul-crushing ways to lose.

Number 10: Hey, Coach, I Thought We Were Trying to Win Here

Coaching in the NFL is a demanding job. No doubt. And you have everyone second-guessing you at all times. So I give a lot of leeway to coaches. But sometimes a coach does something so boneheaded that it defies all logic. One of the most famous examples happened in week 13 of the 2011 NFL season.

At that time, Dan Bailey was a very good fantasy kicker. Averaging almost 11 points a game in ESPN standard scoring, he was among the top three guys at his position in week 13 (and finished fifth highest among kickers that year). So with the score tied and time running down, Dallas drove down the field against Arizona and lined up to kick a field goal, which Dan Bailey knocked through the uprights. Hold on. There's a time-out. We see it a lot—the attempted "icing" of the kicker. Only issue? The guy who calls the time-out is Jason Garrett—Bailey's *own* coach!

After the time-out, Bailey comes out and *misses* the field goal! That four-point swing (lost three points, minus one for a missed FG) caused thousands of teams to lose that week. All because Jason Garrett decided to "ice" his own kicker. The bizarre coaching decision is frustrating not just for the loss it generates but for the complete lack of logic behind it. It never should have happened because *it makes no sense.*

Number 9: **One of *Those* Plays**

Like the top five plays we discussed in chapter 15, every once in a while there is a play so crazy, so out of the norm, so "that-should-never-have-happened," that it boggles the mind. The Brian Westbrook kneel-down is the all-time leader in this category, of course, but as I was writing this chapter a new one just happened. Heading into the 2012 season, the NFL had locked out the referees in a labor dispute. So replacement referees, many of whom had limited experience above Division III or high school football, were called in to, er, replace the real refs. It was a disaster waiting to happen, and in week 3 disaster struck.

On a Hail Mary play at the end of the *Monday Night* game, the replacement refs missed what appeared to be an obvious offensive pass-interference call as Seahawks wide receiver Golden Tate shoved Packers cornerback Sam Shields out of the way. Refs then ruled that Tate, not Packers safety MD Jennings, had control of the ball and that it was a touchdown. Replays appeared to show Jennings had possession, it should have been an interception, and the Packers should have won. But the replacement refs gave the victory to the Seahawks, who then kicked an extra point, making the final score 14–12, Seattle.

The implication of this play was felt in the fantasy world. The Packers defense/special teams had been started by 62 percent of the more than 5 million people who played on ESPN.com that year. By not allowing the interception, the refs cost the Packers D/ST two points (which are awarded to a defense for a turnover). And because they called it a touchdown (along with the subsequent extra point), it pushed Seattle's score past 13 (holding a team under 13 was worth three points), so ultimately that incorrect ruling cost the owners of the Green Bay D/ST five points. The result? Approximately 33,500 players lost their matchup instead of winning that week because of that one call.

Added to the anguish is the fact that controversial plays like this get replayed millions of times on TV. You don't just lose, oh no, you have to relive it again and again and again. Cruel *and* unusual.

Number 8: Can I Just Take a Zero?

Dennis had a decision on his hands in week six of the 2006 season for his 14-team league. Dallas's Drew Bledsoe was Dennis's quarterback, but there were rumors he might not play the whole game so they could let his backup, Tony Romo, get some game action.

So instead, Dennis chose to start the Bears' Rex Grossman against the Cardinals. Rex goes out and has one of the worst fantasy performances in the history of the sport: 144 yards passing, no touchdowns, *four* interceptions, and *two* fumbles for a final score from Rex of *nega-*

tive 7. Dennis lost by four. He'd have been better off starting no one. I've seen it a million times, especially with defenses—the negative points bring such pain when you realize you would have won if you had just started a guy on a bye. Or retired. Or dead . . .

Number 7: Shanahan!!

Do I even need to write anything here? No coach in the history of the NFL has tortured fantasy owners more over the years than Michael Shanahan. First in Denver, later in Washington, it's not the giving unheard-of running backs starts over established veterans despite no visible evidence the vet has lost anything, nor is it the musical chairs at the position. It's not even the running back by committee that drives us nuts. They're all annoying, to be sure, but for me it's the inconsistency about the inconsistency.

It's always something different. The guy named the starter and listed as #1 on the depth chart? Doesn't touch the ball in a game. The guy signed from the practice squad on Wednesday? Twenty carries for 120 yards and a score. Players will "start" and play the first three plays, only to be never heard from again. And then after a guy goes off and we're all like, okay, he's the guy now, the next week that running back goes back to being benched. There's no rhyme or reason to it, and Shanahan's depth charts bear no actual resemblance to what happens on the field. This track record of messing with fantasy owners caused many people to miss Alfred Morris's breakout season in 2012 because no one trusted it. Nor should they have, based on Shanahan's track record. Just when you think you can't trust him, he goes out and starts Morris every week. Every year, every week, every play . . . he's consistently inconsistent. He's a brilliant offensive mind, but as far as fantasy owners are concerned . . . Mike Shanahan is the devil.

Number 6: The Statistical Improbability

Something so improbable that, heading into the matchup, you know, "unless something totally crazy happens," you're winning. Tom Schmidt has one such story.

Going into the last week of the 2011 regular season, Tom needed a win to get into the playoffs in both of his Bismark, North Dakota–based leagues. Heading into *Monday Night*, Tom was *ahead* in one matchup by 23 points, he had no players left, and his opponent had Maurice Jones-Drew.

In the other matchup, he was *down* by 25 points heading into *Monday Night*. His opponent was done, but Tom had, yes, Maurice Jones-Drew. Not ideal, but at least Tom probably wins one league, right?

Nope! MJD goes out and scores *exactly* 24 points!

"I lost *both* leagues!!!!!" Tom remembers. "I needed him to score under 23 or over 24, and I would have won at least one! But 24 points and I lose both. And he hit exactly 24!"

That's like roulette-wheel-level odds of bad luck. You know, I've been playing fantasy sports for 30 years. I thought I had heard of every possible way to lose. But even for me, that story was a new one.

Number 5: But He's *Active!*

We all hate our player being a late scratch due to injury. But it happens, and when the player is declared inactive, you at least have about an hour before kickoff to find a replacement. In 2011, Marshawn Lynch had become a fantasy revelation. After a promising start to his career in Buffalo, it had floundered recently. But a 2010 trade to Seattle revitalized him, and in 2011 he was a midround pick and a sleeper for some, including, ahem, yours truly. Anyways, he exceeded everyone's wildest expectations, scoring a touchdown in *every single game* from week four to week 16. Well, every single game he *played in*, that is. Heading into week seven, Lynch had scored in two straight, was clearly "the guy" in Seattle, and, coming out of a bye in week six, had a terrific matchup with a porous Cleveland run defense.

Now there had been no indication anything was bothering Lynch. And so Sunday morning, on the field warming up, he is declared *active* for the game. I had Lynch in an intense 14-team league involving all the ESPN editors and other analysts that year. So of course I played him, just like everyone else did, and saw . . . my stud running back, standing on the sideline, doing *nothing*. He's completely dressed and yet never gets in the game, never touches the ball, I get a zero, I lose by 1.3 points, and that one loss keeps me out of the playoffs. I was furious, and I wasn't alone.

Lynch had apparently reaggravated something (even though no one knew he had something to aggravate in the first place!) in warm-ups, so he didn't play. When asked about it later, head coach Pete Carroll said, "I guess I should have put him on the injury report this week." Ya think, Pete???!??!

The cruelest part of an NFL star being active but not playing in the game is watching the game itself as the cameras continue to pan over to your stud, dressed in pads, but not in the game, saying things like, "The Seahawks sure could use Marshawn Lynch today," or whatever. Yeah, not just the Seahawks, guys!

Number 4: Wait! Where Are You Going? Get Back in There!

Similar to number five, I decided this was slightly more frustrating because it happens much more often. Because when your star gets injured in a game and leaves early, you still have hope he'll return to the game. It's this hope that really sharpens the despair when they ultimately never return. We've discussed the most famous example of this a few times. Week 16, 2011, the Super Bowl for many leagues, and Tony Romo hurts his right hand, leaves the game, and doesn't return. He is 0-for-2 with zero yards. Having to spend the rest of the game hoping he returns and getting knots in your stomach as the guy you benched for him goes off is the part of the player's injury they never mention, but it hurts just the same.

Now we've all had bad-luck seasons, when all your guys get banged up and there's nothing you can do to plug the holes. You just limp along, desperately wishing the season would end and put you out of your misery. Even worse is when the injury happens to your first-round stud. It's one thing to lose a midround wide receiver. But your first-rounder? The anchor of your team? There's nothing to do but ride it out and wait until next year.

But what if next year the same thing happens? And the year after that? And after that?

Graig Harris would *still* have you beat. Because he had the greatest string of bad luck I've ever heard of. Check out his draft history in the Andover, Minnesota–based Husky Ballas league. Remember, these are mostly *first-round picks*. Supposed to be the safest of the safe.

2004—Priest Holmes: 8 games played

2005—Deuce McAllister: 5 games played

2006—Clinton Portis: 8 games played

2007—Larry Johnson: 8 games played

2008—Tom Brady: 1 game played

2009—Steve Slaton (second-round pick): 11 games played

2010—Ryan Grant (also second-round): 1 game played

2011—Jamal Charles: 2 games played

As Graig notes, "My fantasy curse has never failed in eight years."

Number 3: **Can't He Just Suck at One Position?**

Justin Ring, GM of the Debutante Ballbusters, plays in the Mac 'n Cheese league, a league that uses Individual Defensive Players (IDP) and where a missed extra point is worth negative 15. That's a lot of points, but hey, they are hard-core. So, okay, in 2010 Jets were playing the Lions, featuring Justin's IDP star, rookie defensive tackle Ndamukong Suh. Justin remembers, "The Jets stop the Lions at their 3-yard line, and they decide to kick a field goal on fourth-and-goal." The Jets get a roughing-the-kicker penalty on the play, which injures Lions kicker Jason Hanson, but also gives Detroit an automatic first down at the 1. Lions QB Matthew Stafford runs it in for a touchdown. But their kicker's hurt. Who's going to kick the extra point?

"Do they go to their punter?" Justin asks. "No. They go to 300-plus-pound defensive line rookie Ndamukong Suh, using the logic that 'he played soccer in high school.' I swear this is true. Of course, Suh shanks the extra point." So Justin lost 15 points because he had Suh in there for IDP. He then loses his fantasy matchup by three points, the loss costs him the playoffs, and, as it turns out, he would have made the championship and won a few thousand dollars.

"And as an awesome postscript, Hanson returned in the fourth quarter to kick another extra point just fine."

Yeah, those IDP leagues can be tricky like that. Brendan Meyer, owner of The Tolbert Report, thought he had won a super-close game in week seven of the 2010 season, having survived a huge game from his opponent's Hakeem Nicks, who had 108 yards and two touchdowns. Until the next morning when he woke up and the dreaded "overnight scoring adjustment" had happened. You see, Nicks's quarterback, Eli Manning, had also thrown a few interceptions in this game, and Hakeem Nicks *made two solo tackles on those plays!* Those tackles counted as points for Hakeem's owner in their IDP league, and Brendan lost, 184.1 to 185.1. The margin of two Hakeem Nicks solo tackles.

Having a player score (or not score) points in a way they normally don't is the third most soul-crushing way to lose at fantasy.

Number 2: Defies All Logic

Mike W. is dominating the Buggy Jockeyz league from Orlando, Florida. As he enters his week 16 Super Bowl in 2007, he's the number one seed.

He is facing a guy they call "Four Leaf" because he is so insanely, consistently lucky. Four Leaf isn't going to be there for the playoffs. He has to go visit family doing a mission in Sarajevo, Bosnia. He'll have no Internet access. So before leaving, Four Leaf has to set his lineup in advance. Against all logic, he benches the red-hot running back Fred Taylor (four scores and 100 yards in each of his last five games) for Najeh Davenport, the *backup* running back on Four Leaf's beloved real-life NFL team, the Pittsburgh Steelers. Davenport is *not* getting any kind of consistent work at this point.

At worst, Mike thinks, maybe Davenport will vulture a TD or something, but anyone looking at it would agree. Mike's got this in the bag. And yet . . . on the very first carry of the game, the Steelers' starting running back, "Fast" Willie Parker, is tackled and breaks his leg. And yep, here comes backup Najeh Davenport, who rumbles for 167 total yards and *two* touchdowns. He outscores Fred Taylor by 10 points that day, and it's enough for Four Leaf to squeak by Mike for the title.

That would have driven me up a wall. You lose in fantasy, it happens. You make the best decisions you can, so does your opponent, you see what happens. But when your opponent makes a decision that clearly has significantly fewer odds of happening than the alternative . . . and it works out!?!? Arghhhh.

The woman from accounting who doesn't follow sports at all but wins the NCAA pool. The guy who leaves three injured players in his lineup and still wins. The person who starts his pitchers who are playing in Denver and Arlington—and gets two shutouts.

It shouldn't work out. It defies all logic. And yet it works.

You lose a title because a guy starts a *backup* who gets two scores and over 160 total yards? That's pull-your-hair-out time.

Number 1: The Combo Meal . . .

Sometimes it's not just one thing, like an active player who doesn't play, a QB kneel-down, or getting Shanahan-ed, which is too a verb. No, if you've truly angered the fantasy gods, you get a combo meal where multiple things happen to crush your dreams.

Just such a moment happened in week 13 of 1998. I heard from a lot of people about this moment, and the story of Jeff Waltz's father Dan was typical. Dad was playing for a playoff spot in Saline, Michigan's own JTFFL, and his team, the Ransackers, were done. All his opponent had left was Patriots kicker Adam Vinatieri. The Ransackers were hanging on to a one-point lead as the Patriots-Bills game was winding down. On the second-to-last play of the game, Patriots quarterback Drew Bledsoe completes a fourth-down pass to Shawn Jefferson to the Bills' 26. Questionable call. Looks like Jefferson was out of bounds, but the refs rule it a catch. Six seconds remain.

Bledsoe throws for the end zone, it's incomplete, but the Bills are called for pass interference! So now there has to be one last untimed play, as the game can't end on a defensive penalty. But the Ransackers still have this fantasy game in the bag. Even if the Patriots score a touchdown and Vinatieri kicks an extra point, the Ransackers will finish with a tie in their matchup and they held the tiebreaker.

But here's the combo meal. On the untimed play, Bledsoe finds Ben Coates for a touchdown, Patriots win. So disgusted are the Bills (they feel they got jobbed by the refs), they *head to the locker room before the extra point is kicked.*

But the play still needs to happen, so Adam Vinatieri *runs in unopposed for a two-point conversion,* which means Vinatieri scores two points instead of one for kicking an extra point, and the Ransackers have an improbable one-point loss.

"My Dad looked like he saw a ghost," Jeff remembers. "Just total silence."

Think about all the different gut-wrenching aspects of what just happened. You have a number 19 ("Really?!? *Him?!?!*") for the kicker being the one to score a two-pointer, you have a number 13 ("They Called What?!?") for the very questionable catch call, you have a weird version of number 4 ("Wait! Where Are You Going? Get Back in There!") for the Buffalo coach not having enough class to stay and just defend the extra point, you have a second number 13 ("They Called What?!?") for the pass interference in the end zone (replay wasn't in the league at that point, but later that week the NFL stated the game-extending pass-interference call was incorrect), and you add all of those to the fact that this was a number 9 ("One of *Those* Plays").

The combo meal is a multi-play parlay of losing, and it sucks because of the infinite odds against it and because it has so many different ways to torture you.

No scientific study has proved that a loss like that takes years off your life. But I assure you it does.

It's because the losses stay with you longer. I've had plenty of them over the years, and a few stick with me. Maybe the cruelest loss happened in the Fat Dog league, my longtime 12-team NL-only keeper league in Texas that I wrote about in chapter 1.

Heading into the last day of the season in the year 2000, my team, the Hollywood Phonies, were tied for first with the Country Hix, owned by David Hicks. The tiebreaker was most categories leading in, and I was beating David there, five categories to three. So all I needed to do was maintain a tie and the title was mine.

In each category, David and I were very set at our spots. No matter what our teams did on the last day, we were not gaining or losing a point in any category. Except pitcher wins, where the Hix were three wins behind the Faux Pas, owned by Warren Faulkner.

But wins are very hard to get, and even better, Hicks only had two starters going on that last day. (The league doesn't allow daily moves, so his lineup was set.) Even better than that? His pitchers were terrible. And even better than that? The terrible pitchers were ice-cold: Adam Eaton (4.13 ERA) and Andy Benes (4.88 ERA) had combined to lose 12 of their previous 15 games heading into the last day.

Of course, Eaton throws six innings of shutout ball to beat the Dodgers, and Benes beats the Reds 6–2 for a win. Ridiculous. But whatever. It's only two wins. He needs three and doesn't have any more starters. Well, you see where this is going, right?

Hicks also has a young middle reliever for the Cubs named Kyle Farnsworth. He appeared in 46 games that year in middle relief, compiling a 6.43 ERA. He won only two games the *entire* year. Wanna guess when the second win came??????

The Cubs were playing the Pirates that day, and Pittsburgh starter Kris Benson is given a *seven-run lead*. But Benson and his relievers can't hold—again—a *SEVEN-RUN LEAD*—so Farnsworth comes into the game for the Cubs only down 8 to 7. Farnsworth doesn't give up any more runs, so when Scott Sauerbeck, the Pirates' middle reliever who had 107 career holds and 13 holds that particular year, *can't hold the lead,* Farnsworth gets the stupid, cheap win to finish 2–9 on the season.

Hicks's three wins gave him an extra half-point, and he ended up beating me 68.5 to 68.0. I've hated Kris Benson ever since, well before it was cool to do so. Kyle Farnsworth played 14 more seasons (and counting) after that. I've never owned him. In any league. And I wouldn't want to be Scott Sauerbeck at a bar with me after I've had a few.

It's been 12 years. I'm still not over it.

One of the beauties of fantasy is that it's a microcosm of life. Highs and lows, surprises and disappointments, laughter and anguish. Fleeting interactions and lifetime relationships. The truest form of the good, the bad, the ugly.

And memories to last a lifetime.

Fantasy sports helped me develop a thick skin for events I could not control. I didn't know it yet, but as I packed up my life and my dog and moved to central Connecticut in the spring of 2007, I was gonna need it . . .

PART NINE

THE CHAMPIONSHIP

18.

Trash Talk

—————————— *or* ——————————

At Which Point Monty's Wife Walks In, Holding a Sharpie: "Now's Your Chance"

Chris Brzinski is not what you would call a "good loser."

Competitive? Sure. Smart? You bet. Hilarious? Definitely.

But being a bad loser is, no question, among his personal failings.

Chris plays in the PDC Ceeper League ("Our commissioner is so dumb, he spelled *keeper* wrong—not a joke," Chris says), a longtime PPR league comprising close college friends from the University of Wisconsin–Stout.

In 2011, Chris made it to the championship game. Where he lost by less than one point. 0.93 points, to be exact.

He did not take it well. And he desperately wanted to get back at the guy who won the league.

What Chris did next would not have occurred to anyone. Which is why it's borderline genius. Semi-cruel and crazy, but definitely hilarious and undeniably creative.

Chris went out and bought an URL/domain name with the winner's name. Something like www.MatthewJBerry.com, but with the winner's name instead of mine. And after buying the URL, Chris, what did you do?

"I launched a simple website with a picture of a piece of poop in a gutter."

That's right. The above image is *all* that's on the website that had the URL of the guy's actual name. Note the ability at the top to tweet, share, or "like" it on Facebook.

Chris sent out the link to the site in a league message board post, where "I congratulated the winner and told him I blew all my winnings on 10 years of domain ownership and hosting to commemorate his win."

A few days later, Chris was asked to take it down. The guy was VP of a bank and apparently "Googling his name wasn't providing the rich, professional details that you'd expect from such a prestigious man."

Chris said he would take down the website and have the URL redirect to this guy's LinkedIn profile under one condition: the champ would post on the message board that his win over Chris was a fluke and apologize for calling his own team a dynasty.

Of course, the winner complied and posted the message. I don't know about you guys, but I'm pretty sure Chris won *that* league.

As funny as it is, I can totally appreciate the bank VP being upset. It's weird and uncomfortable to have someone, even someone you know, trashing you in public. League message boards are one thing, but here was this site that anyone Googling his name would immediately find.

It makes you feel embarrassed, and you're wondering who else has read it. And then you run into people and you wonder if they read it. *What do they think? Do they think I'm a piece of poop? Do they realize it's the work of a semi-crazy guy who lost to me in fantasy football?*

It's such a bizarre sensation and one that I had never experienced. Until I got to ESPN, where I found out one fairly important thing about myself.

I wasn't ready.

They say hindsight is 20/20, but in my case it's more like 20/10. With the luxury of time to reflect and more years of experience to do so, it's only now I am reminded of the old saying, "I didn't know what I didn't know."

I had spent so much of my life both practicing and preaching "being prepared," you'd think I'd be ready when I got the biggest opportunity of my life. Wrong. And I didn't know I wasn't prepared, which made things even worse.

ESPN hired me to do two jobs. The first was as an on-air analyst, doing fantasy sports for the network. ESPN also hired me as its senior director of fantasy sports. That's a management position focused on things like helping grow the audience and revenue from our online portfolio of fantasy games and increasing fantasy content offerings on ESPN's many platforms: TV, radio, the magazine, non-fantasy sections of ESPN.com, and so on.

I was actually management, had direct reports, a P&L to oversee, and open positions for hiring. That is an awesome opportunity—if you know what the hell you're doing. I thought I could handle it and I had told ESPN I could. Yes, I had run some profitable websites, but running two small, successful websites where I'm the only full-time employee is *very* different from leading a division of a major corporation. Decisions are different; the stakes are different. And the daily, in-person oversight of full-time staff is very different from managing a bunch of free-lancers over the Internet. The only similarity is that both jobs are on planet Earth. Seriously, that's about it.

Forget running a major corporate division. I had never even *worked* at a major corporation before. I was from Los Angeles. Show business. I worked on sitcoms. Working on a sitcom as a writer is different from any other job in the universe. Dress code, hours, expected behavior— everything is different.

Add to that the fact that obviously Los Angeles is not Bristol, Connecticut. For all those reasons and many more, I was basically a fish out of water. I had no clue what I was doing and, worse, had no idea I had no idea. It was a very challenging situation—and I didn't handle it well.

I made many, many mistakes in new, spectacular, never-before-seen ways. I invented new things to screw up.

I won't get into the details because it's a fantasy sports book, not a "How to Screw Up in Business Without Really Trying" kind of thing, but suffice it to say my first year was really difficult in my new surroundings. And at every opportunity I unwittingly made it worse.

Also, I was alone. I moved there as a single guy, not knowing anyone, and who wants to go have a beer with the boss? Oh, they'll go, but do they *want* to? I never wanted to be that guy, so I tried not to force that.

It's different in metropolitan areas like New York or LA, but in small-town Connecticut most adults have spouses and kids, and they aren't really interested in grabbing a bite or hitting the bars with a newly single 37-year-old dude. So early on, I had only a few friends, especially as I was busy with a full-time job where I was trying to hire folks, help build up our fantasy business, and constantly put out the fires I'd set.

But while the management piece of it was a challenge, the biggest thing I wasn't ready for . . . the part of the equation that I misjudged . . . the thing that, frankly, I just had no idea about . . .

. . . was the whole ESPN-ness of it.

I wasn't prepared for the size of ESPN's audience. Yes, I knew it was big, but until you're in the middle of it, you don't realize how many *millions*—yes, between TV and online—*MILLIONS* are aware of every single pick you make. Obviously, you can't tell the future, so you're gonna miss sometimes. Before ESPN, when I got a pick wrong, not that many people were paying attention. But when you swing and miss on a national stage like ESPN, *everyone* knows. At least it seemed like it. The amount of attention was unsettling, and I was not ready for it. To this day, people will bring up calls I missed from 2007 or 2008.

I wasn't prepared for the power of the ESPN brand. "The Worldwide Leader in Sports" isn't just a slogan, people believe it. The ESPN brand resonates with sports fans from all over the world. And when I was introduced as the senior fantasy analyst, people expected me to be the greatest fantasy analyst alive. "If he's on ESPN, he must be the best in the world." I thought I was a guy who knew what he was talking about and presented it in a fun, goofy manner. Not some fantasy Rain Man, which is what people expected from the senior director of fantasy of ESPN.

I wasn't prepared for the scrutiny. It wasn't just my picks or my knowledge going under the microscope once I got to ESPN. It was *everything*. It's not like I'm some big star or something, I'm not. (Unless you're a woman who turned me down in high school, then yes, I am actually a crazy big MEGA-STAR. Your loss.) But there's a certain group of people interested in *anyone* working for ESPN, especially if the story could embarrass the company. So suddenly there were stories about who I was with or where I was. They were always some weird and very distorted version of reality. I'd be at a bar, and suddenly there'd be a flash as some stranger was taking my picture. One guy filmed video of me at the airport with my family and posted it to YouTube. It took getting used to.

I wasn't prepared for the reaction to my style. I was and have always been different from other fantasy analysts, but many people felt someone on ESPN should be just the stats and nothing else. I did a humor column for my college newspaper—I'd been writing the same way for more than 15 years—and humor/pop culture/writing about my life was my thing. But a lot of people disagreed and weren't shy about telling me.

I wasn't prepared for social media. Facebook and Twitter exploded during my time at ESPN. They are amazing tools for fantasy sports in terms of news reaction, analysis, and immediate fan interaction, but social media is also, as a comedian once said, "like everyone on the planet having your cell phone and being able to text you whenever they want." I was learning as I went on social media and I definitely made some mistakes. But you get a lot of tweets on a Sunday afternoon, and not all of them are positive; well it's hard to ignore sometimes.

I wasn't prepared for the jealousy and lack of support from some within the fantasy community. Maybe I was naive, but my thought was that all of my fellow fantasy analysts would be rooting for me. A "Hey, another one of us made it!" kind of thing. Especially since among my big goals was to help promote and make fantasy sports more mainstream and popular, something that would benefit everyone in the community. But while my longtime friends in the industry were kind and supportive, others were not. I was shocked by the vitriol spewed toward me on message boards, Twitter, Facebook, and other fantasy sites by other fantasy analysts. No matter where I was in my career, I have never taken shots at others because I know the challenges of predicting the future for more than 200 football players every week, just like everyone who does fantasy analysis should.

I wasn't prepared for how every aspect of my personal appearance would come under fire. I wasn't prepared for people being angry with me that I wasn't Eric Karabell or Tristan Cockcroft, two guys who had been doing fantasy at ESPN for a long time. People thought I was replacing them, not adding to them, so there was resentment there. And I wasn't prepared for the fact that (at the time) some hard-core ESPN sports fans thought fantasy was a stupid nerd game and had no place on ESPN's airwaves or pages.

But mostly, I just wasn't prepared for the anonymous anger and venom. I would be lying (and frankly, wouldn't be human) if I didn't say stuff like that bums me out sometimes. Not all the time, and of course, a logical part of my brain says, hey, these people have something wrong with them or are massively unhappy. They are cowardly to hide behind a screen name. Plus, let's be honest: there's part of me that brings this on myself because I was following the "Howard Stern style" in my writing. Printing some of the hate mail only encouraged more of it to come in. And, to be fair, I probably came across as too cocky early on, trying to overcompensate. So it's definitely my fault on some level. But still. I wasn't ready for it.

So imagine you are me: You move across the country to a new town where you know no one. You have never worked in a corporate environment, you've never done this full-time in your life, and now you're working for the biggest company in the world for your profession.

You handle criticism and authority very poorly. You have what you thought was your dream job, but now you are alone, confused on how to act and proceed, you have many eyes on you, and you live in a town with few single people your own age.

My first year at ESPN was among the toughest of my life.

I ended up getting used to it as part of the job. Things bother me a lot less these days and thick skin is a must when you're in the public eye. Just as it is in any fantasy league of friends who have been together for a while. In fact, the hate mail, extreme and crazy as it may be, does remind me of one of my favorite parts of fantasy sports.

Trash talk. There is a difference, of course, between crazy hate-filled emails and fun fantasy league trash talk. When done right among people who are all in on the joke, there's nothing better. The best leagues are the ones where a close-knit group takes the smack talk to epic proportions.

Trash talk takes many forms: face-to-face, emails, message board posts, texts, photos, "gifts," pranks, you name it. The only thing consistent is the message: You suck. I rule. But mostly, you suck.

And like everything else, trash talk starts at the draft. I've mentioned before that Jacksonville Jaguars running back Maurice Jones-Drew is an avid fantasy football player. In his main league, a bunch of Jaguars teammates and staff, there is no shortage of trash talk. MJD explains, "During the season, if I have a bad game, people will paste articles talking about how terrible I am on my locker."

Now, most leagues let MJD draft himself. Most. So draft day comes, and in the first round it's the pick right before MJD. The guy stands up, looks right at MJD, and says, "From the Jacksonville Jaguars, I pick running back . . ." Maurice is shaking his head. He can't believe the guy is gonna do him like this. ". . . Rashad Jennings."

Yes! MJD's backup. Drafted ahead of MJD. It was the 2012 season, MJD was in a very public holdout over a contract dispute, and while MJD was publicly telling fantasy owners not to worry and to draft him as a first-round pick, his teammates still drafted his backup over him. And laughed their butts off as MJD just sat there and stewed. "It was definitely messed up," Maurice recalled.

There's a lot of benefits to being well known, but one downside is that it's that much easier to talk trash about you. Sports anchor and political commentator Keith Olbermann is a longtime, hard-core fantasy player. He once had a keeper baseball league with a two round high school and college draft before they auctioned off 40-man rosters.

Another time, he did a football draft from the back of the Wrigley Field press box.

But among his many leagues is a secret fantasy football one comprised of various political media types, a league where they had all agreed to keep its existence quiet. Until one week when NBC News' Chuck Todd upset Keith in a matchup and decided to talk trash on Twitter. So much for keeping it quiet. Oh sure, Chuck can keep political secrets and news sources, but beating Keith Olbermann in fantasy? That he couldn't shut up about. Thanks, Chuck.

Now, sometimes trash talk is verbal. And sometimes, it's visual. Remember the guys who all wore the T-shirt with the picture of their buddy and a person they thought was a dude? Well, the guys in Sid's Washington, D.C.-based Fantasy Football League scoff at that T-shirt. Cute, they might say. Because they took T-shirt trash talk on draft day to another level.

First, they all wore a particular T-shirt to the draft. On it was a picture of one of the other guys in the league making out with a girl. The pic had been taken at Sid's wedding a few years earlier. No big deal, right? Except the girl was *Sid's sister*. And Sid *never knew* his leaguemate had hooked up with her.

Until the draft.

Think that would make it hard to concentrate? But this league had even more twisted T-shirt trash talk up its sleeve. Another year they all showed up wearing T-shirts that merely said: APRIL 27, 2030.

What's the significance of that date, you ask?

Only the 18th birthday of Sid's daughter.

Oh yeah, these guys play for keeps.

Personally, I love embarrassing others, especially if the whole league is in agreement, but I don't love it when people who have nothing to do with the league get dragged into it. There should be no collateral damage when talking trash, because sometimes it can go horribly wrong.

Daniel McHugh certainly knows that. Years ago, his brother-in-law asked him to join his fantasy baseball league. As Daniel remembers, "They didn't have very much experience, and he knew I was a vet of 20 years."

Daniel didn't need another league, but the brother-in-law was a good kid, so he begrudgingly joined, figuring he would just check in on it every once in a while. After a few months, all of Daniel's other teams were tanking, but lo and behold, this team he had totally ignored was suddenly in second place. He could win this thing.

So he decided to take a closer look at the setup. "Five bench spots! Three DL spots! Who came up with this thing, Mother Teresa? I'd never seen a system more geared toward manipulation."

Daniel realized that he could make up the most ground in saves. So he went to work. "I filled my DL spots with closers still a few weeks from coming off the injury list. I handcuffed. I streamed. Effectively, I cornered the market."

It worked. He rose to first. But a week later, Daniel noticed something: he was still in second.

It made no sense. His DL spots were gone, as were many of his closers, which were now evenly distributed on various teams around the league.

Daniel remembers, "My eye fell on the message board. I saw phrases like 'fun for all,' 'everyone deserves a chance,' and 'we decided in the best interests of the league.' I was seething with rage."

He was officially blocked from making trades, and his bench/DL players had been released back into the player pool. So he took to the message board and unleashed a horrific rant. "You #@%#! losers. You're gonna @&&%ing block me from makin' moves!? I followed the

*BLEEP*ing rules. If you're gonna play %$#&ing Fantasy Baseball, grow a @$&@ing pair before ya start!"

On and on he went, getting nastier and more vulgar. Finally, still angry, he found his wife to get more ammo to write about.

"Your brother," said Daniel, "what school does he go to?"

"Gordon-Conwell," she said.

Those dweebs didn't even attend a college he'd heard of. "What the hell is that?"

"A seminary."

"What?"

"John and his buddies are studying to be ordained ministers and missionaries."

That's right. Daniel had just unloaded profanity-laced insults on a bunch of guys studying to help and feed the poor.

Daniel went back to the league message board. This time he read more closely, scrolling through the league's history. It read like a '60s love-in.

"Anyone have an extra catcher? My guy is out for six weeks."

"Sure, I've got one on my bench. I'll drop him tonight."

"Hey, a little help. I forgot to rotate in my starters and I'm in class."

"No worries, bro. I got it. What's your password?"

"John, that guy I traded to you yesterday is out for two weeks. Sorry, just send him back in a trade request. My bad."

"No worries. I'll keep him. The news wasn't out. Not your fault."

That's the group Daniel cursed out. As he read further, he saw lots of gentle questions about Daniel's tactics, questions that he had never answered. "Why would he hoard closers on his bench or in the DL? Was he aware others had lost their closers and were in need? Why wasn't he offering them up?"

And Daniel, not having seen these, had remained silent until the day he unleashed more hate than these guys had ever seen in their lives. They must have thought he was possessed. And maybe that wasn't too far from the truth. As Daniel said, sheepishly, "Fantasy baseball makes me do some really stupid shit."

That's a pretty good segue to Greg Davis and his buddies. Started in Americus, Georgia, they've been in the Basketbeer fantasy league for 12 years now. They meet every August for a one-night bender at their buddy Monty's place way out in the country, playing cards and drinking beer until four in the morning.

After some trash talk, Monty bet John that he would beat him in fantasy hoops. The loser not only had to pay $100 but, in front of the entire league, announce: "[Winner's name] is the greatest."

Lots of trash talk went back and forth during the bet. It was very close, but ultimately Monty lost. The next year, at the party, Monty gave the $100, but swore he'd *never* tell John he was the greatest. They tried to get him to pay up, but he wouldn't budge.

However, by 1:00 AM, Monty was passed out drunk. At which point,

Monty's wife, possibly the greatest sport ever, walked in. Holding a sharpie.

"Now's your chance."

Bet? Paid. OFF.

Logan Dorrell plays in a deep 12-team, two-QB work league in San Diego, which means, with bye weeks, every starting QB is owned and played at some point in the year. Logan remembers week one of the 2009 season. He was down six points and had no one left. His opponent, however, still had Jake Delhomme. Albert should have just benched Delhomme to guarantee the win but total points is a tie-breaker, so he left Jake in.

You see where this is going, don't you?

In a 38–10 loss to Philadelphia, Jake Delhomme threw for 73 yards with four interceptions, a fumble, and no touchdowns for a total of *negative 7 points*. Logan won by one, and Albert missed the playoffs by one game. Since Logan sits next to this guy at work all day, is he compassionate about the tough loss?

Of course not.

"To this day, I will print out giant pictures of Jake Delhomme and hang them by our cubicles every other month or so, and he'll furiously tear them down."

I like how it's not constant, but every once in a while, just when you think Logan is done with it. The six-weeks-to-two-months thing is sort of genius. Plus, as Logan notes, "It's amazing how many different sad pictures of Jake Delhomme there are out there."

Logan has the right idea. It's not just about the trash talk in the moment. It's about making your buddy relive the loss over and over and over and over. A group of guys who completely understand that are the STP All-Stars League, a 12-team fantasy football league of high school buddies from St. Peter, Minnesota. They've been together for more than a decade, and in the 2010 playoffs, Chris Germscheid and his I'm Getting Schaubbed was playing the second seed, Matt Mogensen and the SJU All-Stars. Truth be told, Chris didn't think he had a great chance against Matt, who had a very strong team.

But Chris ended up cruising to a victory when Matt's team put up a 15.1. That's not a typo. In the semifinals, the number two–seeded playoff team scored *just 15.1 points*. Check it out:

Matt's team, week 15, 2010:
Aaron Rodgers—0.9
Adrian Peterson—1
BenJarvus Green-Ellis—4
Michael Crabtree—0.5
Mike Thomas—0
Jacob Tamme—3
Tashard Choice—0.5
Broncos D/ST—1
Josh Scobee—8
Total: 15.1

A crushing end to a season if ever there was one—just a complete and utter failure. I'm sure Matt was very depressed after having such a good team completely tank during the playoffs. So what does the league do? Never let him forget it, of course. You see, Chris's league gets together every year after the playoffs to play an annual football game in the snow. And what'd they do? They all had T-shirts made.

As Chris remembers, "Right when we were about to kick off the football game, we all took our jackets off and had our 15.1 shirts on and continued to mock him the whole game. Classic." And 15.1, of course, continues to come up every year in the league.

I love the expression on Matt's face. He's the one in black, of course, and frowning. But if you look closely, there's a hint of a smile. Like, he *wants* to be upset, but it's too funny and he almost can't help himself. Sometimes that's all that's left: laughing at yourself.

Something that was good to remember as I started my second year at ESPN . . .

TIME-OUT:

Punishments for Losing Your League

Sometimes, in fantasy, it's more important to play to *not* lose the league. Because of all the things that bring leagues together, of all the funniest, most outrageous, most talked about traditions, it's punishments for losing the league that are the most memorable.

Consider the tale of Dan Panton's No Bitchassness standard 10-team league from Charlotte, North Carolina. Their tradition is to vote on the end-of-the-year punishment for the loser. Dan explains: "In 2011 some cruel and unusual ideas were tossed around, from frosted tips in the hair to full body waxes. However, one option stood well above the rest."

I'm listening.

"The loser had to get a butterfly tattoo."

Wait, there are *two* tattoo leagues?!

"Yep. The 'Battle for the Butterfly' came down to the wire in week 16 of 2011. There were cheers of celebration, sighs of relief, and so much swearing that a drunken sailor would blush. But in the end, Zack Garcia manned up and got the tattoo."

Got the tattoo where, Dan?

"Near the top of one of his butt cheeks, right below his back."

Hold on. Zack had to get . . . *a tramp stamp???!??*

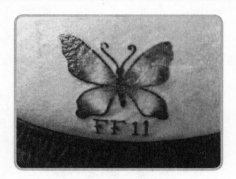

"If this doesn't exemplify dedication to fantasy football, then I don't know what does."

I'll tell you what does, Dan. Pretty much the rest of this Time-out. Because you'd be amazed at how many leagues have punishments for losing.

A popular choice is to force someone to dress as a woman. This is Jim Lavin, who lost his Northeast Florida–based league in 2008.

And here's Clint Hoffman with Josh Browing. After Clint suffered through a 2–12 season in their Cape Girardeau, Missouri–based league, "I manned up, wearing one of my mother's dresses, and even let my girlfriend do full-blown makeup. The good news is apparently I make a beautiful woman," Clint says.

On behalf of beautiful women everywhere, Clint, no you don't. But you have guts. I'll give you that. It's not just dressing as a woman, however . . .

Ben Sharbel's HRA league in Nashville, Tennessee, requires the loser to draft in a Speedo. Tobin Olson's Aztec Edition league takes it one step further: loser has to attend a party wearing a Speedo. And nothing else. When his buddy Dave lost one year, Tobin remembers, "he waxed his chest and got a spray tan. It was one of the funniest moments of our fantasy league, for sure." The loser in Jody Blakley's Liberty, Indiana–based league has to draft the next year in his underwear. Josh True has the "Puppy Dog Bet" with his best friend Don when they play head-to-head. Hot and scratchy, the loser "is required to wear a dog head costume from the moment he leaves the house in the morning until he arrives home at night. At work, at home, at a restaurant, or anywhere else during the day, the puppy dog hat is to be worn."

In their league, Scott LoMurray and his best friend Aaron Doverspike have weekly, head-to-head bets where the loser has to do some pretty terrible things, including swallowing a tablespoon of cinnamon while getting slapped in the face by a fish, getting a leg wax, and sitting in the back of a pickup truck as it goes through a car wash wearing only a Speedo, swim cap, and goggles. And, as Scott shows, there's also a bet that involves a sign that says I SUCK AT FANTASY FOOTBALL.

You know, it's possible both guys lost a fantasy league bet.

Humiliation in public is a common theme. In Luis's league, the loser has to go to a supermarket on a busy Friday night. And what does the loser have to do there, Luis? "Pick up three items only: a large cucumber, lube, and condoms. And pay for them in the busiest line he can find," Luis explains. "It's the most uncomfortable you can feel."

Speaking of public humiliation, I play in a fantasy summer movie league with a bunch of friends, including TV personality Michelle Beadle. While talking about the league on her podcast, we got into an argument about how much money *The Smurfs* movie would make, betting over/under $90 million. Loser had to go to the most popular bar in West Hartford dressed as a Smurf. Guess who lost?

I've heard of requiring the loser to take the SATs as an adult, to get a job at a fast-food restaurant (it's not that it isn't honest work, it's more making the guy wait on them while wearing a polyester uniform), or to shave all their hair off. I repeat. All.

The loser in Tony Brun's League of Mediocre Gentlemen out of Hawaii has to place a special license plate border on their car for a whole year. It's pink and reads, I SUCK ASS IN LIFE & FANTASY FOOTBALL.

Humiliating? Sure. But at least it's only one guy. Travis Knoll's BIG League in Bigfork, Montana, wonders why only one guy should be punished. Remember them? They're the rubber duck race guys. Well, they don't just stop with illegally trespassing to race plastic ducks. No, these guys are nuts. They decided it's not just last place who gets punished. It's *everyone who didn't win the league.*

Travis explains: "Whoever finished in second place gets to choose from the list of punishments, then third place, and so on, until the last-place member is stuck with the worst punishment. These include getting slapped on the inner thigh four times, eating worms, eating a small jar of mayonnaise, and finally, standing about 15 yards away from the rest of the league wearing nothing but your underwear and a mask while each owner gets one shot at you with a paintball gun. Needless to say, these punishments cause much bruising, scarring, and vomiting . . . as well as plenty of laughter."

You know the old saying. The league that vomits together stays together. Turns out it's not just about *eating* disgusting things. Paul Wood Jr.'s Bergen County, New Jersey–based Tecmo Bowl Fantasy League forces the loser to draft the next year from this throne. Here's Matt "Meats" Lucivero, owner of "Unexplained Mayhem."

Wow, the thumb is not the finger I would've used here.

And the loser of Aris Vasilopoulos's New Hampshire–based high school fantasy league goes in front of everyone at their school and gets kicked in the balls.

For the record, we were 18 whole chapters into this thing before someone got kicked in the balls. And you were worried we wouldn't stay classy. Of course, the violence doesn't end there. Permanent tattoos, humiliating outfits, disgusting acts . . . and now, things that hurt.

Pat's Boozehound Fantasy Football League is a 14-team PPR from the Bronx with this simple ritual: "The week before the draft, the last-place finisher is taken to a paintball location, where he has to dress as a lion and be hunted by everyone else in the league."

It's not the dressing as a lion that gets you, and it's not the hunted-by-paintball-gun that's that bad, but the combo? Kinda genius.

The DJ and Pasta League out of Brooklyn is a seven-year-old keeper league that harkens back to vaudeville for its last-place loser. As "Raffa the Gaffa" explains, "Every year before the draft the last-place team will stand for one minute and all the league members launch tomatoes at him."

More than 200 pounds of tomatoes are thrown at the loser and Raffa adds, "DJ Black's wife clocked in a faster tomato throw than he did. It is imperitive that this info is not looked over." We have different definitions of the word "imperative," Raffa, but duly noted. Incidentally, for you kids out there thinking of doing this, Raffa offers this helpful hint. "Microwave the tomatoes so they soften up a little, bringing the grime level to a 10."

And so here we are at the end of the Time-out. We've seen tramp stamp tattoos, leotards on street corners, and being pelted with tomatoes. We've learned of being hunted by a paintball gun while dressed as a lion and having to draft on the toilet.

And now, the Panda League. They are a fantasy football league of 10 high school buddies from the Central Virginia area, and August 23, 2012, was the fifth annual draft for the league. After discussions and votes on rule changes and amendments to their governing document, the "Panda Carta," the guys got down to the last piece of business at hand. Voting on this year's punishment for last place.

Options included the loser performing stand-up or buying a cat. They wanted to top the previous year's punishment, when a league member named "Pillar" had to dress up in a full clown suit and wear it for an entire weekend, including out in public. Commish Walker explains, "He was unable to give an explanation while at bars. When asked why he was in a clown suit, Pillar's only allowed response was, 'Don't worry about it.'"

Clearly, this is a serious league. In addition to the "Panda Carta," they have a roughly three-foot-tall, over-20-pound trophy. They sponsor two underprivileged children to attend the Russell Wilson Passing Academy in Richmond, Virginia. And they have a league where, in 2012 . . . the loser had to get his belly button pierced.

With . . . you guessed it . . . a Panda.

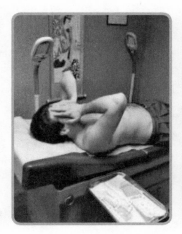 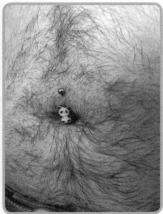

No words.

For hours, I stared at that picture, trying to top it. I couldn't. No words.

So I'll just say that happier times are ahead. Because for every league that has a loser, there is also a winner. And the rewards for that are just as fun.

19.
Trophies

or

"That, My Friend, Is the Rusty Tromboner"

One thing.

There might be only one thing more frustrating than being in a longtime league and never winning that league.

And that would be being in a longtime league and never winning the league that *is named after you.*

The members of Marsh's Rotisserie League are all buddies from college who have been playing together for well over a decade. The league got its name from commissioner and league founder Ryan Marsh, who named it after himself. And it appeared the fantasy gods did not appreciate that hubris. Because, as league member Steve Sherman tells me, "Ryan had gone through 12 tough seasons without getting his name on the trophy."

Sure, Ryan was aware he hadn't won the league in 12 years, but his buddies wanted to *make sure* he remembered.

So Steve and a league-mate, Rob Cordle, made T-shirts with a picture of the league trophy on the front and a list of the champions on the back. However, Steve says, "instead of the actual champion, we put the year and NOT MARSH."

Steve recalls: "When I walked into the draft that year, I remember Marsh pointing at me, laughing, and saying, 'You son of a bitch!'" Marsh, to his credit, took it in good spirit. Steve continues: "That year in May, when Marsh decided to give up and essentially play for next year, he sent out an email saying, 'You can add another "Not Marsh" to the shirt.'"

In fact, Marsh was not only a good sport but actually played along, adding NOT MARSH to his own shirt in 2009 and 2010 when he didn't win those seasons. Properly appeased by his good humor and humility, the fantasy gods finally let him off the hook. In year 15 of Marsh's Rotisserie League, Ryan Marsh finally won it all.

"So," Steve explains, "now our league trophy shows 14 years of NOT MARSH and one year of RYAN MARSH."

Good for those guys, and good for Ryan for hanging in there. I can relate to the story on many levels. Because at the start of 2008 at ESPN, I had become Ryan Marsh.

I had gotten my ass kicked from all directions since getting there, and I'm sure much of it was my own fault. But I didn't quit. I kept working hard. I tried to learn from my mistakes and correct them when I could. And, it did get better.

I started to figure out how to be a manager. I don't have a ton of skills, but I've always been able to identify talented people. The secret: hire smart folks from the outside and some good people within ESPN who were in other departments but wanted to get into fantasy. My job then: get the hell out of their way.

The tech guys kept improving the game, and many smart, hardworking people just kept kicking ass at their jobs, from marketing to technology to sales to integration to content to support, and so on. We were growing and growing.

And by late summer of 2008, *ESPN Fantasy* had grown so much and things had gone so well that we all agreed my job should become two separate jobs. We also all felt I was better at being an expert. So I happily put down the P&L to concentrate on writing, radio, and, uh, putting on makeup.

People started to get used to my style, I got better (not great, just better) at dealing with, well, everything that comes along with being on ESPN, and for every hate tweet and angry email, truthfully, I got 10 positive notes. I didn't publish them because it always seemed self-serving, but I appreciated every one of them.

And as the fantasy football season started in 2008, I no longer had to be anyone's boss, but rather just had to be the best I could be at my new title:

ESPN's senior fantasy analyst.

Goofy title, sure, but seeing that on a business card for the first time was heady stuff. All of it—my business card, my company ID, an *ESPN Fantasy* computer bag—none of it really meant anything in the grand scheme of things. But the symbolism wasn't lost on me. They were objects. Solid, touchable objects that showed changing my life at 35 had been the right move, that it had paid off, that I had, well, won the league that mattered most to me.

The moment you twirl that card in your hands, hold it, look at it, hand it out . . . it's a great moment. And everyone who has ever won a fantasy league has experienced a similar feeling. That card was my trophy.

There are few things more cherished than a fantasy sports trophy. It's so hard to win a league. You've gone through a roller coaster of emotions over the course of a year. From injuries to pickups to trades to sweating out the standings and matchups . . . it's a marathon, not a sprint. And when you finally finish and you are at the finish line as the last one standing, you are exhausted. Thrilled, joyful, ecstatic, overwhelmed, and *exhausted*. You want something to show for that other than a screen-shot that displays you had the higher score on the final week. You want something physical. Something you can cradle, take pictures with, hold above your head, or, in the case of the FX TV show *The League*, simulate sex with.

Think of the iconic "trophies" throughout the world of sports. The Lombardi Trophy. The Stanley Cup. The Green Jacket of the Masters. The Million Dollar Man Ted DiBiasie's Million Dollar Championship Belt. A trophy in your fantasy league will inspire even more jokes, even more camaraderie, and an even greater sense of history in your league. And the "trophy" can be whatever you want, as long as it's a symbol of excellence to display proudly.

The lack of something to display was an issue in Charles Clark's TECH FFL League in Ann Arbor, Michigan. They'd played for 10 years, and the winner didn't get a piece of hardware—just cold, hard cash. But after Jason Speer's Kicking Ass Is My Forte took home the title in 2010, Jason wanted a little something to commemorate his win. Unfortunately, just three days after his victory, as he was mulling over what to buy, his wife Amy informed Jason that their washing machine had died. And so was born one of the greatest fantasy football trophies ever. (To see this, and all the other trophies in this section, flip to the photo insert.) ①

Don't know if you can see it, but the inscription says, WASHING AWAY

THE COMPETITION. Not sure how you top a washing machine trophy. Certainly, many leagues don't try. Some leagues just have a solid, impressive, but fairly traditional trophy. I've taken the liberty of assuming you know what a traditional trophy looks like. So there aren't any in here. Plus, it's no fun to look at traditional trophies. Which maybe explains why so many leagues go the extra mile, like the Drawing Guy Fantasy Football League from Pittsburgh. They've been around for 11 years and Jason Fickley loves his trophy from the 2010 season. "It's actually a great representation of how I felt the night I finally broke through nine years of futility and two previous championship game losses." ②

Naturally, many leagues make their trophies a replica of famous real-life trophies. I've seen exact replicas of the Lombardi Trophy, the Larry O'Brien Trophy, and the Stanley Cup. And it's not just trophies. Lots of leagues do something uniquely their own. I've seen rings, mugs, championship jerseys, and belts. Not belts, mind you. *Belts.*

Dustin Williams and his Schaubshank Redemption is a back-to-back champion of the Chesterfield, Michigan, C-Town Fantasy League. The belt is attached to leather like a real WWE belt, and they have removable nameplates on either side so as to engrave each year's winner in their league. ③

A lot of times, leagues will use a totally random object as a trophy. Like a 126-pound golden pelican. That's right. Meet Nick Anthony, current champion of the seven-year-old Pelican Keeper League, a situation that the owner of "Whatever, Dude," James Wickham, is not happy about. "Nick is definitely the guy you don't want to win. If you lose, you lose, but to him it's unbearable. The picture is him, his wife Patty Anthony, and her friend (the blonde) Jade McBride." ④ Yes, James tells me, the women had the pelican T-shirts made. "It wasn't enough that the kids run around saying things like 'The Pelican lives here, Daddy is never going to lose.' No, they needed shirts to symbolize it.

It's an all-around terrible situation." Nick agrees with you, James. "There will be no living with me in our league after this book comes out!" he laughs.

The guys in the league live in St. Petersburg, Florida, where the city logo has a pelican on it, so the trophy makes some sense. But there's nothing to really explain the trophy in Ricky Garcia's Backyard Ballhawks league from Naperville, Illinois, except, er, past high school "glory"? All of Ricky's best friends from Neuqua Valley high school are in the league, and the winner gets the Brothel Bowl.

Why "the Brothel Bowl," Ricky?

"Because around the ring of the bowl are the initials of all our past girlfriends, none of whom we are dating anymore."

So I guess there *are* other ways besides winning the league to get your name on the trophy. Matt Hoefle's 12-team PPR Manly League of Manliness had this bad boy custom-made. ⑤

From custom-made to, uh, nature-made. Drew Diehl sent along this picture, as Andy Joseph holds what is given to the winner of the James Chapman Fantasy Football League. ⑥

Brad DeBoer's Des Moines, Iowa–based League of All Leagues has been around for 25 years, so you know they needed something sturdy. ⑦

Jordan Skelton's Tuesday and Company Football League in Little Rock gives out a bronze bust of former president Jimmy Carter to whoever finishes third. Why Jimmy Carter? "Because you were good enough to get into the playoffs but really sucked once you got there," Jordan explains.

There is no good transition from former presidents to a stuffed rooster, but is there *ever* an elegant way to get to a giant stuffed rooster? Here's the El Gallo of Brent Barnett's College Station, Texas–based Wings League. League champs are listed on one side and

Vince Lombardi's "What It Takes to Be Number One" speech is on the other. ⑧

Speaking of stuffed animals, Nate Butcher's "Rowdy Group Brings Danger to the Hood" league from Derry, New Hampshire, awards this rare armadillo to the total-season-points winner. ⑨

Many, many leagues like draft beer. But most don't use it as a trophy. The 10-team PPR TX Football Rules League that Corbin Miles is in with a bunch of fellow bartenders, however, is unlike most leagues. ⑩

Some prefer beer from a tap and some prefer it from a keg, including DJ Calligaro and Ryan Sula of the Men of Steel League from, naturally, Pittsburgh. Ryan explains: "The trophy is made of an Iron City keg, Midget football trophy, Steeler helmet, and a beer bong. The keg has inscribed plaques with each year's champion." ⑪

And oh yeah . . . it actually works. ⑫

That's Shane Ball holding it and Darren Watt is the one drinking. The defending champ of the Men of Steel has to do an honorary beer bong before the draft. Meanwhile, I think it's safe to assume that Brian Chamberlain's Power Thirst League likes something a little stronger than beer. ⑬

The members of Kevin Sparkman's Claywell Cougar Den League have known one another since their time at Claywell Elementary School in Tampa. As a result, he and Ryan Trainor (on the right) want to make sure there is no confusion whatsoever about who won. ⑭

I'm guessing they didn't buy that off the shelf. They're not alone. Many creative leagues take matters into their own hands to design a trophy. In Detroit, Eric Sadowski's Rusty Football League trophy features, as he describes it, "the Legendary Rusty Tromboner and Rusty Trombone Football League insignia, all made of 100 percent copper, slated on a half-inch thick of aged and fully rusted steel." Apparently it weighs nearly six pounds. ⑮

Power Twist Champion

15

16

17

18

19

20

21

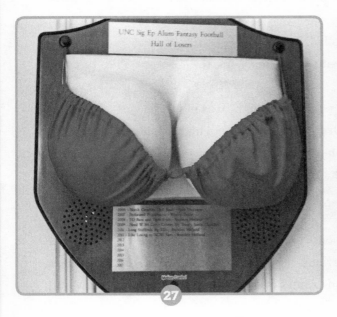

Eric adds, "Wish I had a dollar for every guest who went to the trophy owner's house and asked, 'What the hell is that thing?' . . . To which we simply reply, with a satisfying grin, 'That, my friend, is the Rusty Tromboner.'"

You're damn right it is. As Eric opines, "It's not a trophy unless you get your hands dirty."

Tom Hergert knows about getting his hands dirty. Tom runs a classic car restoration shop. And his League of Extraordinary Gentlemen has been around since they were all at Gonzaga University 10 years ago. So he took matters into his own hands for their trophy. Tom explains that he "welded all the parts together from parts I found around the shop. The base is a ring gear, the top is a pinion, the football is made out of pushrods with rubber control arm stops for the ends. LOEG is also spelled out with pushrods around the ammo box. It weighs about 25 pounds." **16**

If there's nothing manlier than making a trophy out of car parts, then there's nothing girlier than a trophy bedazzled in glitter. Here's the trophy for Sarah Garner's all-female Balldazzler's Fantasy League out of Denver. **17**

Football Jesus? Football Jesus. **18**

Chad Spinks explains the trophy for the 12-team PPR the 760 League:

"A common theme permeated the boards of our league—that of an omnipotent Football Jesus. Suggestions of a higher fantasy power were scoffed at but soon became embraced after countless unexplained events took place. Acts or words against the Football Jesus received the harshest penance. The worst offender ended his season with a 3–10 record."

After learning about www.catholicshopper.com, where statues depicting Jesus in various sports activities are sold, Commissioner Ryan T. Kirk knew this would make the perfect trophy for his Vista,

California–based league. Once it showed up, Chad went to work. "The base was made with a Dremel tool, miter box, and a six-pack by the league rookie." "Not completely square but at least structurally sound, 'the FJ' serves as an homage to the divine power that makes the game of fantasy football so unpredictable, improbable, and irrational. The FJ is not only an object to be desired, but feared."

Around Albany, New York, in 2007, Steve Lawton and his buddy Rob Matt set up the PorkChopSandwiches League after an old GI Joe Internet video they all made fun of. After looking and finding nothing, they approached a friend from high school to build a trophy for them.

As Steve notes, "What's better than a 10-pound concrete pig in a sandwich?"

The answer, of course, is absolutely nothing. ⑲

From a fake sandwich as a trophy to . . . a real sandwich? Yes. Nelson Johnson explains: "This sandwich is packed with turkey, ham, and American cheese. It was made three years ago by the top chef at the local diner and is considered prestigious around these parts. The winner gets to take one delicious bite and then has to store it in his freezer until another victor is crowned."

I thought it was made up, but, no, Nelson insists it's real. It's a two-QB league out of Butler, Pennsylvania, started by a bunch of high school friends. The sandwich, Nelson relays, "came about when multiple people wanted the same sandwich at the draft, which was at a diner, and there was only enough meat in the kitchen for one." There is, however, concern in the league. Current champ Jennings Graham explains that his mom is starting to complain. "It makes the freezer stink." Jennings is trying to hold tough, but they may need to get a new trophy.

Speaking of smells . . . trophies in fantasy leagues aren't just given for first place. No, many leagues also give out trophies to the last-place finisher. And perhaps none are as creative—or as stinky—as the one for Commish Kevin Leary's Beer Boy League. The Charlotte, North

Carolina–based league has been around for 19 years, and since 2002 the last-place team has had to sign this shirt, retire its team name, and then wear the shirt during the draft. While serving everyone drinks. 🔘 🔘

It's *never* been washed. *NEVER*. 2002. Just saying.

Speaking of wearing smelly things that have never been washed, at least Nathan Baker-Lutz and his West Side Football Club had theirs bronzed. As Chicago fans know all too well, nothing says last place like Curtis Enis. 🔘

It seems that almost all the last-place trophies have to do with smells, specifically from the toilet. And more on point, the toilet itself. Lots of leagues have a small bronze toilet trophy for last place. But it's not just toilets. It's also toilet-seat-shaped objects. Like a mug.

The loser of the Leavenworth Correctional Conference out of Wellington, Kansas (16 years and going strong!), has to drink all beverages from this "trophy" on draft day and whenever at least four members of the league are watching football together. GM of The Moose, Heath Freeman adds, "And a picture of the person drinking from the mug is the league's home-page picture for the first week." 🔘 🔘

From the toilet-shaped objects to an actual toilet seat. I've seen many versions of this, but the one in Brian Cook's GLITW (Greatest League in the World) was my favorite. 🔘

Here's Brian: "The loser of the league has to hang the Pink Leaf in a prominent place in their house for one year, bringing shame upon the loser and convincing the wives to allow us to spend more time improving our teams. Having that thing hang on your wall all year is a good reminder to put in waiver claims, set lineups, and check injury reports."

We move on from toilet seats to toilet-related accessories, like the toilet paper used in Eric Schoonmaker's 12-team Jay Cutler for MVP

Fantasy Football League. League headquarters are in Morris Plains, New Jersey, and they offer this up to last place in the loser's bracket. Loser is required to display it at work and prove it with a photo. ㉖

And of course, if you have toilets and toilet paper, you have a plunger. Right, Corey McDonnell? The Marple Newtown Fantasy League, out of Philly, has been awarding the last-place plunger to the previous year's last-place finisher at the draft for five years now. It too must be on display all year.

There's no easy transition to the word "balls," so I'll just say . . . huh. Easier than I thought, actually. Balls. Lots and lots of last-place trophies feature balls. In Jake Walton's league, the Balls-of-Defeat trophy comes to every draft (always in a crowded bar), where it sits in front of the loser. The chrome balls hang over a light that changes between eight colors. And whenever there is a dumb or questionable pick by anyone, the loser has to ring the balls like a bell.

Christopher M. Curran's Chicago–based Crotch Buffet Fantasy Football League gives out the Balls in the Basement Award to its last-place owner. The "winner" has to "proudly" display it in his house and change all of his social media pictures to include both his face *and* the trophy. Most important, the trophy features a removable set of realistic-looking balls. When the loser leaves the house, he must remove them from the trophy and carry them with him. If a fellow league member calls him out and he doesn't have the balls on him, he loses one draft spot in the next draft for each infraction.

Of course, it's not just balls featured on last-place trophies. Let's be honest: there wasn't a safer bet for this book than finding a "booby prize" trophy in it.

Carter Cordes's 12-team Sig Ep Young Alum Fantasy Football League has been together since they graduated UNC–Chapel Hill in 2005 and gives a literal "booby" prize to the last-place finisher, who has to display it in his home. It's actually a pair of dancing breasts retrofitted with plaques for the last-place team each year. I would have enjoyed being there when they brought this into the engraver's shop. **27**

Speaking of trophies that might give you pause upon first seeing them, Nicole Ansaldi shares the story of the Gardner Trophy, so named for the woman who gave it to Nicole as a wedding present. "Apparently it was a fertility statue. We were pretty creeped out." A creepy odd piece of art? Sounds like a fantasy trophy to me.

As the symbol for winning the Rochester, New York–based league that Nicole and her husband are in, it holds powers beyond just recognizing a champion. "My brother-in-law won it the first year, and my sister won it the second year. Well, guess what happened? While they were in possession of the masterpiece known as the Gardner Trophy, they had a baby boy." **28**

Now *that's* a trophy. Nicole and her husband won in 2011, and now *they're* expecting. See? The birth of a baby. We're ending on an up note. What could be nicer than a trophy where the punch line is a new baby being born? Everyone loves babies.

We started this whole section with smack talk, and I saved one last smack story for the end. Todd talks about a league he played in with his 10-year-old son. Todd did most of the work for his son in year one but had to stop in year two—his son was in the championship game against him. "Of course, he wins and is now the champion of the league. I hate to lose, but I'm also glad it was my kid instead of my brother-in-law."

Todd's league has no trophy, but the winner can ask anyone in the league, at any time, for the whole next year, "Who's the champ?" And everyone else has to answer, "You are."

Todd remembers the day after he lost. "The next morning I roll over to look at the clock because I have to get up at 6:00 AM for work. Taped to the clock is a piece of paper. 'Who's the champ, Dad?' Be careful how you raise your kids."

That's what's great about fantasy sports. Winning and losing, dad teaching son and then son getting revenge, them spending time with each other and talking trash. Sounds like you're raising your kid completely right, Todd.

Stories like Todd's were the ones that had me, well, a bit wistful.

By 2009, I had been at ESPN for almost three years. Things were going very well professionally. My transition from a management/on-air expert hybrid to just pure analyst had worked well. In 2007, ESPN started a live Sunday morning show, *Fantasy Football Now* (we even won an Emmy), which proved so successful online that it eventually moved to ESPN2 and became one of the highest-rated shows on that channel. My ESPN.com columns and the "Fantasy Focus 06010" podcast kept growing in audience each year, and I was making regular appearances on some of ESPN's biggest shows, like *Sunday NFL Countdown*, *SportsCenter*, and *NFL Live*.

When I started at ESPN, the question had been: how do we get fantasy players to switch to ESPN.com from our competitors? My answer was: it's *hard* to get people to switch. Fantasy players are creatures of habit, and leagues tend to like where they play. Instead, we've got a much better shot at just convincing new people to play fantasy. Instead of trying to get a bigger piece of the existing pie, let's just grow the pie. ESPN reaches pretty much every sports fan one way or another. So let's convince people who already like sports to try fantasy.

The way we did that was to get rid of the stereotype that fantasy's a nerdy or a niche thing. We needed to make fantasy sports seem like it's just one of those things that people do. Look, everyone fills out a bracket, everyone likes Vegas, everyone likes the new big superhero movie—and everyone has a fantasy football team. Make it seem like everyone does it and if you don't, you're missing out. That should be the message.

To that end, every year, thanks to lots of hard work by many people and tireless support from management, we kept making progress, getting more and more people at ESPN to play fantasy, to talk about fantasy on TV and radio, and to promote the game. When *SportsCenter* anchors and *Monday Night Football* analysts would make casual mentions of their fantasy teams, it kept chipping away at the "nerd" label and people realized it was cool.

And it started to work. Every season our game and content on ESPN .com showed significant growth, both in general and specifically compared with others in the industry. We always strive to be better, but by 2009, we were very happy with where we were in the fantasy industry.

Thank goodness my career was going well. Because my personal life was, um, basically the same as work, except I did it in my apartment. I had made some nice friends, but mostly I worked. And worked some more. And then slept a little so I could get up early and work even more.

And as the calendar flipped to 2009, it was starting to get old really quickly.

PART TEN

THE
OFF-SEASON

20.

Husbands, Wives, and Fantasy

or

"I Paid a Therapist $100 to Hear Me Explain How the Waiver Wire Works"

"I have three kids."

The drinks have not been ordered yet. The menus are still closed. We are less than 60 seconds into our first date.

"Before we get any further," she says, "I just thought you should know I was divorced five years ago and I have three kids." Half-joking, she adds: "This is the part of the date where you run away screaming."

Now it's time for the big smile. "Noooo. What are you talking about? I love kids."

The part I fail to mention, of course, is that the reason I love kids is because they are never around me. The ex–Mrs. Roto and I never had children, just my dog Macy, and at that point in my life very few of my friends had kids, even the ones back in Los Angeles. I didn't live near any relatives. My interactions with kids were limited to stopping at lemonade stands and reading misspelled tweets by socially awkward 12-year-olds.

She grins and says, "Well, I didn't want to go too far without mentioning it," and opens her menu.

I didn't think another thing about it because, truth be told, as soon as she told me that, I knew I wouldn't be around long enough to ever meet her kids. Yes, I lied to her about liking kids. But it's not my fault. She's really hot. Guys will nod and agree to anything crazy a woman says if she's hot. And so began our relationship.

Date one goes well enough to lead to date two and then three, and eventually we're seeing each other a few nights a week. She is funny, it turns out. Loves a good dirty joke. She's got this wonderful empathy and nurturing side. She's whip-smart. She's adventurous and open-minded and has incredible energy. She's the first to laugh at herself or make fun of something she does. An amazing cook and a Howard Stern fan. She's an old-fashioned girly-girl and makes no apologies for it. Doesn't understand basketball yet roots for my Lakers with the passion of a season-ticket holder. We have the same morals and point of view on most everything. She just . . . gets it. Whether we're at a corporate event with my bosses or at a dive bar with friends, she's totally comfortable. Everyone, including my dog, likes her more than they like me. But the thing I like the most? She's positive. Always, always positive and smiling. Super-happy, laughs easily, and rarely complains or gets annoyed about anything. For a curmudgeon like me, that's a breath of fresh air.

So that's why, after we had been dating for a while, we had a problem. The kids.

I hadn't met them. By design. She didn't want me to meet them until we were serious and she knew it was going somewhere. I agreed completely. I'm certainly no expert, and every situation is different, but to generalize on a subject I know nothing about (okay, fine, *another* subject I know nothing about), I think it screws kids up if they're constantly meeting new adults their single parents are dating. I've caused and been in enough therapy in my own life—I don't need three kids' neuroses on my conscience too.

She told me she was worried. She was starting to really fall for me because—and I can only guess here—she's human. To know me is to love me. Ask anyone. Wait. Just ask her. Actually, better just take my word on this one.

"Where is this going?" she wanted to know, and considering the amount of time we had been spending together, it was a legit question.

In a rare moment of adult clarity, I said . . . "I don't know." I told her she had every right to ask that question, but the honest answer was . . . I wasn't sure. I didn't want to lie to her and say, "Yeah, I'm willing to commit," because, well, she had three kids. Three kids I didn't know. Three's a lot, you know? I had no idea what that life was like. We only dated when the kids were with their father. A life with her and three kids would be very different from a life with just her.

What if the kids hated me? What if I hated them? What if I discovered what I've always suspected is true—that I'm fairly selfish and like being on my own a lot more than with kids? I told her that I was willing to try, but I wanted to be honest. If I discovered I didn't enjoy life with the kids—for whatever reason—I would have to bail. She respected my honesty, but her kids, rightly so, were more important. She wasn't going to introduce me to them and take things to the next level without more assurances.

So she broke up with me.

But even while we were apart and going about our normal lives, we kept in contact, a rarity for her. I'm actually friends with almost all of my exes. She, however, never looks back. Except this time. She would text or call me from time to time, and we would have lunch or talk and catch up.

Eventually, she said she wanted to get back together and give it another shot. She would slowly introduce me to the kids, and we would see. If it wasn't a fit, then she'd deal with it and at least we'd know. I decided the shot at love was worth more than some sort of stand based on useless pride or ego, so . . . I said okay.

So we got back together, and it was then that I got the biggest surprise since she first told me she had three kids.

I loved her kids. *Loved.* Smart, good-natured (mostly), well-behaved, hilariously funny, energetic boys who were four, eight, and ten when we met. They're all into sports, so I'm sure my job helps some, but they quickly embraced me. More important, I quickly embraced them.

What I discovered was that I enjoy being around kids. Love it, in fact. Stereotypically neurotic, I get in my own head a lot. Except when I'm around the kids. Because you can't be anything but focused on them. And when I'm focused on them, I'm not thinking about myself. Which is nice.

Dating a woman with children at a vulnerable age can go a lot of different ways in terms of whether they accept or reject the new guy. In my case, their love of sports is huge. Plus, their father remains very involved in their lives and has never been anything but gracious to me, and they had been raised well before I ever showed up. They are filled with love, have no bitterness, and are just normal, upbeat kids who want their mom to be happy and like having someone else around who can shoot hoops with them or take them to the movies.

I can't describe the feeling as anything other than "freeing." I'm amazed at how quickly my priorities changed once I had stepkids. That's right. Stepkids.

Because, you see, once I got to know the kids, the rest was very easy, and there was no reason to waste any time. Within six months, we owned a house together and were married.

Crazy, right? I didn't see it coming. I never saw myself as a stepfather, let alone to three kids. But in a way, it makes sense. When I started my journey, I never saw myself making a living at fantasy sports, never saw myself living in Connecticut, never saw myself working for ESPN.

So perhaps it's fitting that when I started this book, I never expected to have husband-and-wife stories. The original book pitch included many of the chapters you've read—stories about draft day, trades, obsession, work. Until I started reading my email. And just like I was blindsided by love, so too was I overwhelmed by how many people play fantasy sports with their spouse. Or play in leagues with family members, or even people who play in a league that includes a married couple. And just like anything else that involves family, it doesn't always go smoothly.

In 2011 a man who would like to be referred to as "Ricky L." was in a 10-team non-keeper league with a husband and wife who were each managing their own teams. Very normal.

The husband owned Buffalo Bills running back Fred Jackson, who was having a breakout season. The wife had Eagles running back LeSean McCoy, who was in the middle of a monster year. Still normal. On the Sunday of week 11 in the 2011 season, however, Fred Jackson broke a bone in his leg and was lost for the season. A tough break, to be sure, but sadly, injuries are a part of both football and fantasy football.

And this is where the normal ends.

Because two days later, on Tuesday of that week . . . tragedy. The wife suddenly and tragically passed away. Heartbreaking, right? Just devastating. As Ricky recalled, "It was a very sad and awkward and weird situation to be in a fantasy league with someone who dies. We all felt bad for the husband."

Of course, Ricky. There are no guidelines on how to deal with something that horrible. But here, gentle reader, is where the story takes a turn. You see, while there is a horrific event in this story, that is not why it is in this book.

It is here because it turns out funny.

On Friday of that *very* same week, just three days after the wife passed away, a new transaction pops up on the league message board. The husband trades out-for-the-year Fred Jackson. To the dead wife's team. For LeSean McCoy!

What? *What?!?* Now what do you do??? It's a terrible trade, obviously, as no one would ever trade a stud for a guy who's done for the season, but beyond that, the owner of McCoy is, you know, *dead!*

Clearly, the husband is controlling both teams. But the guy just suffered a tragic and horrific loss. "Who wants to criticize a guy who just lost his wife?" Ricky asks.

Of course. An awkward situation is now even more uncomfortable. So the league comes to a decision. "You know what? People grieve in different ways. There's not a ton of money on the line. It's just fantasy football, doesn't compare to the death of a loved one. It's weird, but whatever." They're just gonna look the other way.

Except, as I described earlier in the book, some leagues have a jerk—That Guy. And in Ricky's league, we'll call him "X."

X doesn't care. He starts blasting the husband all over the message board, emailing him privately, calling him names, and yelling about the trade. "I don't care if she's dead! It's a bullshit trade!"

NOW WHAT DO YOU DO???

But then, finally, the husband responds: "Hey!!!" he says. "It was her dying wish."

Ball game, husband.

For the record, I don't believe it was the wife's deathbed wish for her husband to have Fred Jackson, but I'm not arguing it. Neither did the league. They let him have McCoy and the husband didn't make any more questionable moves. And because fantasy karma is a real thing, the husband's team didn't make the playoffs, "X" was kicked out of the league at the end of the year, and the wife's team *still* ended up making the playoffs, with the husband just setting the best possible lineup for her.

Crazy story. The whole thing, honestly, sounds like something from a daytime talk show. A feeling that Dan Press knows all too well.

In 2007, Dan's draft day in the Toth-Lacotte Bath House Fantasy Baseball League winds up falling on the same weekend as a trip Dan promised to take to Boston with his girlfriend Sara. Dan can't get out of the trip, so it's agreed that he'll draft on the phone. It's not ideal, but Dan will make it work.

So when they go to a bar with her friends on draft day, Dan sets up shop and starts drafting. He remembers, "Forty-five minutes into it, I start getting flak from the girlfriend. Two and a half hours later, we're wrapping up and I'm in an all-out fight and had no idea. We argued, and she ran out of the bar, disgusted at how rude I was with her friends."

Dan had to search all over the streets of Boston to find her and eventually calm her down. So, okay, a big fight that started because of fantasy sports. We've all been there.

Except for the part where Dan's girlfriend went on *The Rachael Ray Show* to complain about him.

It was a "Girl's Guide to Football" episode with Valerie Bertinelli (really? . . . really), and Dan's girlfriend complained on the show about his obsession watching football (for fantasy). Next time your significant other rags on you about your fantasy obsession, remember Dan. It's one thing to get grief about fantasy; it's another to get nagged on *national TV.*

Tough times.

But proving love is bigger than fantasy, Dan ended up marrying her, and they have two beautiful children. As Dan says, "We are still madly in love . . . but she'll never understand just how much fantasy sports mean to me."

One person who finally understands what fantasy means to her husband is Katie. You see, her husband, Kyle, is into it. How into it are you, Kyle? "I like to save my waiver spot as much as I can, so I have determined what time players become free agents every week. It's at 3:00 AM Thursday and 12:00 AM on Wednesday in respective leagues."

Kyle tells me he would set his alarm, wake up, and make his picks. "I would bring the laptop to the bathroom so as not to wake my wife, make the pickups, and go back to bed."

Katie didn't like how much time Kyle spent on fantasy sports, so he often hid it from her. One night, midseason, Katie walked in on him and he quickly closed his computer. Suddenly, Kyle found himself in couples therapy. She thought Kyle was looking at porn!

"Basically, I paid a therapist $100 to hear me explain how the waiver wire works."

Even funnier is that when Katie found out the truth, she was disappointed. She told the therapist that "she would have preferred an Internet porn junkie over an obsessive fantasy nerd." Apparently, she just hated fantasy sports since it took Kyle away from the family so often. Now out in the open, things got better. At least until the end of the year. Kyle won the league, you see, so he wanted to trash-talk his leaguemates. Kyle explains: "I sent the league a picture of myself wearing nothing, with the trophy covering my junk."

"A week later my wife and I went out on a date. The next morning my son asked why I took a naked picture with my trophy. Turns out the 15-year-old babysitter was using the iPad camera with the kids and that photo came up."

I can see why a wife might get upset at that. Luckily, you already know a good therapist for the babysitter. You know she's scarred.

But, Kyle reports, there is ultimately a happy ending.

"She loves the show *The League* and will watch with me and repeatedly say, 'That is so you,' throughout. We can now laugh at my fantasy addiction rather than fight over it." The other positive is that Kyle smartly made a deal. Whatever he won from fantasy, he would spend on her. So when Kyle won two of his leagues this year, Katie finally got a Tory Burch purse.

Katie eventually learned what many of us have known for a long time. When husbands, wives, significant others, and family members decide to play fantasy sports together, it's a wonderful thing. Whether you're playing with your wife or against your brother, the theme is the same. Fantasy football, as great as it is, is better when you share it with family. In often the most surprising ways . . .

TIME-OUT:

Playing Fantasy Sports While Your Child Is Born

Of course, sometimes the mixture of fantasy sports and family happens immediately. In the hospital, in the delivery room, or in the case of Jason Stack, *on the way to your child being born*.

Jason had his Alcohol All-Stars league draft scheduled on the same day his wife Bekki needed to be induced, so he left his draft early to take her to the hospital and planned to finish it from his cell. He picked up his wife, and as they were driving, Bekki's contractions start. Suddenly, Jason's phone rang.

"You're up." Jason explains he's not even past the house where they are drafting, let alone at the hospital yet. What happened to them waiting? "So just stop on your way and make your pick!" And in the background Jason hears other owners yelling, "C'mon, Stack! You're holding us up!"

Which is when Jason hears the little voice in his head. Hmm, the draft *is* on the way to the hospital. . . .

So with his pregnant wife in the car starting to have contractions and *about to give birth,* Jason stops at the draft to make a pick. That's right. He delayed the birth of his child for fantasy.

Only by about ten minutes and her contractions were still fairly far apart, but still. I repeat.

He delayed the birth of his child for fantasy.

Jason adds that his daughter was born that day with no complications (save for some dirty looks from the nurses), and that "I *love* my wife. She understood my obsession with fantasy football and still married me!"

After hearing that story, perhaps no husband should love his wife more than you, Jason. Of course, at least Bekki knew what was happening and begrudgingly allowed it. Dave's wife, Kim, went into labor, right on David's draft day. Since his son was early, a stay in the neonatal ICU was required. At the ICU, David was told his son was totally healthy. So then what did he do?

"I came to Labor and Delivery to 'check' on my wife. She was passed out, so I pulled out my laptop and logged on to the hospital's wi-fi. I drafted from the daddy pullout chair, with birthing guts around, as my wife stayed passed out the whole time. And as I am writing this, she just turned to me and said, 'You did what?' She had no idea."

Why do I think there's gonna be a lot of wives saying that after this book? Someone who is not in the dark, however, is Jennafer. She remembers exactly what happened on the day her son was born. As does Jim. Of course, there are two sides to every story....

JENNAFER: I enjoyed the heck out of college, went to Mardi Gras twice, ran with the bulls in Pamplona, and still managed to graduate. Then I became a teacher, backpacked through South America for a year, joined a rescue squad, and continued to do my best to help make the world a better place. But first and foremost, I've always wanted to be a mom.

JIM: I started playing fantasy baseball in 2002.

JENNAFER: When I met Jim, I tried to scare him away on our second date, but it didn't work. We got married, and we were going to have children. They would be raised Jewish and Boston fans. And I continued to regale friends and family with tales of mystery and adventure, victory and defeat. I made them laugh and cry. But above all, the one constant, to the very core of my being, I wanted to be a mom.

JIM: My draft that year was scheduled for the morning of March 16.

JENNAFER: I reveled in my body's determination to tip the scales at a buck-eighty before the big day. I marveled at the way my belly would ripple as the baby got bigger. I *loved* being pregnant! The months were rich with powerful, funny, life-changing moments. But those stories would have to wait until the baby was born. My water broke at 4:15 AM, and we had nothing packed, nothing prepared.

JIM: I was prepared. I had all of my ESPN rankings printed out with each position tiered in color-coded highlighter.

JENNAFER: Cameron Joseph Curran was born on March 15, 2002, weighing 8 pounds, 11 ounces.

JIM: In 2002 we still didn't have a laptop, and the hospital only allowed in-house phones, so I made sure to get the telephone number to my wife's recovery room.

JENNAFER: Cameron was magnificent. His hair was a platinum color that drew in visitors from all over the ward. He was peaceful and princely and pudgy. He rocked.

JIM: I had arranged to have my brother Brian call me every five picks so I could keep up with the draft.

JENNAFER: I was a mom. Jim was a dad. And I had so many stories to tell!

JIM: I explained to Jennafer that it was very important to keep the line clear in case my brother needed to call with an update or for my picks.

JENNAFER: The phone was off-limits. I couldn't share the news. I couldn't tell any stories.

JIM: What would we have done if he was trying to call and she's hogging the phone?

JENNAFER: I couldn't shout from the mountaintops or the comfort of my hospital bed that I was a mom. We had to keep the line open so Jim could get updated on who had been drafted.

JIM: The last thing I wanted to do was establish a bad reputation with my league as one of those guys who tries to pick already taken players. Quite honestly, I felt I was being very thoughtful about the whole thing.

JENNAFER: After Brian updated Jim on who had been drafted, Jim would go outside to use his cell phone to call in his draft pick.

JIM: My brother and the rest of the league commended me for not holding anything up.

JENNAFER: Then he would return to stare at the spreadsheets and agonize over who would go next, who would be available when his next pick came around.

JIM: Her parents were there, and Cameron was requiring her full attention anyway.

JENNAFER: I think his first pick was Ichiro.

JIM: I had Ichiro in his prime and felt great about the categories he fills.

JENNAFER: His newborn son was there for the whole thing, to hear his dad regale him with the stories about who he'd chosen as his retainers, his strategy, how he was going to hornswoggle his league-mates.

JIM: I was very happy with my team.

JENNAFER: Our day *was* filled with phone calls and stories, only I wasn't the one making or telling them.

JIM: I finished last in batting average and therefore out of the money by a couple of points. I got what I deserved.

JIM: My in-laws, it was their first grandchild, were mortified. That was, of course, until my father-in-law hired me to run his high-end doctors' league team.

JENNAFER: Our equally magnificent daughter, Michaela Hope, was born at 10:39 AM on June 17, 2005, weighing in at 6 pounds, 9 ounces. Her dad chose Johan Santana in the first round for his fantasy baseball team in the draft that year . . . and he won his league.

JIM: As I email this to you, Cameron is now ten years old, loves your podcast, and is my co-manager.

Considering you were doing it when he was born, it's only fitting that fantasy baseball has brought you guys closer together, Jim. Fantasy sports has a way of doing that with a lot of families . . .

21.

Fantasy Brings Families Together

or

"I Vowed to Always Support the Guinness Bowl Draft Day, from That Day Forward, 'Til Death Do Us Part"

In 1983 the Austin Franchise Football League (AFFL) was started among eight friends in Texas. Theo Thompson III was three years old. His parents were already separated.

Theo remembers, "My mom moved my sister and me to south Texas, so I would only see my dad sporadically over the next seven years as he battled drug and alcohol addiction. I don't remember thinking too much about it as a child. Some kids had a dad around; I didn't. Whatever."

But Theo does remember when his dad came back into their lives. "He and my mom showed up one Friday at my school. Apparently we'd be going to visit my dad in Austin every third weekend for the next eight years. He was required to pick us up after school on Fridays of his weekend and bring us back by five on Sunday."

Theo continues: "I don't remember much about those first few years, except for the car rides. As an adult, I can appreciate how much of a commitment it took for him to pick me up at 3:00 PM on a Friday, two hours from home—four hours round-trip—and then do the drive again on Sunday. But as a child, all I remember is that I'd never seen a football game before (even though I live in Texas . . . that's what happens when you grow up with only a mom)."

But luckily for Theo, in 1990 his dad introduced him to both football and fantasy football. You see, his dad was a founding member of the AFFL. And young Theo latched onto it. "I wasn't good at sports," Theo remembers, "but I was really good at math. So while I wasn't very interested in throwing the football, I was happy to pore over predraft magazines with my dad, looking for hidden gems."

So every third weekend Theo and his dad had a Sunday ritual. "We'd look at the matchups in the paper at 11:30 and decide on our starters. We'd watch the noon game on TV, then get in his truck for the drive to Victoria, Texas, for kickoff of the 3:00 game. My sister would complain about listening to the static-filled game as we switched stations as we traveled, trying to find either the Oilers or Cowboys. And I would sit next to my dad, roster in hand, estimating the score every time Warren Moon threw a TD or a game break came on to give us stats from other games. Of course, two weeks would pass before I saw him again and could see our record, but I reveled in those hours with my dad."

Theo must have been good luck. His dad won his first AFFL title that year. And in 1995, when Theo was 15, his dad made him GM of the Black and Tans. The commissioner of the league started mailing Theo the weekly scoring sheets, and Theo got to attend the draft. Most important, Theo and his dad would talk on the phone each Sunday (a first for them) about setting their lineup.

"Fast-forward to 2003. My dad was rushed to the hospital by ambulance. The first one to call and let me know was the league commissioner." Theo's dad would be in the hospital for three weeks. "Every time I would come in to check on him, there'd be Owen or Steve or Terry or one of the other AFFL owners talking to him, holding his hand, reminiscing about the past. No one said it, but we all knew that the years of drug and alcohol abuse had caught up to him. During those three weeks, I was at the hospital every Sunday, going over the lineup with him and then tracking our players on the 17-inch hospital TV."

When Theo's father passed away, the other AFFL owners were pallbearers. "He didn't leave much of an inheritance," Theo remembers, "but I did get to keep the Black and Tans. And with Tom Brady, Randy Moss, and LaDainian Tomlinson—all holdovers from those drafts with my dad—I was league champion in 2007. And after my dad's passing, the members of the AFFL voted unanimously to rename the trophy the Theo Thompson II Memorial Trophy. So, with all due respect to everyone else in your book, I'll take the AFFL trophy over any of theirs."

I get it. I 100 percent, completely, fully, totally, get it. Not that I needed Theo's story to understand the importance of fathers and sons, the challenges of a divorced couple with kids, or the ability of fantasy football to help heal wounds and bridge gaps. No, I've understood it for a long time.

After I got married, everything sort of hit me at once. Two jobs, three boys, and a dog made for total chaos. Wonderful chaos, but chaos nonetheless. And I finally *felt* what it was like to be in a family that had a lot of moving parts to it.

As I sit here writing this chapter, my parents are a week from celebrating their 47th wedding anniversary. They dated for two years before getting married, so they've been together for about half a century. I was very lucky in that I never grew up having to deal with divorce. But now that I've married into a family that's gone through one, my life and focus have shifted.

Look, I can barely take care of myself. And other than my dog, I'd never really been responsible for any other living being before I got married. Now I've gone from seeing the kids a few times a week when their mother and I were dating to living in the same house with three boys ages 7, 11, and 13.

It was a huge transition, but not just for me. Think about it from the kids' point of view. They'd already been through a lot in their young lives, and despite spending a lot of time with me before the wedding and all of us getting along, it still had to be a big adjustment to live full-time with your mom and her new husband, right?

I tried to walk a fine line. I wanted to be there for them but also didn't want to come on too strong, show them I cared but not seem like I was trying to replace anyone. The big decisions were their parents' call, but I could be a sounding board, an advocate, or, when necessary, a disciplinarian. I tried to be positive and involved but not too pushy.

A guy who had probably seemed new and fun to them when their mom and I were first dating was now in their face 24/7. So it was a bit of eggshell-walking for me and probably for them too. Everyone got along fine, of course, but it was more like we were all roommates than a true family, if that makes any sense. And although all three boys are sports fans and knew what I do, even occasionally watching me on TV, none of them had ever shown a real interest in my work. Until one day David, the 13-year-old, surprised me with this:

"I want to play in a league with you."

"You do?"

"Yeah. Actually, I want to do a team with you. Can we? Is it too late?"

I looked at him, and I smiled. "No, it's not too late," I said. "We'll start a league."

And start a league we did. My wife and I are friends with the parents of all the kids' close friends. So I decided we should do an eight-team extended-family league. We'd invite parents to co-own with their kids and do it up. I would co-own with David.

The next day we had just finished watching Matt's (the 11-year-old) youth football game. As we were walking out, we ran into Matt's father (my wife's ex) and his longtime girlfriend. And a thought occurred to me.

"Hey, uh, don't know if you'd be interested, but, uh, I think we're gonna do a little fantasy football league with all the kids. You wanna play? You could co-own a team with Matt."

He looked surprised by the invitation. We had always had a very cordial relationship, but it's not as if we ever socialized or anything. And this whole thing had to be an adjustment for him as well. There's some new guy living with his kids. He's always been respectful of me, and I of him, but it's still awkward, you know? Divorce is never easy on anyone, and new partners entering the equation don't make anything simpler.

But he looked at me and said, "Sure. Sounds fun."

And that weekend we all gathered at a friend's house. The kids and their friends, their parents, my wife and I . . . and her ex-husband and his girlfriend.

I was the only one who had ever played fantasy football before, so I printed out a bunch of cheat sheets and roster forms, explained the rules, keeping it super-simple, and suggested that, if they were unsure, they should just go down the list and pick the next available guy. David would draft for us.

I have to tell you, doing a draft with a bunch of 11- and 13-year-olds who know nothing about fantasy football is *hilarious.*

The kids grew up in Connecticut, so they've mostly watched just the local teams. That led to this exchange in the second round.

KID 1: I'll take Mark Sanchez.

KID 2: Aw, man! I wanted him. He's so good.

KID 1: I know. I can't believe he didn't go in the first!

Totally genuine. (If you're reading this book years after it was written, understand that New York Jets quarterback Mark Sanchez is terrible, both in real games and especially in fantasy. He would never be drafted in any eight-team league, let alone early.)

The kids would help each other out: "You need a running back? Oh look, no one took Michael Turner yet. You should take him." "Oh, thanks!" Michael Turner was a top running back, and it was, like, the 12th round.

Kickers went in the third. Kids took back-to-back quarterbacks in the first two rounds. I just smiled a lot. It was great.

But best of all, it was *normal.*

We were in a big circle, the adults with beers, the kids with cheat sheets trying to figure out what tight end to pick now that Dustin Keller (another Jets player who should not have been drafted) was off the board. In the fourth round. And most important, the kids saw their mom and dad and their parents' current significant others all hanging out, having fun. It wasn't weird at all.

I can't exactly describe it. It's like there was this collective sigh of relief. Everything had always been pleasant and cordial, but now it was more than that. All of our mutual friends now realized it would be fine to have the four of us at the same party or out to dinner. The kids realized they didn't have to tiptoe around anything. And the good feelings from the draft continued through the season. If their dad and I are at one of the kids' Little League games or whatever, we'll sit next to each other. They've come over for drinks or parties. He'll text me pictures or video of the kids at a game I can't make, and I'll do the same for him. As opposed to having two different households, we're all raising these kids together. It's terrific.

During the season, whether it was picking up free agents, reviewing trade offers, setting our lineup, or going over the matchup scores the next day, my stepson and I always had something to talk about and look forward to. Something for us to do together.

Just like at the draft, being in a league with a bunch of young kids who had never played before was fantastic. Kids at that age are so blunt and honest.

KID 1: Dude, your team sucks.
KID 2: I know. (hangs head)

No attempt at a comeback, just acknowledgment that he was right.

Thanks to the crazy numbers Matthew Stafford and Calvin Johnson put up in week 17 of the 2011 season in that 45–41 loss to Green Bay, David and I won it all. Watching that comeback together was a great moment. The league continued into 2012: David joined forces with his dad, Matt and I co-owned a team, and my wife and Connor (our eight-year-old) got into it, finishing a surprising middle of the pack, considering neither of them had ever watched football seriously before. We watch all the games together now, iPads out, as we check the league scores and celebrate or curse with every score. Just like a family playing fantasy football together should.

What was a silly little eight-team league turned out to be my most important one. When you say yes, you never know which one will be a throwaway league and which one will help transform a group of people into a family.

That's been the best part of writing this book. Hearing and reading all the great stories of how fantasy has brought people together, especially families. Of course, sometimes you don't need to play with a family member to enjoy fantasy. Sometimes it's just enough to know they understand . . . and they care.

Mike Brake would agree with that. He started the Gatorball Fantasy

Football IDP League with some University of Florida buddies in 2001. His team, the Afterbirth, won that first year, but soon he was wandering in the fantasy desert. "From 2002 to 2009, it was mostly disappointment," Mike laments. "I won the regular season three times in that span, only to be bounced in the first round of the playoffs each time . . . heartbreak."

Mike had another strong regular season in 2010 as he advanced to the championship game. But he was worried he would fall short yet again. That's when his wife, Julie, decided to give him an extra boost by, you know, re-creating Mike's entire starting lineup in gingerbread.

Yep.

#18—Peyton Manning, #84—Jacob Tamme,
#4—Adam Vinatieri, #80—Andre Johnson,
#23—Arian Foster, #34—Rashard Mendenhall,
#89—Santana Moss, #13—Stevie Johnson,
#52—Chad Greenway, Atlanta Defense

That's awesome. And Mike agrees. "In the 10-plus years of marriage and three years of dating, she has put up with my fantasy football shenanigans time and time again. Making her miss TV shows, putting up with me checking my lineup during family dinners and weddings. I never really thought she cared that much or knew how much this silly little game with friends meant to me until she made those gingerbread men. In my mind those cookies are what won me the title."

I think we've all learned a valuable lesson here. Never underestimate the love of a woman or the power of gingerbread.

But Mike's wife may have competition from Katie, wife of Costas. They were married in December 2011. While Katie spent months before the wedding picking out flowers, trying on dresses, and tasting entrée selections, Costas "scouted players during the preseason, completed mock drafts, and watched NFL fantasy coverage."

On their wedding day, Costas found that he liked the flowers, band, venue, Katie's dress, and the entrée—but especially the cake.

"A total surprise. In a sea of elegance, champagne, and filet mignon— an oasis for my inner dude. The three loves of my life: Katie, beer pong, and fantasy football. In the end, Katie got her fantasy wedding. I got my fantasy football cake. And got to eat it too!"

Think *that's* a supportive wife? Adam Squires sees that and raises you one. Adam, remember, is in the Guinness Bowl League from chapter 2. They're the ones who pull out the previous year's draft boards and look at them.

Well, Adam's wife, Jennifer Janka Squires, showed her love and devotion by not only being supportive of Adam's fantasy addiction but actually *making it part of her wedding vows.*

"On that unseasonably warm New Year's Day, in front of friends and family," Jennifer remembers, "I vowed to always support the Guinness Bowl Draft Day, from that day forward, 'til death do us part."

You don't have to talk to Adam, Mike, or Costas for very long to know how much they appreciate their wives' support of their fantasy football madness, but the best is not when your significant other merely tolerates fantasy sports or even supports it, but rather . . . joins in!

Of course, if you do get your significant other to play, Drew Thomas from Cleveland has a cautionary tale. "I love two things in this world. Fantasy sports and my wife. Possibly in that order."

Having played for over a decade when he first met Shana, Drew hid his fanaticism. "The last thing I wanted to do was scare this girl away. How would she react if she knew about my compulsive participation in three different fantasy football leagues?"

But you can only hide something like addiction for so long. "As our dating progressed she sensed how big a part of my life fantasy football actually was. One day while preparing for an upcoming draft she came in and told me that she signed up for an all-girls fantasy football league at work so we could have more to talk about. We were only dating a few months, but Matthew, I swear to God I would have married her on the spot."

Drew helped her with her draft and lineup decisions, but soon she became more confident and eventually stopped asking for help. She finished third. "By the end of that season, the depth of her knowledge had increased so dramatically I was afraid I had created a monster."

And the next year Drew was right. "Subscriptions to *ESPN Insider* and *Rotowire* replaced watches and purses on her Christmas list. Sunday mornings were no longer for the gym, but for plopping down to watch you and Tim Hasselbeck on *Fantasy Football Now*. On our honeymoon, we skipped a moonlight dinner on the beach to watch *Monday Night Football* because she was down eight and had Matt Forte to play. That's a true story."

You see that, gang? The couple who plays together stays together.

"Our relationship has only become stronger now that she is a part of this world, and we have a whole new way to relate to one another. At first, I was scared to let her see how much I loved fantasy sports. But now I realize the only scary part would be joining a league with her. Because honestly, she terrifies me."

I love how fantasy sports has brought Drew and Shana even closer together and how it's a big part of their family. I'm sure if they ever have children, their kids will be fantasy fanatics as well. It's definitely a hope I have for my twin daughters.

You read that right. Twin daughters. Because you'd think that getting married to a woman with three kids and all moving in together

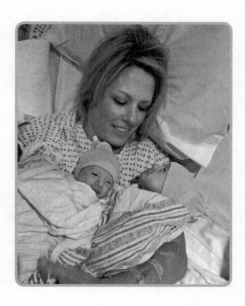

would have been enough change for a while, right? But, of course, anytime you think you're done with surprises, that's when life just laughs at you.

Apparently, it was meant to happen, because right out of the gate she got pregnant. Pregnant with . . . you heard correctly . . . twins. There are three sets of twins in our family, so this wasn't out of the blue, but it was still unexpected.

So I went from zero kids to five in about a year. I'm like a sitcom. Except it's my life and I love it. On October 25, 2011, my wife gave birth to two beautiful, perfect, amazing daughters. Being 100 percent objective, I can assure you they are only the cutest things that ever lived.

Saying that my life is very different these days might be the understatement of the century. My weekends are no longer spent out on the town but during the day on playgrounds. I have to watch a lot more *Barney* and get to listen to a lot less Howard Stern these days. But I've never been happier.

If you've paid attention while reading this book, you know how I struggle with happiness. Despite my unbelievable luck to have careers in two different professions that many people want to get into, relatively good health, and a terrific group of family and friends, long-term, consistent happiness had eluded me.

Notice I used the past tense. No longer the case.

It's weird. I wasn't sure I would ever solve the issue, but if I ever did, I knew—I *knew*—it would *not* be this way. I was not seeking anything remotely serious. She is everything I wasn't looking for and the same is true for her. She never wanted to date someone without kids; she needed someone who understood what her life was like. She's not into sports and had no idea what I did for a living until our second date. To this day she doesn't totally understand it, though between playing in our league this year and this book, she's getting closer. Of course, she still doesn't get the guys in the tattoo league.

Once I was with her and the kids, however, my perceptions changed. You know, when you draft a fantasy team, you are, in essence, taking a leap of faith. That this player will perform as expected or better. You're choosing this player over many other potential players with no assurances that it will turn out all right. But you do it anyway. You open yourself up with cautious hope and optimism that your fantasy heart won't be broken.

Just like I've done in my personal life. Taking on three kids and having two more is, for a single guy, by any reasonable account, a crazy leap of faith. But you know what? I can't imagine my life without them, and my life seems much more normal than ever, despite what may seem nuts to anyone on the outside.

A friend who read an early draft of this book said, "It's like a love letter to fantasy sports." I hope he's right. Because it should be.

It's not hyperbole to say fantasy sports changed my life. Forget that it puts a roof over my head. I've met lifelong friends because of fantasy sports. It has given me amazing experiences I never thought possible. I've even gotten to act on TV sitcoms and soap operas because of fantasy sports (and I can't act). Hell, I got to write a book.

It's been a blessed, insanely lucky, unreal journey.

But there is no greater testament to what fantasy sports has meant to me than my family. Without fantasy sports, I'm not at ESPN. Without ESPN, I don't meet my wife. And if I don't meet my wife, I don't have my family. You have just read a whole book about fantasy sports, and the underlying theme of every single story is that the person was ultimately trying to win a league. Chasing one of those trophies you saw in chapter 19.

But this right here is the greatest fantasy trophy of all time.

Ball game.

Throughout my career, I have tried to be loyal to people who helped me, to make those who took a chance on me proud of their decision, and to leave fantasy sports better than I found it.

Because man, it sure has done right by me.

THE CRAZY LONG LIST
OF ACKNOWLEDGMENTS

This book was a labor of love for me and doesn't exist without the generosity, intelligence, and friendship of many people who probably should have said "no" instead of "yes." And since a decent part of the book is about my life, there's many people who deserve thanks for their part in that as well.

We don't often get a chance to show our gratitude publically, so I'm going to make sure I take full advantage of this opportunity. As you just read, I have a lot to be grateful for and it's due to a lot of great people. So sit back, this is gonna take a while.

My undying gratitude and reams of good fantasy karma to Geoff Kloske and the entire gang at Riverhead Books, including Helen Yentus and Alex Merto for the cover. Super editor Matt Boyd answered calls, texts, emails at all hours with edits, suggestions, hand-holding, encouragement, grace when pages were late, making the tough cuts that I didn't want to, and if any of you ever need someone to look at male strip club websites and chase down the photo rights, he's your guy. Love me the Matt Boyd.

The book doesn't even get sold and would not be nearly as good without the guidance and help of Richard Abate and 3 Arts throughout everything. If you ever want to do a book, he has to be your first call. He's a rock star.

Doing the book isn't possible without the amazing people at ESPN. Starting with our fearless leader John Skipper. John is a longtime fantasy player who, thankfully for me, is not scared to try new things or people. John Kosner has been a great friend, supporter, boss, confidant, and his courage when many others would have thrown in the towel will never be forgotten. His early feedback on the outline for this book was incredibly helpful. I'm not always the easiest guy to be in charge of but Rob King has been much better than I deserve. It's an honor to both work for him and call him a friend. HTTR, Rob.

He'll hate it, but I want to specifically single out John Walsh. After Daniel Okrent formed the very first fantasy baseball league in 1979, he pitched an article about the league to John, who was then the editor of *Inside Sports* magazine. John bought the article, loved it, and immediately formed a league, the second ever fantasy baseball league in existence and one that continues to this day. Given that the original Rotisserie League is no longer together, John is in the longest-running fantasy baseball league in the world. Kind of cool. He's been an unbelievable mentor to me, a dear friend, gave notes on every word of this book, and is one of the most kind, loyal, and genuine people I have ever met. John is the creative person's best friend. Lucky are those of us who have John Walsh in their life.

I feel very lucky that among my first "jobs" at ESPN was that I got to be the auctioneer for George Bodenheimer's personal fantasy league. Despite the enormity of his responsibilities and demands on him, he always found time to check in on me, counsel me, and I'll always cherish our advice meetings. There's a reason George is beloved by all who worked under him at ESPN.

It's an amazing group of people who comprise ESPN Fantasy, starting with Nate Ravitz, who is actually very un-weasel-like. He's done a fantastic job running the entire fantasy department and has been a good on-air partner and great friend for a long time, before either of us were at ESPN. I always say, best part of my day is doing the podcast. So, yes, a shout-out to Jay Soderberg, "Podvader," who is a good sport and even better at his job. I, uh, may exaggerate a little. Pierre Becquey, Keith Lipscomb, Brendan Roberts, James Quintong, Andrew Feldman, Eric Karabell, Tristan Cockcroft, Christopher Harris, AJ Mass, Ken Daube, KC Joyner, Dave Hunter, Shawn "C-Dub" Cwalinski, Todd Zola, Brian Gramling, (and formerly Jason Grey) . . . proud to call you all colleagues.

On the TV side, Seth Markman not only has the hardest commish job of any league in America, but he also oversees all of ESPN's NFL coverage, including *Fantasy Football Now*, with a strong, smart, and patient hand. I work (and have worked) with many, many great people on the TV side, but special mention to Greg Jewell, Amina Hussein, Mike Cambareri, Mike Epstein, Todd Snyder, and of course, the *Fantasy Football Now* gang, led by the incredible Scott Clark and the tireless Sid Wong.

I hope I never have to do *Fantasy Football Now* without Tim Hasselbeck next to me. He's smart, works his ass off, is a great on-air partner and an even better person. Robert Flores, Stephania Bell, and Sara Walsh are awesome to work with and make the mornings fly by.

Chris Berman sat with me when I first got to ESPN, patiently answered all my questions and has continued to do so for seven years. He is beyond gracious and supportive, both on air and off, and I have learned much from him. Thanks for everything, Boomer. Getting to watch football every Sunday with him, Tom Jackson, Mike Ditka, Cris Carter, Ron Jaworski, Keyshawn Johnson, Chris Mortensen, Adam Schefter, Trent Dilfer, Merril Hoge, John Saunders, Herm Edwards, Tedy Bruschi, and Eric Mangini is one of my favorite parts of my job. They teach me something new every Sunday and I appreciate all of them sharing with me.

Thanks to my friends Chris Bishop, Heather Cocks, John Cregan, Steve De-

Maio, Nando DiFino, Greg Erb, Tucker Max, Chad Millman, Jason Oremland, and Bobby Patton for their early thoughts, suggestions, jokes, and brainstorming.

Thanks to Don Smith and all the Fat Dogs and Lone Star League gang. Tommy Connell, Rick Hill, Woody Thompson, Randy Malazzo, Warren Faulkner, David Hicks, Frank Smith, Carl Jaedicke, David Ellis, David Schrank, Wade Kusler, and the new guys Todd, Tim, and Tanner. Thanks to all the guys in the Doug Logan League, and thanks to everyone, everywhere, that's ever played in a league with me.

Thanks to Steve Mason for giving me my first shot on air and being a great friend. To the late great Ray Kalusa, John Ireland, and David Singer for going along with it. Thanks to the late Andrew Ashwood and Harry Gore.

There are no thanks big enough for the amazing Adam Silver and the NBA. Brenda Spoonemore, Steve Hellmuth, Steve Grimes, and everyone at NBA.com and NBA Entertainment. FOREVER. INDEBTED.

I don't know where my career is without having Bill Simmons's early support and friendship, but it's not anywhere close to what it is now, I know that much. Thanks, Bill. You're like Brandon and Dylan rolled into one.

The years we did the TMR site were a very special time to me and I will never forget it. It was truly a labor of love for many people, starting with Pierre and Janet Becquey, who, as I said earlier, basically ran the site, edited everything, handled customer service, were the heart and soul, they worked many late nights. Without them, none of this happens. Big leap of faith for parents of four young kids. Thank you.

The TMR core: Dave Hunter, Shawn "C-Dub" Cwalinski, Brad Evans, Christopher Harris, Andy Behrens, Tom Herrera, Nando DiFino, Heather Cocks, Brian McKitish, David Young, A.J. Mass, Bob Schenks, Guy Lake, Dan Cichalski, Wade Alberty, Shawn Peters, Adam Madison, Ken Daube, Will Brinson, Jim McCormick, John Cregan, Mike Bornhorst, Tommy Landry, Sean Allen, Matthew Greber, Ken Weitzman, Will Harris, Josh Whitling, Pravin Bhandakar, Dale Normanson, Ben Ice, Trace Wood, Jonathan Phillips, Candice McDonough, Victoria Matiash, Chris Cates, Anthony Targan, Bo Levy, Jon Loomer, Todd Whitestone, John Pereira, Chuck Landzdorf, Tim Kavanagh, Neil Tardy, Josh Whitling, Chris Carlson, David Srinivasan, John Hunt, Tyler McLean, Drew Belzer, Dan Sullins, Ian Ferguson, Eric Maltais, Sam Gaines, Robert Poe, Charlie Wilke, Brian Hughes, Brian Sykes, Jon Phillips, Drew Belzer, David Ohayon, Max Work, Mike Thornburn, Dave Gawron, Jim Stechschulte, and many, many others. Thank you, thank you, thank you.

I take extreme pride that many on that list have gone on to do even bigger and better things in the fantasy industry. Thanks for keeping the flame alive.

Thanks to all my friends in the fantasy sports industry: Matthew Pouliot, Rick Wolf, Rick Cordella, Ron Shandler, Peter Schoenke, Jeff Erickson, Chris Liss, and the whole Rotowire gang, Ryan Houston, Whit Walters, The Huddle and all the current and past sites and owners in RotoPass, Mike Narhstedt, Kenny Gersh, Gregg Klayman, Mike Beacom and the FSWA. Glenn Colton, Stacie Stern, Paul Charchian, Greg Ambrosius, Charlie Weigert, and everyone at the FSTA. Lawr Michaels, Jason Collette, Steve Moyer, Rob Leibowitz, Larry Schecter, Peter Kreutzer, Joe Sheehan, and all the members of Tout Wars, past and present. Joe Bryant, David Dodds, Sigmund Bloom, and the gang at the legendary FootballGuys. Jeff Ma, Larry Tobin, Rick Kamla, Scott Engel, Brandon Funston, Evan Silva, Jason Kint, Nathan Zegura, Cory Schwartz, Mike Siano, Ryan Bonini, Michael Fabiano, Jason Smith, Gregg Rosenthal, Jeremy Ellbaum, Brian Schwartz and the team at DraftStreet.com, Mike Harmon, Scott Pianowski, Mike Clay, Josh Moore, Frank DuPont, Ray Flowers, Louis Maione, Steve Gardner, Howard Kamen, Matt Deutsch, and the gang at SiriusXM Radio fantasy sports, Dave Gonos, Emil Kadlec, Scott Philip, John Hansen, the gang at NumberFire, and the ton of people I am sure I am forgetting because I am writing this late at night and it's past due so I'm writing quickly. Frankly, everyone who has ever written about, talked about on air, promoted, done business in or with fantasy sports. Thanks for helping grow our game. You know, none of us can rest until every man, woman, and child plays fantasy.

Thanks to everyone who took the time to write up a story, send it in, answer multiple questions. I got way more great stories than I had room to use, so I apologize to those that didn't make the cut for one reason or another. Hey, there's always the paperback! Or the column. It'll get used at some point. But special thanks to Mike Davis, Michael Hepburn, Paul Kangas, Jill Maloney, Dave Windham, Sam Jesse, Ian Thompson, Joe Treffiletti, Michael Treffiletti, and Farhan Zaidi for helping track down certain stories that are in this book.

Thanks to everyone who so graciously gave their time to read an early copy and give me a blurb, including the people who are not mentioned elsewhere in this section, Harlan Coben, Dale Earnhardt Jr., Matt Holliday, Maurice Jones-Drew, Peter King, Seth Meyers, Keith Olbermann, Jeff and Jackie Schaeffer.

THANKS: Patrick Stiegman, Marie Donoghue, the wise and sage-like Marc Horine, the late, great John Zehr, Jason Waram, Kevin Jackson, Aaron LaBerge, and everyone at ESPN digital media, including my dear friends Anthony "Big Man" Mormile, Raphael Poplock, Bimal Kapadia, and Michael Cupo. Salil Mehta and Daniel Chiu for early navigation help, Brian Dailey and Quinn Emmett for keeping Poplock in line. Mike Polikoff, John Diver, Jamie Carlson, Dave Fishel, and the entire ESPN Fantasy Games team. Norby Williamson, John Wildhack, my fantasy tag team partner Ed "The Champ" Durso, Mark Gross, Steve Anderson, Chuck Pagano, Mike McQuade, Traug Keller, Mo Davenport, Scott Masteller, Stephanie Druly, Jay Levy, and everyone else helping fantasy at ESPN TV and Radio. The entire gang at ESPN PR, helping promote our game, with special thanks to Chris LaPlaca, Bill Hofheimer, Mike Soltys, and Kevin Ota. If the ESPN ad sales team isn't selling fantasy, none of us get paid. Huge shout-out to Ed Erhardt, Eric Johnson, Mike Maguire, Lisa Valentino, Trevor MacArthur, and everyone in ESPN ad sales—way too many to mention. Scott Burton at the Magazine for that first shot and his friendship. Stacey Pressman at the Mag for friendship, advice, and looking at way too many cover options. Laurie Orlando, Tim Scanlan, Maureen Hassett-Lindsey, and everyone in the ESPN Talent office. The SWAN Zach Jones, John Parolin, and everyone at ESPN Stats and Information. Barry Sacks and Pete McConville for carrying the fantasy on TV torch early and Ivy Abrams, Geoff Reiss, and Chantre Camack for opening those doors and fighting to keep them open. The early *FF Now* crew: Kieran Portley, Anthony Spadacenta, Zach Candito, Gregg Colli. Marcia Keegan, Diane Karagheusian, Molly Qerim, and the people who actually make ESPN run and have saved my bacon way too many times to count: Tina Pagano, Denise Pellegrini, Dominie Dickens, and Pam Chamberlain. Thanks to all the hair and makeup people at ESPN who perform daily miracles on me.

THANKS: Jamie Horowitz, Kevin Wildes, Jack Obringer, Gabe Goodwin, Peter Coughter for their friendship and professional navigation advice. Whit Albohm and everyone at SportsNation. All the on-air talent I get the privilege to work with at ESPN but special mention to Trey Wingo, Mark Schlereth, Michael Smith, Michelle Beadle, Jemele Hill, Buster Olney, Charissa Thompson, Ryen Russillo, Bram Weinstein, Prim Siripipat, and Michele Steele for their friendship and support. Gary Horton for our weekly lunches.

THANKS: My friends Adam "Jellyroll" Shapiro, Melissa Masse, Justin Rosenblatt, Heather Ankeny, Chris and Jeanne-Marie Lindsay, Eric Abrams, especially for carrying the load toward the end, Kevin Mock, John Portnoy, Joanna Lovinger, Andy Wichern, John Bravenec, Brittany Horine, Tory Zawacki, and Erin McParland for their friendship during both good and tough times.

THANKS: Sandy Silver Stutman, Rachel Bendavid, and the late, great Joe Bendavid, for telling me to go for it when they had every reason not to, Les Firestein, Jared Hoffman, super agent Matt Rice, Ryan Hayden and everyone at UTA, Derek Bacon, Darryl Kanouse, and Mark Farris for their help and hard work in the early days of TMR/RotoPass.

THANKS: To the King of all Media, Howard Stern, for over 20 years of inspiration and laughter for a long time. To the Stern Show Fantasy League—Gary Dell'Abate,

Jason Kaplan, Jon Hein, J.D. Harmeyer, Will Murray, Steve Brandano, Scott Salem, Ben Barto, and David Heydt—for great stories, much fun, and support.

THANKS: To the makers of Diet Coke, to the late night cafeteria staff at ESPN, and everyone who sat outside my office and waved their hands when the lights would go out every 20 minutes. I spent A LOT of long nights at the office writing this thing.

THANKS: Bruce Springsteen (rockin'), Eminem (angry), Jimmy Buffett (relaxing), and Suburban Legends (keeping me young). You guys were the backbone of my soundtrack while writing this.

THANKS: To anyone I've forgotten. You do a list this long and still, I know there are people that should be here but who aren't, but my brain is fried. Thanks for understanding.

THANKS: To everyone who has ever read my column anywhere I have written, joined the Yahoo group, listened to the podcast, subscribed back in the day to TMR or RotoPass, or even signed up for the TRUM, posted on our message board, followed me on Twitter or Facebook, watched me on TV or heard me on radio. None of this is possible without you. I don't take it for granted. From the bottom of my heart—thank you.

And finally . . .

THANKS: To my brother, Jonathan, who is, simply, my best friend. He's read way too many drafts of this book and has always been there for me. Love you, J.B. Much love to him, his amazing wife, Mimi, and my super-cute nephew Jacob. And to my parents, Nancy and Len. Thanks for the love, support, advice, notes on the book (my Dad has written several books), not laughing or yelling when I said I wanted to start over at 35, and you know, the whole giving me life thing.

To David, Matt, and Connor—thank you for barging into my office and telling me it was time to play or shoot hoops, thank you for understanding when I had deadlines to meet, thank you for yelling at each other to be quiet because "He has to write his book!" You're all great kids. I love you.

To Samantha and Brooke—my little beans. Thank you for never failing to put a smile on my face, no matter how many hours I worked or how frustrated I might get at certain points. I hope I can make you as happy as you make me. You two are magic.

And finally, to Beth—I highly discourage everyone from writing a book within the first year of twins being born unless you happen to be married to a saint. Luckily, I am, as she spent way too many nights putting the kids to bed alone as I was in front of a computer screen. Thanks for giving me a final chapter.

Matthew Berry · March 17, 2013